CAMBRIDGE T.
HISTORY OF POLITICAL THOUGHT

———

COMTE
Early Political Writings

CAMBRIDGE TEXTS IN THE
HISTORY OF POLITICAL THOUGHT

Series editors

RAYMOND GEUSS

Lecturer in Philosophy, University of Cambridge

QUENTIN SKINNER

Regius Professor of Modern History, University of Cambridge

Cambridge Texts in the History of Political Thought is now firmly established as the major student textbook series in political theory. It aims to make available to students all the most important texts in the history of Western political thought, from ancient Greece to the early twentieth century. All the familiar classic texts will be included but the series seeks at the same time to enlarge the conventional canon by incorporating an extensive range of less well-known works, many of them never before available in a modern English edition. Wherever possible, texts are published in complete and unabridged form, and translations are specially commissioned for the series. Each volume contains a critical introduction together with chronologies, biographical sketches, a guide to further reading and any necessary glossaries and textual apparatus. When completed, the series will aim to offer an outline of the entire evolution of Western political thought.

For a list of titles published in the series, please see end of book.

AUGUSTE COMTE

Early Political Writings

EDITED AND TRANSLATED BY

H. S. JONES
University of Manchester

PUBLISHED BY THE PRESS SYNDICATE OF THE UNIVERSITY OF CAMBRIDGE
The Pitt Building, Trumpington Street, Cambridge CB2 1RP, United Kingdom

CAMBRIDGE UNIVERSITY PRESS
The Edinburgh Building, Cambridge, CB2 2RU, United Kingdom
http://www.cup.cam.ac.uk
40 West 20th Street, New York, NY 10011–4211, USA   http://www.cup.org
10 Stamford Road, Oakleigh, Melbourne 3166, Australia

© in the introduction, translation and editorial matter
Cambridge University Press 1998

This book is in copyright. Subject to statutory exception and to the provisions
of relevant collective licensing agreements, no reproduction of any part may
take place without the written permission of Cambridge University Press.

First published 1998

Printed in the United Kingdom at the University Press, Cambridge

Typeset in Ehrhardt 9.5pt [W V]

A catalogue record for this book is available from the British Library

ISBN 0 521 46511 7 hardback
ISBN 0 521 46923 6 paperback

Contents

Introduction

I

By a happy coincidence, the publication of this edition of Comte's early social and political writings coincides with his bicentenary. But, two centuries after his birth, Comte is rarely encountered at first hand by today's readers. He still enjoys an important place in the history of ideas – as Saint-Simon's ablest disciple, as a formative influence on John Stuart Mill's *System of Logic*, and as the author of the doctrine of positivism which, a generation after his death, shaped the work of the founding fathers of the Third Republic in France. Above all, he coined the word 'sociology', and is still commemorated as one of the makers of that discipline. He inaugurated an important sociological tradition – best represented by Durkheim – which took consensus, rather than class conflict, as the discipline's central focus. But few read Comte today, and those that do tend to encounter him in such a ludicrous form – the founder of a secular religion of humanity, with himself at its head as the self-appointed high priest – that the experience brings them no closer to an understanding of the potent influence his ideas exerted in the nineteenth century.

Comte had a host of disciples in his own century, especially after his death; not only or even mainly in France, but dispersed as far apart as Newcastle and Rio de Janeiro. His followers were to be instrumental in the establishment of republics not only in France but also in Brazil, Portugal and Czechoslovakia. The first objective for a modern edition of his writings must be to impress upon readers some sense of the qualities that enabled Comte to speak so powerfully to his own age. The absurdity of many of the liturgical and doctrinal prescriptions of his later works is so blatant as to obscure the force of his more fundamental ideas. But one obstacle that prevents the modern mind 'accessing' Comte is the sheer scale of his major works: the six volumes of the *Positive Philosophy* and the four volumes of the *Positive Politics* seem destined to gather dust in any modern library. Yet it was precisely the encyclopaedic character of his mind that spoke most eloquently to the nineteenth century – an age that thirsted for new certainties and systematic doctrine.

This is the main reason for turning to Comte's youthful writings, and for constructing a presentation of his work around the 'fundamental essay' he wrote, initially under Saint-Simon's direction, in 1822–4. The *Plan of the Scientific Work Necessary for the Reorganization of Society* has a number of advantages for the modern editor, but the main one is that it combines brevity with encyclopaedic ambition. It does not, to be sure, aim to present the whole of Comte's doctrine: it was conceived as the first part of a much longer work which he did not complete. But it was Comte's first attempt to expound a systematic doctrine. And he continued to regard it as a fundamental work, an essay which set the agenda for his whole intellectual career. It was the work that established him as a major intellectual force, for though a young man's essay, it circulated widely among the intellectual elite of the time. It was distributed to prominent liberals of the stature of Constant and Guizot, Sismondi, Dunoyer and Say; and while Constant was critical of Comte's illiberalism, Guizot and others were deeply impressed. Furthermore, Comte's first disciple, Gustave d'Eichthal, took it upon himself to distribute the essay internationally, and brought it to the attention of both Hegel and Mill. Both read the essay and found much to commend in it. The essay was written at a time when Comte's concerns were at the heart of European political theory. This was not always the case. Later in life, towards the end of the composition of the *Positive Philosophy*, Comte subjected himself to a regime of 'cerebral hygiene': he vowed to preserve the purity of his intellectual vision by insulating himself from the ideas of contemporary thinkers. This regime necessarily had the effect of cutting him off from the European mainstream. But in the 1820s he was addressing questions that were central to European political theory, which was preoccupied, above all, with this question: how can any kind of political community be forged in a society peopled by individuals shorn of traditional social bonds? In France, more specifically, the most urgent question of all was how to 'close the revolution' – how to construct a new form of legitimacy that would transcend the conflicts that had plagued France since 1789 – and Comte constructed one of the most arresting and distinctive answers to that question.

This is the pre-eminent reason why the time is right for a new appreciation of Comte's place in the intellectual history of early nineteenth-century France. For the tradition of enquiry concerned with closing the revolution has been brilliantly excavated in recent years by François Furet and his collaborators, who have set out to build a decisively new alternative to the 'Marxist' paradigm of French revolutionary studies upon a recovery of France's lost liberal tradition. Precisely because Furet's ideological commitment was to the rediscovery of such liberal writers as Constant, Staël, Guizot and Tocqueville, he has given only fleeting attention to Comte. But if historians need a comprehensive 'mapping' of the exceptionally rich debates in France in the 1820s, we must give due space to the terrain occupied by Saint-Simon and Comte. For their approach rested on an original synthesis of the conservatives' sense of the systemic nature of the social order with the liberals' understanding of the revolution as the product of long-term and hence irreversible social change. Their sense of fundamental historical change, which they shared with the liberals, precluded an acceptance of the counter-revolutionary project. But because, like the conservatives, they saw that society was an organic whole, they were suspicious of the liberals' fondness for constitutional fixes: Comte in particular maintained that the practical and political work of reconstruction must build upon a prior theoretical work of reconstruction, which would depend crucially upon the formation of new kinds of intellectual and spiritual authority. That, in short, is why the positivist intellectual system should be seen as the realization of what was, from the outset, a political project.

II

This edition presents the *Plan* as part of a collection of Comte's early writings, spanning the period 1819–28. This corpus of texts is pre-selected, in the sense that these were the texts that Comte himself chose to reprint as an appendix to the final volume of his *Positive Politics* in 1854, and which at one time he had hoped to append to his earlier *Positive Philosophy*. This collection therefore possesses a sort of retrospective authorial approbation. At the same time it is worth commenting on why Comte chose to reprint these texts. His aim was to rebut the allegation that the *Positive Politics*, with its fondness for the elevation of positivism into a secular religion, constituted a betrayal of the 'scientific' character of Comte's first system, as he expounded it in the *Positive Philosophy*. The appendix was intended, Comte informed his readers, 'to demonstrate the perfect harmony of the efforts that characterized my youth with the works accomplished by my maturity' (*Ecrits de jeunesse*, p. 197). What Comte meant by this remark – here anticipating subsequent lines of criticism developed most notably by Emile Littré and J. S. Mill – was that these early essays, considered together, displayed 'the necessary relation between the philosophical base and the religious construction' in his thought (*Ecrits de jeunesse*, p. 197). The latter was not a late accretion, but held a central place in Comte's thought from the outset, as was demonstrated above all by the essays dealing with the 'spiritual power' and its necessity in modern society.

Before we proceed to a detailed examination of the early essays and their significance, we need to begin with a brief survey of Comte's system, as it developed in his two great multi-volume treatises. In these works, Comte addressed the political crisis of the age of revolution, and he analysed that crisis as, at root, an intellectual and spiritual one. He explained the political disorder of the age in terms of the spiritual void that had afflicted Europe ever since the fragmentation of western Christendom at the Reformation. This was, no doubt, an egregious instance of overdetermination – cause and effect were separated by two centuries; and in practice Comte plugged the holes in his argument by invoking the corrosive influence of Enlightenment philosophy, which completed the work of the Reformation. If political unity were to be recaptured, it had to be preceded by the establishment of a new spiritual unity; and Comte's central contention was that the only possible foundation for that spiritual unity was the authority of the positive method.

It has frequently been asserted, most famously by John Stuart Mill, that a wide gulf separated the Comte of the *Positive Philosophy* from the later Comte of the *Positive Politics*. The later Comte – so the argument goes – betrayed the rationalist objectives of his earlier work, and elevated imagination, emotion and the 'social sentiment' above reason. Positivism ceased to be a philosophy and was transformed into a secular religion, in which the worship of humanity supplanted that of the Christian God. Comte even prescribed in notorious detail the trappings of his religion of humanity: a hierarchy of priests, with Comte at the head; a calendar of positivist saints; social sacraments; and quasi-religious festivals celebrating social relations.

There is no doubt that Comte's emphasis did shift in his later work. The priority he now attached to sentiment rather than to reason was quite new, and overturned explicit assertions in his earlier work. But Mill's interpretation as a whole is difficult to sustain. Comte always insisted on the necessary interdependence of *Positive Philosophy* and *Positive Politics*; and by his lights it is easy to see why. The former alone could not serve as a principle of unity, for as we shall see Comte denied the objective unity of knowledge. It was only in the subjective synthesis of positive knowledge in its application for the good of humanity – that is, in the polity, and in the formation of the new spiritual power – that positivism acquired a unifying power. And it is Comte's early essays that demonstrate that his objectives were from the outset spiritual and political rather than narrowly philosophical. From the start, the exposition of the positivist philosophical system and the formation of positive sociology were conceived as means to the development of a positive spiritual power which would serve as the centrepiece of a positive polity.

III

The biographical significance of these early texts lies above all in the fact that they coincided with Comte's break with his mentor, Saint-Simon; indeed, it was the 'fundamental essay' and its publication that played a critical role in the rupture of the relationship of master and disciple, since Comte felt, with some cause, that

Saint-Simon was unwilling to give him sufficient credit for the authorship of the text.

It was in 1817 that Comte met Saint-Simon, one of the intellectual geniuses of the age of revolution and reconstruction. The moment was opportune for both men. Saint-Simon had just lost the services of his valued secretary and collaborator, Augustin Thierry, who was soon to make a name for himself as one of the luminaries in France's emergent school of liberal historiography. Saint-Simon was notoriously difficult as an employer, and it was his authoritarianism that finally overcame Thierry's patience. The loss was a grievous one, for Saint-Simon, possessed as he was of one of the most brilliant and fertile intellectual imaginations of the age, was almost wholly lacking in any sort of talent for organization or system. He needed able collaborators who understood the train of his thought and could weld his sparkling insights into some kind of order. This was Thierry's gift; still more so was it Comte's. The young Comte, meanwhile, had been searching for a direction to his career ever since his dismissal from the Ecole Polytechnique, along with the entire student body, in April 1816. The opportunity to work for Saint-Simon put an end to sixteen months of uncertainty in his life.

The intellectual legacy Saint-Simon was to bequeath to Comte was a composite one, 'a bricolage of the organic social theory of the theocrats with the scientism of the Enlightenment, in the guise of a systematic general doctrine that would finally bring the moral and political crisis of the revolutionary period to a close' (Baker, 'Closing the French Revolution', p. 329). Saint-Simon had been deeply impressed by his encounter with the Idéologues, those liberal heirs of the Enlightenment who were the dominant intellectual voice in France between the fall of the Jacobins and the advent of Napoleon. They taught that the key to rational social reorganization lay in science, and specifically in knowledge of the physiological generation of ideas, which would become the foundation of a science of morality and politics. Under their influence, Saint-Simon conceived the project of deploying the physical sciences as a basis for the reconstruction of society. Meanwhile, a celebrated encounter with Mme de Staël, herself close to the Idéologues, both reinforced the notion that the route to certainty in politics lay in the application of 'the philosophy of the positive sciences' to the moral and political sciences, and introduced a number of new and fertile ideas into Saint-Simon's thinking. These included a concern with the essential role for an intellectual elite in the scientific reconstruction of society: for Staël, men of letters must constitute a sort of 'lay ministry' to guide the people and to defend them against tyranny. She also awakened in Saint-Simon an awareness of the religious basis of social order. This made him receptive to the influence of the conservative social theorists Joseph de Maistre and Louis de Bonald. Maistre's emphasis on the need for systematic doctrine as the foundation for a stable social order, together with Bonald's notion of society as an organic whole, together constituted the second great formative influence on the development of Saint-Simon's thinking.

These lines of thought were developed by Saint-Simon in a series of brilliant works which were, however, wildly disorganized and largely unread before the advent of Thierry, who served as his secretary from 1814 to 1817. Under his influence, Saint-Simon wrote much more lucidly and with greater literary success, for instance in his *De la réorganisation de la société européenne*, published in October 1814. He also moved much closer to the liberals, whom he had formerly looked upon with a measure of contempt. His works were favourably reviewed in the liberal press, and under the influence of the liberals he became increasingly interested in political economy. It was through the influence of Jean-Baptiste Say, the pre-eminent French economist of the time, that the word *industriel* entered Saint-Simon's vocabulary. The new direction to Saint-Simon's thought was marked by his foundation of the periodical *L'Industrie* in 1816. Its subscribers included eminent scientists, businessmen, bankers, peers and deputies, as well as Say himself. The nineteenth century, Saint-Simon declared, was destined to be 'the industrial century'.

Most of the central themes in Comte's philosophy can be found in Saint-Simon's work. Already in Saint-Simon we find the argument that social reconstruction depended upon intellectual reconstruction, and that the foundation of this intellectual reconstruction must be found in the application of scientific method. Further, we can find the seeds of Comte's doctrine of the spiritual power in the Saint-Simonian notion that in a rationally ordered modern society public opinion must be directed by an intellectual elite of scientists. Many commentators have inferred that Comte's significance lay not in his intellectual originality but in his skill as an expositor. This was the position taken by the Saint-Simonians after Comte had broken with them: for them, Comte's early work was only a commentary on Saint-Simon's *Lettres d'un habitant de Genève*. But this inference would be misleading for a number of reasons.

The first is that, though Comte was not twenty years old when he entered Saint-Simon's employment, his mind was far from being *tabula rasa* at that time. Already he was dividing his reading between two fields of study, the physical sciences on the one hand and the moral and political sciences on the other. In the former he was reading such authors as Monge and Lagrange, while in the latter he was considering the works of Montesquieu and Condorcet, Adam Ferguson and Adam Smith (*Correspondance générale* I, 19). In other words, he was already equipping himself with the intellectual artillery with which, five years later, he would tackle his 'fundamental essay'; in Lévy-Bruhl's words, Comte 'already possessed a large portion of the materials for his future system' (Lévy-Bruhl, *The Philosophy of Auguste Comte*, p. 6). Indeed, though we do not know the precise circumstances that brought Comte and Saint-Simon together, there is a suggestion that it was the convergence of their ideas that was responsible for their encounter, rather than vice versa (Pickering, *Auguste Comte*, p. 101; Gouhier, *La Jeunesse d'Auguste Comte* III, 168–70). The second point is that many of the ideas for which Comte was indebted to Saint-Simon can themselves be traced back to Mme de Staël, to Condorcet or to Turgot. Thirdly, the works produced under Saint-Simon's name during the period of his collaboration with Comte were to a large extent Comte's: he was employed to synthesize his master's ideas, but his role went far beyond that. It was he who undertook the hard work of literary and intellectual craftsmanship, and it was he, too, who contributed greatly to shaping Saint-Simon's intellectual agenda. Indeed, it may be no coincidence that, just as the advent of Thierry coincided with a redirection of Saint-Simon's work, so the same was true of the arrival of Comte: the new working relationship coincided with Saint-Simon's abandonment of his growing preoccupation with the politics of production as he reverted to his earlier concern with the spiritual power.

We are dealing, then, with a case of mutual influence rather than a one-way relationship. Comte was open to Saint-Simon's influence because Saint-Simon provided what he was looking for: chiefly, he suggested the possibility of synthesizing his twin interests of the natural sciences and the moral and political sciences into a single project entailing the creation of a social science and a scientific polity. But Comte provided the methodical rigour and concern for system which Saint-Simon lacked. Comte was not by nature a searcher after novelty but a searcher after system: he was a hedge-hog and not a fox, he knew 'one big thing' and not 'many little things', and Sir Isaiah Berlin's categories might have been invented to describe the contrasting intellectual gifts of Comte and his mentor. And it was the systematic credentials of positivism that largely contributed to its sustained appeal in the nineteenth century. It is in that sense that it is indisputably true to say that without Comte there would have been no positivism.

IV

What clearly was central to Comte's project, in his early writings and throughout his career, was the idea of subjecting moral and political phenomena to scientific investigation. But this idea in itself was by no means new. It had been a central ambition of the thinkers of the Enlightenment, especially in France and Scotland. In France, thinkers in the Physiocratic tradition, such as Turgot, deployed the idea of the rational cognition of the natural order of society as a corrective to the disorder and injustice produced by the arbitrary assertion of political will. In the era of the French Revolution, Sieyes coined the term 'science sociale'; and the idea of a rational social science that would serve as the basis for reconstruction was a familiar theme to the members of the Société de 1789 and to readers of the *Journal d'instruction sociale* – in both of which Sieyes and Condorcet were prime movers. After Thermidor, Condorcet's disciples the Idéologues used the newly founded Class of Moral and Political Sciences at the Institut de France as a forum in which to develop their ideas for a rational reconstruction of society on the basis of a scientific study of the origins of ideas.

Saint-Simon and Comte owed much to Condorcet and his understanding of what a science of society had to look like. They agreed, above all, that it must be progressive, and founded on a history of civilization. But they also wanted to move beyond Condorcet:

indeed, Comte's *opuscule fondamental* was originally conceived as an attempt to rewrite Condorcet's celebrated *Esquisse* along truly positive lines (Baker, 'Closing the French Revolution'). If we are to appreciate how Saint-Simon and Comte moved beyond the conception of social science inherited from the Enlightenment, we have to understand that they saw themselves as *synthesizing* the ideas of Condorcet and the Idéologues on the one hand with those of the conservatives Maistre and Bonald on the other. This synthesis generated a wholly new conception of how a progressive social science could serve as the basis for a process of social reconstruction which would effectively 'close' the revolution.

Saint-Simon and Comte had come to see Enlightenment philosophy itself as radically corrosive of social order. In its negative aspects it had been invaluable in sweeping away the relics of the old order; but it possessed no positive, constructive capacity of its own, as the entire experience of the revolutionary era demonstrated. Its defects were most apparent in Condorcet's sweeping denunciations of the Middle Ages from the absolute standpoint of the inexorable progress of the human mind. Through reading the authors of the counter-revolutionary school, Saint-Simon and Comte came to see medieval Europe in a new, more positive light, and came to see that institutions that were good in one era could be bad in another, and beliefs that had once been true could become the errors of a succeeding age. This historical relativism, amounting to the doctrine that all knowledge is relative to a particular stage in the development of civilization, contrasted starkly with Condorcet's unilinear vision of history as the progressive victory of truth over error. It was this *organic* conception of the stages of history that constituted the chief novelty of the positive conception of social science.

Comte shared Maistre's and Bonald's understanding of the structural features that any stable social order had to possess: above all, there had to be an authoritative moral and intellectual order which would serve as the indispensable foundation for social order. But he disagreed with them on the substantive question of what distinctive features a modern social order must possess. For all the complexity of their thought, Maistre and Bonald believed that only one kind of social order was possible, namely one based on church, king and landed aristocracy. The French Revolution, then, did not entail the formation of a new kind of society, but was simply the dissolution of society. It is clear from Essay 2 in this collection that Comte did not accept this interpretation of the place of the Revolution in French history. That essay constitutes a pioneering contribution to the kind of liberal historiography that was to become fashionable in the 1820s in the hands of such men as Guizot, Thierry and Sismondi. Their basic strategy, which took its point of departure from Madame de Staël's posthumous *Considérations sur la Révolution française* was to distinguish 1789 (good) from 1793 (bad) by setting the Revolution in the context of the more general movement of national and indeed European history. The central thread of that movement of history was the rise of the middle class, and specifically, for both Thierry and Comte, the 'emancipation of the communes'. This was the first 'social interpretation' of the French Revolution; and its polemical point was to demonstrate that, even though consensus about political institutions had remained elusive ever since 1789, nevertheless the basic principles of the social order inaugurated in 1789 were irreversible. They were the product, not of one generation's whim, but of a centuries-old process. If the 'Restoration' meant an attempt to restore a pre-revolutionary social order founded on privilege, it was doomed to failure.

Comte had a good deal in common with the liberals. Like them, he deployed history as a weapon against the counter-revolutionaries, who failed to see that the revolution could not be overturned because it was the product of long-term social evolution. But he departed from the liberals over their belief that the new society had essentially come into being, and that the only task remaining was to devise appropriate political institutions. Most liberals of Comte's generation followed Constant in thinking it anachronistic to believe that an ordered society had to have a determinate common purpose. But for Comte this notion was absolutely fundamental, and it lay at the heart of his project in the next of his early essays, the so-called *opuscule fondamental*.

It should be clear from this account that this essay should be understood as an answer to the deepest quandary that confronted French political theorists of the early nineteenth century: how to 'close' the revolution. This is the significance, for example, of the important passage that Comte added at the end of the introduction in 1824 (pp. 59–62 below). Liberals such as Madame de Staël and Guizot were also centrally concerned with how to break the cycle of anarchy and despotism by making at least some of the achievements of the Revolution serve as principles of reorganization. Comte sets out the errors made by both Restoration government and popular opposition, and sees the need for a constructive doctrine to steer a middle course. This echoes the liberal project, which he regarded as less harmful than either the revolutionary or the reactionary project. But whereas liberals tended to see reconstruction as largely a work of statesmanship, Comte's originality lay in his insistence upon its theoretical dimensions, which he had identified as early as 1819, when in Essay 1 of this collection he first stressed the importance of separating theory from practice in politics. The fundamental features of the new social order had to be grasped before the practical work of reconstruction could begin. The claim that 'spiritual' reconstruction had to precede temporal reforms was basic to Comte's break with liberalism, and it marks out some distinctive territory for him in the history of political thought. Guizot and his fellow liberals prized moral and institutional pluralism as the mainspring of progress. Comte, by contrast, was the quintessential anti-pluralist, the archetypal exponent of the conception of society as what Michael Oakeshott, who thought it a fallacy, termed an 'enterprise association'. That is, it was an association bound together by a common purpose, like a golf club or a trade union. This belief that '*society* exists only where a general and combined action is exerted' (below, p. 66) underpinned Comte's conception of social reconstruction. The basic assumption of his *Plan* was that social reconstruction would be in vain if it was not to be grounded in the theoretical work of rethinking the goal of human activity in society. This assumption – 'that government and the social union exist for the purpose of concentrating and directing all the forces of society to some one end' – alarmed John Stuart Mill right at the outset of his encounter with Comte's writings. (Mill to Gustave d'Eichthal, 8 October 1829, in *Collected Works of John Stuart Mill* XII, p. 36).

V

The main reason why Comte always identified the *Plan* as a fundamental work was that this was where, for the first time, he expounded his famous law of the three states, in which he asserted that all branches of knowledge pass successively from the theological state through the metaphysical to the positive. The originality of this law has been much discussed. Its authorship is sometimes attributed to Turgot, sometimes to Condorcet, and sometimes to Saint-Simon, who in his *Mémoire sur la science de l'homme* (1813) reported some remarks made along similar lines by the physiologist Jean Burdin some fifteen years previously. Certainly Comte was drawing on some dichotomies that had long pedigrees in the history of ideas: that between imagination and observation, for example, and that between cause and law. The idea of the progress of the mind was certainly Condorcet's. One obvious innovation made by Comte in his 1822 work was to introduce the second state, the metaphysical, which had not been present in Burdin or Saint-Simon; and even after reading Comte's text Saint-Simon continued to draw the simple contrast between 'the new system' and 'the old'. But this was hardly sufficient to establish Comte's fundamental originality, since he was not inclined to dwell at much length on the metaphysical state, which he always regarded as merely transitional.

A much more important point is that in Comte's work the law of the three states was inextricably linked to his differential theory of science, according to which the different sciences have distinct subject-matters and must therefore employ distinct methods (Heilbron, *The Rise of Social Theory*, pp. 225–6). This differential theory makes it quite clear that Comte's positivism did not entail a doctrine nowadays regarded as constitutive of positivism – namely, the belief that the human and social sciences must be modelled on the methods of the natural sciences. For Comte, if the scientific claims of sociology were to be demonstrated, it had to mark out both a distinctive subject-matter and a distinctive method for itself. But it is crucial to see that the logical relationship between the law of the three states and the differential theory of science was ambiguous, and that this ambiguity explains why that law itself contains an important equivocation. Comte had two different accounts of this relationship. In the first, the differential theory of science comes first, and the law of the three states is an inference from it. Comte's work in the philosophy of mathematics had taught him that the sciences differed in their subject-matter and in their methods; from which he inferred that the social sciences too must have a distinctive method based on the distinctive features of their subject-matter.

How does the human world differ from the plant and animal kingdom? The answer, for Comte, was that human beings possess the ability to learn from the experience of previous generations, so that each generation is not doomed to repeat the experience of its predecessors. This was the chief reason why 'society' was not a constant in the same way as nature. The subject-matter of social science was distinctive in being progressive, and methodologically it should be based upon a historical law.

On this account, the law of the three states is this historical law: it is, in other words, the principal substantive finding of sociology. But Comte's other account depicted this law not as a substantive law of sociology but as the law that shows the necessity of sociology. Here, it is the law of the three states that comes first, and the differential theory of science is a further specification of the law. The law of the three states showed that all branches of knowledge passed from the theological through the metaphysical to the positive state. But the point of the differential theory was that it showed that the fact that the study of society had not yet reached the positive state did not prove that it was incapable of doing so. On the contrary, the differential theory explained why the study of society had to be the last science to become positive, since its subject-matter was the least abstract and the most complex. So the significance of the law of the three states for Comte was that it on the one hand demonstrated that a positive social science was possible and necessary, and on the other hand demonstrated that it already existed. It was on the one hand a law proving sociology to be necessary; on the other hand, it was the essential law of sociology.

VI

Comte's *Plan* has long been acknowledged to be an important work. Less well known are his essays dealing with the question of the spiritual power – Essays 4 and 5 in this collection – and yet they are in their way just as revealing of the cast of his mind. For it was here that he engaged most closely with the works of the political economists and with those of the 'counter-revolutionaries' Maistre and Lamennais. Here he was much more appreciative than he had been previously of the value of the Catholic/feudal system.

Comte's main theme – particularly in Essay 5 – was the need for the institution in modern Europe of the separation of the temporal and spiritual powers, a principle that had first been developed in medieval Christendom, but which had been lost since the dissolution of that system set in with the Reformation. This principle had both authoritarian and liberal aspects. On the one hand, it was in formulating his understanding of the place of the spiritual power in modern society that Comte first expounded in detail his conception of a positivist priesthood – to be composed, not of scientific specialists, but of moral and social philosophers who would be grounded in the sciences without being specialist practitioners of any one science. Benjamin Constant noted that this conception left little room for freedom of conscience. Comte commended faith as a 'fundamental virtue', defined as 'the disposition to believe spontaneously, without prior proof, in the dogmas proclaimed by competent authority; which is indeed the indispensable general condition allowing the establishment and the maintenance of true intellectual and moral communion'.

Constant denounced Comte, and other contributors to the Saint-Simonian journal *Le Producteur*, for advocating a new kind of theocracy. And it is quite true that Comte had no sympathy for *intellectual* liberalism: the principle of freedom of conscience, which was so dear to Constant, was a heresy to Comte. But it would be wrong to infer that the *political* implications of the essay were illiberal. The most obvious implication of the principle of the separation of powers was to contest the absorption of the spiritual power by the temporal. Comte wanted to assert the importance in the modern world of a distinct and autonomous spiritual power which could serve as a force for intellectual and moral governance. He maintained that the separation of spiritual and temporal powers conferred two significant benefits. On the one hand, it permitted the reconciliation of two desirable goals which would otherwise have been incompatible: the increase in the scale of human society and the maintenance of strong government. At the same time, the reconstitution of a moral and intellectual authority independent of the temporal power facilitated the maintenance of order without recourse to the kind of centralization of political power that would stifle progress. What Comte was saying here was that there were two sources of social cohesion, namely moral force and material force; and in the absence of the former the latter must expand to fill the gap. 'In a population where the indispensable co-operation of individuals in public order can no longer be achieved by the voluntary and moral assent accorded by each to a common social doctrine, there remains no other expedient for maintaining any kind of harmony than the sad choice between force and corruption' (below, p. 200). In modern society, then, the reconstitution of spiritual power was a means of averting administrative despotism.

These two essays also have a crucial biographical significance for the student of the development of Comte's intellectual projects following his break with Saint-Simon. The *Plan* of 1824 was described as the first part of the first volume of a projected *Système de politique positive*. The first volume, when complete, would deal comprehensively with the *scientific* work necessary for social reconstruction; that is, principally with 'social physics' or what Comte would later call sociology. Its fundamental idea was 'the application of the positive method to social science' (*Correspondance générale* I, 84). The second and third volumes would, presumably, deal with the other two 'series of works', namely the educational and the political, while the second part of the first volume would present a first outline of a social science by 'presenting a first scientific overview of the laws which have guided the general course of civilization, and in turn a first glimpse of the social system which the natural development of the human race must bring to dominance today' (below, pp. 47–8). The last two volumes seem to have been a longer-term project, but in May 1824 Comte saw the completion of the first volume as an immediate priority, which would take him two months at the most (*Correspondance générale* I, 83). This ambition, needless to say, was one that Comte never fulfilled, but the reasons are not wholly clear. In 1824–5 Comte repeatedly told friends that the ideas for the second part were clear in his mind and that he just needed a good stretch of time to put pen to paper. But the curious thing about his correspondence at this time is that, though he frequently raised the subject of his planned second part, he never discussed in any detail the ideas it would expound. There is inevitably a suspicion that the work was not as fully developed in Comte's mind as he suggested. But he also suffered from financial difficulties, as he repeatedly complained, and these led him to divert into income-earning projects (whether teaching or writing) energies that might have been channelled towards the completion of his major project. The works that appear here as Essays 4 and 5 originated as two series of articles Comte wrote for the Saint-Simonian journal *Le Producteur*; and at the time he made no secret of the fact that he regarded them as a diversion from his main task. They did not develop new ideas, but just served to propagate principles he had expounded in his *Plan* (*Correspondance générale* I, 172–3).

Comte's project in the early/mid-1820s was the establishment of positive politics, or 'social physics'. His assumption at this stage was that the establishment of 'positive philosophy' would not be for his but for the next generation, since it could not be accomplished until all the positive sciences, including social physics, had been established. But on completion of the third part of 'Considerations on the Spiritual Power' in February 1826, he experienced some kind of nervous crisis which led him in a new direction. On his own subsequent account, he now dedicated his life to the foundation of the new spiritual power; and he came to see the need to combine the abstract and the concrete points of view, which were developed respectively in Essays 4 and 5. Finally, he came to see that, whereas from the theoretical point of view it was indeed true that social physics must precede positive philosophy, from the practical and educational points of view positive philosophy had to be developed now, since it was central to the education of the new spiritual power. The result was that Comte now attributed a more fundamental importance to the course on positive philosophy which he had originally planned simply as a means of earning his living and thus being able to complete the *Positive Politics*. That course was to be Comte's chief work of the 1830s and early 1840s (Pickering, *Auguste Comte*, esp. p. 368).

This account cuts at the roots of the thesis of the 'two Comtes'. That thesis rests upon a perception that there was a fundamental shift in Comte's interests between the 1830s, when he was concerned with the classification of the sciences and the logical foundations of sociology, and the 1850s, when his attention shifted to the religious foundations of the social order. Mill, Littré and others could enthuse about the former while deploring the latter. But the error here lies in a confusion between Comte's *subject* and his *purpose*. In the *Positive Philosophy* Comte was not writing about the classification of the sciences out of a purely theoretical interest in epistemology. Rather, it was vital to him to be able to establish positive philosophy because it was a prerequisite for the formation of a new spiritual power, which he had now come to see not as an ultimate goal but as an urgent necessity. If he was not, at this stage, writing *about* the spiritual power, he was most certainly writing *for* it. From the abstract or theoretical point of view, the urgent need was to create 'social physics'. This would in turn make positive philosophy possible. From the concrete or practical point of view, however, the urgent need was to create and educate a new spiritual power, and that demanded the prior establishment of a positive philosophy. Comte's 'theoretical' turn originated, paradoxically enough, in his growing disenchantment with the quietism of the first approach. He now sought to synthesize the two points of view.

Comte identified three 'series of works' necessary for the reorganization of society: the theoretical, the educational and the political. But in the *Plan* he dealt only with the first series, which is why in 1824 he described the essay as simply the first part of the first volume of a projected *Système de politique positive*, and why its principal title identified it as a plan of the *scientific* work necessary for social reorganization. In 1826, at the end of his 'Considerations on the Spiritual Power', he envisaged proceeding to a discussion of the more specifically political aspects of reconstruction. But in the event he did not proceed in this way. Soon afterwards he experienced what he described as 'a veritable nervous crisis', which led him, as he explained to Blainville, to undertake 'a total and, to my mind, truly systematic recasting of my work on positive politics, of which you have the first part' (*Correspondance générale* I, 186). This recasting was what Comte went on to undertake in his *Cours de philosophie positive*. The story of how he set about it lies beyond the scope of this introduction.

VII

There remains one essay, the final one, which has not yet been discussed and which might seem rather out of place in this collection. Comte recognized that the essay marked something of a turning-point in his career – 'the passage from my social debut to my intellectual career' (*Ecrits de jeunesse*, p. 200). We know that he hesitated before including his essay on Broussais in the appendix to the

Positive Politics. Nevertheless, he did decide to include it, and we should take his reasons for doing so seriously. If read in conjunction with the section at the end of the *Plan* where Comte discusses Cabanis and the attempt to found social physics directly on physiology, this text helps us situate Comte in relation to the idea of the 'science of man' which, from the Enlightenment to the Restoration, had furnished so fruitful an idiom in the quest for a rational foundation for politics. This is a complex and technical subject which can be treated only briefly here; but it is nevertheless important for an understanding of both Comte's intellectual development and his originality.

There were many different strands within the discourse of the science of man. Some of its exponents – notably the Montpellier school – tended towards vitalism, and emphasized on the one hand the unity of the phenomena of life and on the other the radical gulf that separated the life sciences from those sciences which dealt with 'dead' matter. Others, such as the Idéologues, leaned further in the direction of sensationalism, but were still more vehement advocates of a unitary science of man that joined the moral and the physical. By the time Comte was writing, however, a philosophical reaction had set in against the sensationalism of the Idéologues, whose ideas were now thought to be tainted with materialism. Cabanis's friend Maine de Biran now repudiated the reduction of the moral to the physical. Others emphasized the active role of the mind, which did not just passively receive sensations. The most influential philosopher of this anti-materialist reaction was Victor Cousin, who denounced the sensationalist principle that all knowledge is derived from the senses and therefore dependent upon the body's sensory apparatuses. Cousin's psychology stressed the innate sense of unity and continuity constituting the self. Sense experience was meaningless without consciousness. For Cousin, one part of psychology – that concerned with the sensory operations of the body – properly belonged to medicine and physiology; the other – the study of consciousness – belonged to philosophy, and must deploy a sort of rational intuition as its distinctive method.

Cousin's liberalism was politically suspect to the Restoration governments of the 1820s, which first dismissed him from his academic post and then imprisoned him. But his was the emergent philosophical orthodoxy of the time, and it was against Cousin's school of 'eclectics' or 'spiritualists' that Comte's essay on Broussais was directed. For F. J. V. Broussais was the best-known exponent of materialism among the medical theorists of the Restoration, at a time when that doctrine was regarded as decidedly heterodox. He made his name in 1816 with his *Examen des doctrines médicales*; but his 1828 text, *De l'irritation et de la folie*, was his most provocative work. Here he expounded a 'physiological medicine' which held that all disease results from a general state of 'irritation'. Broussais's work was read as a rehabilitation of the sensationalism of the Idéologues; and his heroes were indeed such thinkers as Locke, Condillac, Destutt de Tracy and Cabanis. For Broussais, the true 'physical and moral science of man' was dependent upon the insights of medicine. He denounced eclecticism as unscientific; and his book was itself attacked by the Cousinian journal *Le Globe*.

For Comte to write about Broussais, and to take a stance in favour of Broussais against his critics, was thus a deeply partisan act. He admired Broussais partly because, by replacing the 'vital force' by 'irritability', Broussais had clarified the distinction between organic and inorganic phenomena. Broussais showed that physiology was not reducible to the inorganic sciences, and he thus struck a blow against the 'mechanists'. At the same time, in insisting that interior sensations were caused solely by physiological phenomena and therefore could not constitute revelations of moral truths, Broussais launched a frontal assault of the 'psychological' method of Cousin, Jouffroy and their allies.

Broussais was important to Comte because he helped him identify the distinctive place of physiology within the hierarchy of the sciences. On the one hand he had to establish that physiology *rested on* the inorganic sciences, because it was an integral feature of Comte's classification of the sciences that each science rested on the preceding one in the hierarchy – and in that sense it made sense to speak of the unity of knowledge. This was something that the vitalists overlooked. But on the other hand it was still more important to be able to show that it was a distinct science, with its own distinct method and subject-matter – which was something that the mechanists of the Paris medical school tended to overlook. Broussais, who was suspected of materialism, helped Comte establish the existence of physiology as a distinct positive science in its own right; but so too did the Catholic nobleman Henri de Blainville, who became something of an intellectual mentor to Comte – which says a good deal about Comte's complex position on the French cultural map of the time. It was Blainville who introduced Comte to Lamarck's term 'biology' as the new designation for this science.

Comte, however, was no mere disciple of either Broussais or Blainville. He points out that Broussais devotes no attention to the demarcation to be drawn between the sphere of physiology and the sphere of social science; he does nothing to eradicate Cabanis's confusion between 'the study of the individual man and that of the human race considered in its collective development' (below, p. 235). This distinction was the crucial one for Comte, and it shows him breaking decisively with the hegemony of the discourse of the science of man; and thus breaking decisively with Saint-Simon too, for Comte's old employer himself remained in important respects wedded to that discourse. Indeed, one reason why Comte thought it so important to be able to establish the autonomy of biology in relation to chemistry – and why he was prepared to draw promiscuously on Broussais and Blainville in order to do so – was that it was a key stage in the elucidation of his classification of the sciences, the *coup de grâce* of which was the legitimation of social science as a positive science in its own right. Others had asserted the autonomy of biology *vis-à-vis* the inorganic sciences in order to affirm the homogeneity of the science of man. Comte was critical of this view. He agreed that *ultimately* the history of civilization (and hence social physics) was the consequence of human organization, or of 'the natural history of man'. But 'it would be a misunderstanding to conclude . . . that we should not establish a clear division between social physics and physiology properly so called'. Direct observation of social phenomena was necessary because of the progressive character of the history of civilization: in the analysis of that history, 'it would be quite beyond the powers of the mind to connect any term in the series to the primitive point of departure, if we suppressed all the intermediate links' (below, p. 133).

Why, we might ask, was it so important to Comte to establish social science – sociology, he was soon to name it – as a distinct positive science, rather than as an application of physiology? Why could his purposes not be served by the older discourse of the science of man, which itself aimed to supply a sort of rational foundation for politics? The ultimate answer to this question must remain a matter for speculation, but it is surely bound up with the polemical stance he was adopting in the political debates of the 1820s. He wanted to establish the positive credentials of social science because he wanted to delegitimize those other discourses about politics – he labelled them 'theological' and 'metaphysical' – which in his analysis perpetuated the intellectual and political disorder of the age. In addition, as we have seen, the distinctive subject-matter which Comte mapped out for social science – the direct observation of the history of civilizations – had the real advantage of itself furnishing proof of the historical inevitability of social science, and of the political and social order that must result once the intellectual reign of the positive method had been completed by its application to the study of society. For Comte, then, the project of creating a social science was no open-ended intellectual quest; he was interested in intellectual order rather than in a restless and endless pursuit of truth for its own sake. There would be no fourth state, for positive philosophy was to be 'the definitive state of man' (below, p. 154). Its formation was from the outset a political project with a determinate social end in view.

Notes on text and translation

Text

Of the essays translated here, it is the longest and most important one, the *Plan*, that has the most complex textual history. Comte began the composition of the essay in January 1822 and completed it in May. We know quite a lot about the process of composition, since Comte's notebooks containing his manuscript drafts of this essay, formerly held in the archives of the Maison d'Auguste Comte in Rue Monsieur-le-Prince in Paris, are now held in the Bibliothèque Nationale (Nouvelles Acquisitions Françaises 17901–17902). The essay's original title was *Prospectus des travaux scientifiques nécessaires pour réorganiser la société*. In this form it was to have appeared in a series of works that Saint-Simon had begun to publish under the title *Du système industriel*. In the event it was never published in this form, but one hundred proof copies were distributed in 1822. It was preceded by a preface by Saint-Simon in which he compared the work of his 'collaborator and friend' with d'Alembert's *Discours préliminaire à l'Encyclopédie*; it was 'my system presented in a scientific form'. Two years later, a revised and slightly extended version was published, now under the title *Plan des travaux scientifiques nécessaires pour réorganiser la société*, and with the foreword that precedes it in the present edition. Even now, however, there were two distinct editions. One was presented as the first part of the first volume of a projected larger work, the *Système de politique positive*. One hundred copies of this were published. These were the copies that Comte distributed; and this was the publication format to which Comte had agreed. But one thousand further copies had an additional cover, added at Saint-Simon's instigation and without the author's consent. This cover described the essay as the third issue (*cahier*) of Saint-Simon's *Catéchisme des industriels*. Here the essay was preceded by a preface by Saint-Simon (again, inserted without Comte's agreement) in which Comte's mentor commended the essay but voiced two principal reservations: that Comte considered the scientific capacity rather than the industrial capacity to be of primary importance; and that he confined himself to the scientific part of Saint-Simon's system and neglected the sentimental and religious side.

Comte republished the essay in 1854, along with the other early essays presented here, in the General Appendix to his *Système de politique positive*, volume IV. Here the title was *Plan des travaux scientifiques nécessaires pour réorganiser la société*, i.e. the 1824 title, and the text was (more or less) that of 1824; but he gave the date of first publication as May 1822. He also omitted the *avertissement de l'auteur* (foreword) in which Comte had, in 1824, exaggerated his debt to Saint-Simon.

There is a further complication. The essay was again reprinted as volume IX of the edition of the *Œuvres de Claude-Henri de Saint-Simon* in 1875. Since a facsimile of this edition was reprinted by Anthropos in 1966 (where the essay appears in volume IV) this is now one of the easier editions to obtain. It is substantially the 1824 text, whereas the authoritative edition of Comte's *Ecrits de jeunesse* by Berrêdo Carneiro and Arnaud reproduces the 1854 text. Unfortunately, however – and this has not previously been remarked upon, to my knowledge – the 1875 and 1966 editions contain a large number of minor variations, especially in punctuation, from the 1824 edition; it is thus a rather imperfect text. In this edition I have used the 1824 edition, so as to emphasize what the young Comte was saying. But I have indicated important variations where appropriate, so as to give the reader a sense of the ways in which the later Comte wanted to correct the earlier texts.

The 1824 text differed from that of 1822 in two principal respects. There were a number of small word changes, so that, for example, 'infaillibilité sacerdotale' becomes 'infaillibilité papale'. More importantly, Comte added some new text, notably seven pages at the end of the introduction and ten pages at the end of the essay. The first section spelt out the inability of 'kings' and 'peoples' to satisfy the need for social reorganization, and included a critique of the eclecticism of Victor Cousin and his followers. The second section dilates upon the difference in method between the organic and the inorganic sciences, and identifies 'social physics' with the former. The changes introduced in 1854 were more minor. Comte suppressed references to future works which were planned in 1824 but which in the event did not come to fruition; he replaced 'nous' with 'je', so as to remove the impression that the essay was co-written with Saint-Simon; and he suppressed a footnote underlining the difference between the methodological interactions of the natural sciences *before* and *after* they reached the positive state (in this edition, p. 140 n. *i*).

Translation

No twentieth-century editor has attempted a fresh translation of these essays or, indeed, of any of Comte's work to the best of my knowledge. Henry Dix Hutton's contribution to the Victorian translation of the *Positive Polity* has held sway, sometimes in the modified form produced for Frederic Harrison's Everyman edition of these essays. One can easily see why Comte has not attracted new translators, for he had little taste for elegant prose or colourful imagery. Although I have tried to make the text readable within limits, I have striven at the same time to be faithful to Comte's not always readable original. Inevitably these two principles have collided from time to time.

Unlike the Victorian versions, which were the work of proselytizers, this is intended as a scholarly translation. I have not tried to render Comte's text into words that might have been used by an English thinker struggling to formulate similar ideas. In particular, a basic principle I have tried to follow is that where Comte uses a certain word in a technical sense, or in a distinctive or idiosyncratic way, the same English word should be used to translate it on each occasion. One example is the noun 'communes' in Essay 2. Strictly speaking, the best translation of this word would be 'commons' in some contexts and 'communes' in others. But if we are to follow the force of Comte's argument we have to opt for one translation and stick to it. Since the enfranchisement of the communes ('l'affranchissement des communes') is a critical event in Comte's account, I have taken 'communes' as the normal translation. Another example is 'travaux', which appears in the title of Essay 3. Previous translators, wishing to indicate that this word does not bear the meaning 'literary works', have usually translated it as 'operations'. But this often looks just as odd and more cumbersome than 'work' or 'works', which I have usually preferred. Finally, Comte makes promiscuous use of the noun 'combinaisons', especially in Essay 3. In some cases he uses this word to refer to political movements or institutions, where neither the French 'combinaisons' nor the English 'combinations' would normally be used. Nevertheless, Comte chose to use the same word, and its repeated use clearly carries force in suggesting an analogy between political and social phenomena on the one hand and physical and chemical phenomena on the other. I have therefore decided to sacrifice some elegance and readability by sticking to the English 'combinations'.

One other difficult term should be mentioned here. Comte makes frequent use of the word 'savant', and previous translators, in a laudable desire to avoid anachronism, have steered clear of 'scientist', which first appeared in the English language a decade or so after Comte's essays were published, though well before the French 'scientiste'. They have therefore translated it variously as 'savants', 'men of science', and 'scientific men', and have sometimes moved arbitrarily from one to the other. I have formed the view that 'men of science' and 'scientific men' are just too cumbersome to translate a word that Comte uses so frequently; and I also believe 'savants' to be misleading in English. I have therefore risked the accusation of slight anachronism and used 'scientists'.

Chronology

1842   Finally breaks up with Caroline Massin
1843   Publication of *Traité élémentaire de géométrie analytique*
1844   Publication of *Traité philosophique d'astronomie populaire*, including preamble 'Discours sur l'esprit positif'
        Not reappointed to his post as examiner at the Ecole Polytechnique. J. S. Mill seeks to organize a subscription fund to help him financially
        Meets Clotilde de Vaux
1846   Death of Clotilde de Vaux
1848   Publication of *Discours sur l'ensemble du positivisme*
        Founds Société Positiviste
1849   Publication of the *Calendrier positiviste*
        Publication of the 'Appel au public occidental'
        Institutes the Religion of Humanity
1851   Begins publication of the *Système de politique positive* (four volumes, 1851–4)
        Loses his post as tutor (répétiteur) at the Ecole Polytechnique
1852   Publication of the Catéchisme Positiviste
1856   Publication of volume 1 of the *Synthèse subjective*
1857   Dies 5 September. Buried at the Père Lachaise cemetery

Biographical notes

BARTHEZ, PAUL-JOSEPH (1734–1806). Physiologist. Contributor to the *Encyclopédie*, subsequently a leading light in the Montpellier school of medicine, and consulting physician to Napoleon. His major work was *Nouveaux éléments de la science de l'homme* (1778; expanded and revised second edition 1806).

BICHAT, MARIE-FRANÇOIS-XAVIER (1771–1802). Leading physiologist of the revolutionary period, and founder of general anatomy. Showed that the complex structures of the organs of the body were to be explained in terms of their elementary tissues, and that certain tissues and membranes were common to all organs.

BONALD, LOUIS-GABRIEL-AMBROISE, Vicomte de (1754–1840). Emigré noble and counter-revolutionary theorist, author notably of the three-volume *Théorie du pouvoir politique et religieuse dans la société civile, démontrée par raisonnement et par l'histoire* (1796). His organic conception of society had a profound impact on Saint-Simon, but Comte was more influenced by Maistre.

BROUSSAIS, FRANÇOIS-JOSEPH-VICTOR (1772–1838). Physiologist. His *De l'irritation et de la folie* (1828) maintained that vital functions resulted from inflammation or irritation. This and other works established Broussais as a leading exponent of materialism in the sciences of man. He benefited from government patronage after the July Monarchy of 1830, but lost prestige in the later years of his life, especially after the outbreak of cholera in 1832. Broussais treated this as acute gastroenteritis. His best-known patient, Casimir Périer, died as a consequence.

CABANIS, PIERRE-JEAN-GEORGE (1757–1808). Idéologue philosopher, who sought in medicine an instrument for the analysis of the origins of ideas. His best-known work, the *Rapports du physique et du moral de l'homme* (1802), analysed the relationship between the physical and the moral constitution of man. Comte thought this work collapsed the distinction between social science and physiology, and was critical of Cabanis for that reason.

CONDORCET, JEAN-ANTOINE-NICOLAS CARITAT, Marquis de (1743–94). Enlightenment philosopher, mathematician and French revolutionary. His most famous work, the *Esquisse d'un tableau historique des progrès de l'esprit humain*, was published posthumously in 1795. It expounded a theory of the unlimited perfectibility of man. Comte was deeply influenced by Condorcet, and claimed him as his 'principal precursor'.

COUSIN, VICTOR (1792–1867). Fashionable and highly influential philosopher of the era of constitutional monarchy 1815-48. Influenced by the Scottish philosophers Reid and Stewart, and by the German idealists. He expounded the doctrine he termed 'eclecticism', which sought to forge moral and spiritual unity by means of a synthesis of conflicting philosophical systems.

CUVIER, GEORGES (1769–1832). Zoologist and leading academic politician. Pioneered new classificatory approaches to natural history and depicted organisms as functionally integrated wholes. Championed a 'catastrophist' interpretation of the earth's history and opposed the evolutionary ideas expounded by Lamarck and Geoffroy Saint-Hilaire.

ECKSTEIN, FERDINAND D' (1790–1861). Born in Copenhagen, educated largely in Germany, settled in France. Son of a Jewish convert to Protestantism, he himself converted to Catholicism, and achieved prominence as a Catholic convert during the Restoration. He subsequently established himself as an orientalist of note.

GALL, FRANZ JOSEPH (1758–1828). German-born anatomist and psychologist, chiefly concerned with the functions of the brain. He is chiefly renowned for the thesis that specific mental functions had specific cerebral locations, and he is generally regarded as the founder of phrenology. He maintained that mental phenomena should be treated as analogous to physiological functions.

LAGRANGE, JOSEPH-LOUIS (1736–1813). Mathematician who revolutionized the study of mechanics. Professor at the Ecole Polytechnique.

LAMENNAIS (or LA MENNAIS), FÉLICITÉ-ROBERT DE (1782–1854). Religious and political writer and priest. Initially a subtle apologist for ecclesiastical authority, he broke with the church in 1834 and his ideas later moved in a markedly democratic direction. In 1826 a shared interest in consensus briefly brought him close to Comte, whom he regarded as 'the strongest mind of the liberal party'.

MAISTRE, JOSEPH DE (1753–1821). With Bonald, the chief theorist of counter-revolution. Comte was particularly influenced by *Du pape* (1819), in which he insisted that social order rested crucially on the spiritual authority vested in the papacy. Other key works were *Considérations sur la France* (1797) and *Soirées de Saint-Pétersbourg* (1821).

MONTESQUIEU, CHARLES-LOUIS DE SECONDAT, Baron de la Brède et de (1689–1755). Enlightenment philosopher and author of *De l'esprit des lois* (1748), which is renowned for its comparative and relativist analysis of political institutions. Comte saw it as the first significant attempt to create a positive science of society.

SAINT-SIMON, CLAUDE-HENRI DE ROUVROY, Comte de (1760–1825). Soldier, speculator, social theorist and visionary, often regarded as a forerunner of socialism. Comte's employer from 1817 to 1824. His works included *Lettres d'un habitant de Genève à ses contemporains* (1803); *Introduction aux travaux scientifiques du XIXe siècle* (1807–8); *Mémoire sur la science de l'homme* (1813); *De la réorganisation de la société européenne* (1814); *Du système industriel* (1820–2); *Catéchisme des industriels* (1823–4).

SAY, JEAN-BAPTISTE (1767–1832). Leading French classical economist, close to the Idéologues. Author, notably, of a *Traité d'économie politique* (1803).

SPURZHEIM, JOHANN CHRISTOPH (1776–1832). German anatomist, collaborator of Gall. Coined the word 'phrenology', and was one of the leading advocates of that 'science'.

STAËL, GERMAINE DE (1766–1817). Literary and political writer and *salon* hostess who was close to the Idéologues. She exercised an important influence on the development of Saint-Simon's thought, notably through her *De la littérature considérée dans ses rapports avec les institutions sociales* (1800), in which she expounded a vision of politics as a science. Her posthumous *Considérations sur les principaux événements de la révolution française* (1818) played a formative role in the development of liberal historiography.

VOLNEY, CONSTANTIN-FRANÇOIS CHASSEBŒUF, known as Volney (1757–1820). Historian and politician associated with the Idéologues. Author notably of *Voyage en Egypte et en Syrie* (1787); *Les Ruines, ou méditation sur les révolutions des empires* (1791); and *Leçons d'histoire*, in which he took a sceptical line on the possibility of attaining accurate historical knowledge.

Bibliographical note

The authoritative edition of the texts presented here is Auguste Comte, *Ecrits de jeunesse, 1818–1828, suivis du mémoire sur la cosmogonie de Laplace 1835*, eds. Paulo E. de Berrêdo Carneiro and Pierre Arnaud (Paris, 1970). They also appear in the appendix to volume IV of the *Système de politique positive ou Traité de sociologie instituant la religion de l'humanité* (Paris, 4 vols., 1851–4). An English translation of this was published in 1877, the appendix being translated by Henry Dix Hutton. For Essay 3 I have also used the 1822 text, as reproduced by Pierre Laffitte, 'L'opuscule fondamental d'Auguste Comte', *Revue occidentale* 18 (1 January 1895), pp. 1–124. An indispensable source is Comte's *Correspondance générale et Confessions*, vol. 1, 1814–40, eds. Paulo E. de Berrêdo Carneiro and Pierre Arnaud (Paris, 1973).

The standard work on the early Comte was until recently Henri Gouhier, *La Jeunesse d'Auguste Comte et la formation du positivisme* (Paris, 3 vols., 1933–41). But Gouhier, exhaustive scholar as he was, stated his thesis tendentiously (notably in understating Saint-Simon's influence and thus overstating Comte's originality), and while his works remain an invaluable quarry they have been superseded by Mary Pickering, *Auguste Comte and Positivism: an intellectual biography*, vol. 1 (Cambridge, 1993). This promises to hold the field for a long time, and it includes an extensive up-to-date bibliography. Pickering's second volume is eagerly awaited. To this should be added a more polemical work by Johan Heilbron, *The Rise of Social Theory* (Oxford, 1995), which culminates with Comte – perhaps oddly, since Heilbron's argument seems at times to be that Comte's importance was not really as a social theorist at all. There is an admirable sketch of the background to Essay 3 in Keith Michael Baker, 'Closing the French Revolution: Saint-Simon and Comte', in François Furet and Mona Ozouf, *The French Revolution and the Creation of Modern Political Culture*, vol. III: *The Transformation of Political Culture 1789–1848* (Oxford, 1989), pp. 323–39; and to this should be added Gérard Buis, 'Le projet de réorganisation sociale dans les oeuvres de jeunesse d'Auguste Comte', in A. Amiot et al., *Régénération et reconstruction sociale entre 1780 et 1848* (Paris, 1978), pp. 133–48. The most important textual study of that essay is Henri Gouhier, 'L'opuscule fondamental', *Les Etudes philosophiques* no. 3 (1974), 325–37, though even Gouhier was wrong on one or two textual details. There is a perceptive discussion of Comte as sociologist in Raymond Aron, *Main Currents in Sociological Thought* (Harmondsworth, 1965), vol. I.

The Saint-Simonian background may be studied in Georg Iggers, *The Cult of Authority: the political philosophy of the Saint-Simonians – a chapter in the intellectual history of totalitarianism* (The Hague, 1958), and in Frank E. Manuel, *The New World of Henri Saint-Simon* (Cambridge, Mass., 1956); Manuel also treats Comte in his *The Prophets of Paris* (Cambridge, Mass., 1962). For the broader evolution of positivism, W. M. Simon, *European Positivism in the Nineteenth Century: an essay in intellectual history* (Ithaca, N.Y., 1963); D. G. Charlton, *Positivist Thought in France during the Second Empire, 1852–1870* (Oxford, 1959); and D. G. Charlton, *Secular Religions in France, 1815–1870* (Oxford, 1963). The relationship between Comte and Enlightenment conceptions of social science is best approached through Keith Michael Baker, *Condorcet: from natural philosophy to social mathematics* (Chicago, 1975), ch. 6, and through the essay by Baker cited above; but there are also useful essays by Jacques Muglioni and Annie Petit in Pierre Crépel and Christian Gilain (eds.), *Condorcet: mathématicien, économiste, philosophe, homme politique* (Paris, 1989). The best work on 'historicism' and nineteenth-century social theory is still Maurice Mandelbaum, *History, Man, & Reason: a study in nineteenth-century thought* (Baltimore and London, 1971).

Ceri Crossley, *French Historians and Romanticism* (London, 1993), ch. 4, is invaluable as background to the second essay in this collection. So too is Guizot's *History of Civilization in Europe*, which has now been reprinted by Penguin with an introduction by Larry Siedentop (Harmondsworth, 1997). An exceptionally interesting work for understanding Comte's cultural and intellectual context is Alan B. Spitzer, *The French Generation of 1820* (Princeton, 1987). Comte's work on the spiritual power has been unduly neglected, but its context is illuminated by Christophe Charle, *Les Intellectuels en Europe au XIX siècle: essai d'histoire comparée* (Paris, 1996) and by Anne-Sophie Leterrier, 'La notion de pouvoir spirituel au début du XIX siècle', *Revue d'histoire moderne et contemporaine* 35 (1988), 107–22.

There is a growing literature on the medical and biological thought of this period. Works which place this subject in a broad social and cultural context include Elizabeth A. Williams, *The Physical and the Moral: anthropology, physiology, and philosophical medicine in France, 1750–1850* (Cambridge, 1994); John Pickstone, 'Bureaucracy, liberalism and the body in post-revolutionary France: Bichat's physiology and the Paris School of Medicine', *History of Science* 19 (1981), 115–42; and Barbara Haines, 'The inter-relations between social, biological, and medical thought, 1750–1850: Saint-Simon and Comte', *British Journal for the History of Science* 11 (1978), 19–35. The standard work on Broussais is now Jean-François Braunstein, *Broussais et le matérialisme: médecine et philosophie au XIXe siècle* (Paris, 1986).

A student interested in placing Comte in the context of broader debates in social and political theory might with profit turn to F. A. Hayek, *The Counter-Revolution of Science: studies on the abuse of reason* (Glencoe, Ill., 1952) and Herbert Marcuse, *Reason and Revolution: Hegel and the rise of social theory* (Oxford, 1941). To these should perhaps be added Karl Popper, *The Poverty of Historicism* (London, 1957). In addition, two classics must be mentioned: John Stuart Mill's *Auguste Comte and Positivism* (London, 1865) and Lucien Lévy-Bruhl's *Philosophy of Auguste Comte* (London, 1903). Both are admirable and fair-minded expositions written from very different standpoints. Finally, cyberpositivists might be interested in visiting the Auguste Comte website, maintained by the International Positivist Society. This is currently at the following URL: http://www.mygale.org/04/clotilde/home.htm.

Essay 1
General Separation between Opinions and Desires[1]

Rulers would like us to accept the maxim that in politics they alone are capable of clearsightedness, and that it is therefore for them alone to have an opinion on this subject. They certainly have their reasons for speaking thus, and the ruled have exactly the same reasons for refusing to accept this principle, which in fact, considered in itself and without the prejudices of either ruler or ruled, is indeed totally absurd. For, on the contrary, rulers – even if we suppose them to be upright – are by their position the most *lacks clarity* incapable of forming a just and elevated opinion on general politics; since the more one is immersed in practice, the less one is able to have a clear view of theory. A necessary condition for a publicist who wants to form broad political ideas is strictly to abstain from any public office or employment: for how could he be at the same time actor and spectator? *can't be both*

But in this regard men have gone from one extreme to the other. In combating the rulers' ridiculous pretension to exclusive political wisdom they have engendered in the ruled the prejudice – no less ridiculous, though less dangerous – that any man is capable, by *unqualified* instinct alone, of forming a just opinion of the political system, and each of us has asserted the duty to set himself up as a legislator.

[1] This essay was submitted to *Le Censeur* in July 1819, but was not published.

As Condorcet observed,[2] it is a singular fact that men think it impertinent to presume to know physics or astronomy, etc., without having studied these sciences; and yet that they believe at the same time that anyone can understand political science, and have a settled and trenchant opinion on its most abstract principles, without the necessity of taking the trouble to reflect about it and making a special study of it.

That stems, as Condorcet should have added, from the fact that politics is not yet a positive science: for it is obvious that, when it has become such, everyone will realize that to understand it it is essential to have studied the observations and deductions on which it is founded.

However, to achieve a synthesis, to exclude this prejudice without falling back on the principle of political indifference so dear to rulers, it would be right to distinguish, more than we have yet done, between opinions and desires. It is reasonable, it is natural, it is necessary for every citizen to have political desires, because every man has an interest of some kind in the conduct of social affairs; it is, for example, straightforward to understand that all citizens who do not belong to the privileged class, and who live off the product of their labours, desire liberty, peace, industrial prosperity, economy in public spending, and the proper use of taxation. But a political opinion expresses more than desires; it is, besides, the assertion – most often decided and absolute – that these desires can only be satisfied by such and such means, and by no others. And it is on this sort of thing that it is ridiculous and unreasonable to pronounce without special thought. For it is obvious that, in the question of whether such a measure or such an institution is capable of achieving a given goal, there is a chain of reasoning and of reflection which, to be undertaken properly, demands a special study of this kind of consideration. In the absence of this, we should believe certain means capable of attaining a goal, whereas they would in fact have a wholly opposite effect. Thus many people sincerely desire liberty and peace but at the same time have such a false idea of the appropriate means to obtain them that, if these means were

---

[2] Here, as elsewhere, Comte overstates the similarity of his own views with those of Condorcet. See Keith Michael Baker, *Condorcet: from natural philosophy to social mathematics* (Chicago and London 1975), p. 340.

put into practice, they would lead, on the contrary, to disorder and arbitrariness.

Two important political consequences follow, I think, from this analysis of opinions and desires.

First, by looking at things in this way, and considering the political opinions of unenlightened men as the expression of desires confused with that of means, we can see that there exists more uniformity than is ordinarily imagined in the political wills of a nation. In France, for example, among the individuals who profess retrograde opinions, there are only a small number, composed of those who were formerly privileged, who really – that is, with full knowledge of the facts – desire the re-establishment of the old institutions; the great majority basically want, with everyone, liberty, peace and economy. They associate the idea of the feudal regime with this desire only because they regard it as the only kind of regime capable of securing these ends for them.

Secondly, it seems to me, we can see how from the same analysis we can determine the share which the mass of a nation must take in government. The public alone should indicate the goal, because, if it does not always know what it needs, it knows precisely what it wants, and no one should take it into his head to will on its behalf. But as for the means of attaining this goal, it is for political scientists[3] alone to concern themselves with this, once it has been clearly indicated by public opinion. It would be absurd for the masses to seek to reason about it. It is for public opinion to form a will, publicists to suggest means of execution, and rulers to execute. As long as these three functions are not distinct, there will be a greater or lesser degree of confusion and arbitrariness.

In short, when politics has become a positive science, the public will have to accord publicists – and will necessarily accord them – the same confidence in politics that it currently accords to astronomers in astronomy, to physicians in medicine, etc.; but with this difference that it will be for the public alone to indicate the goal and the direction of the undertaking.

This confidence has had the most serious disadvantages whilst politics has been vague, mysterious, indeterminate, in a word theological; but when politics is a positive science, that is a science of

---

[3] The French here is 'savants en politique'.

observation, it will have no more drawbacks than the confidence which we every day fearlessly accord to a doctor, to whom we are nevertheless often entrusting our life.

In this state of things, the submission which is due to reason, and the precautions which must be taken against arbitrary power, will be perfectly reconciled.

Essay 2
Summary Appraisal of the General Character of Modern History[1]

The system which the course of civilization calls us to replace was the combination of spiritual (or papal and theological) power and temporal (or feudal and military) power.

As regards spiritual power, the birth of this system should be traced back to the emergence of the preponderance of Christianity in Europe, that is around the third or fourth century. As for temporal power, we should place its origin around the same period: in the first great attempts by the northern peoples to settle in the South of Europe, and in the earliest dismemberments of the Roman Empire.

These two powers were definitively constituted in the eleventh and twelfth centuries. At that time, on the one hand feudalism was universally established on settled foundations, as a national power; and on the other hand, the authority of the Holy See was fully organized as a European power.

Let us dwell for a moment on this notable period, to make two important observations.

In the first place, this dual organization was brought into being in a short time and without much difficulty, because it had been gradually prepared during the seven or eight hundred years that had passed since the birth of the two powers.

---

[1] This essay was first published, under Saint-Simon's name, as the eighth and ninth letters of *L'Organisateur* in April 1820.

5

The establishment of the temporal power was the consequence of the overthrow of Roman authority by the northern peoples. If this power was not constituted immediately after that authority had been totally annihilated, this was because for that to happen it was obviously necessary first of all to put an end to the pattern of irruptions, which happened with the victories of the first invading settlers over later invasions. This was the object of Charlemagne's wars against the Saxons and the Saracens, and then of the Crusades.

The constitution of the spiritual power had been prepared by the overthrow of polytheism, and by the establishment of the Christian religion, whose numerous clergy were spread throughout Europe.

When, in the eleventh century, Pope Hildebrand directly proclaimed the superiority of pontifical authority, as a European power, over national powers, he was only summing up a principle whose foundations had already been established in all minds, or, in other words, formulating a belief all the elements of which had long been accepted.

In the second place, the coincidence of the two powers, in respect of the period of their origin and in respect of that of their definitive constitution, deserves to be noted. We shall be able to observe the same analogy in relation to their decay, and this constant correspondence tends to prove (independently of our reasoning, which demonstrates that these two powers rest on each other) that they must disappear at the same time; that the temporal power could not be replaced by a power of a different kind, without the occurrence of an analogous replacement of the spiritual power; and vice versa.

This social system was born during the lifetime of the preceding system, and indeed at the time when the latter had just attained its full development. Equally, when the feudal and theological system was constituted in the middle ages, the germ of its destruction was coming into being and the elements of the system which is to replace it today had just been created.

Indeed, as regards the temporal power, it was in the eleventh and twelfth centuries that the enfranchisement of the communes began. As regards the spiritual power, it was roughly at the same time that the positive sciences were introduced into Europe by the Arabs.

Let us focus all our attention on this capital fact, which is the true point of departure for the series of observations by which we must today enlighten our politics.

It is industrial capacity, or the manufacturing arts and crafts, that must be substituted for the feudal or military power.

At a time when war was and had to be regarded as the primary means to prosperity for nations, it was natural for the direction of the temporal affairs of society to be in the hands of a military power, and for industry, classed as subordinate, to be employed only as an instrument. By contrast, when societies are at last convinced by experience that the only means for them to acquire wealth consists in pacific activity – that is in industrial activity – the direction of temporal affairs must naturally pass to industrial capacity, and military force in turn can only be classed as subordinate, as a purely passive force, probably even destined one day to become wholly useless.

The enfranchisement of the communes laid the basis for this new state of things; it made it possible and even necessary; and as we shall soon prove it subsequently became increasingly necessary. This enfranchisement brought about industrial capacity, since it established for the latter a social existence independent of the military power.

Before this period, quite apart from the fact that artisans taken collectively were absolutely dependent upon the military, each of them was wholly subject to the individual whim of the possessor of the land of which he formed a part.

Enfranchisement, while allowing the first kind of arbitrariness to remain, annihilated the second, and consequently created the germ of the destruction of the first. Previously, artisans possessed nothing of their own; everything they possessed, themselves included, belonged to their lord; they had only what he was willing to allow them. Enfranchisement created industrial property originating in labour, a distinct and independent kind of property which soon came to rival territorial property, which was purely military in origin and character.

Through this memorable innovation, industrial capacity could develop, progress and expand, and nations could organize themselves in all their parts on an industrial basis; only the head of society remained military, along with the general government which remained in its hands.

Let us make observations about the spiritual power analogous to those we have just made for the temporal power.

In the same way, it is positive scientific capacity that is to replace the spiritual power.

At a time when all particular knowledge was essentially conjectural and metaphysical, it was natural for the direction of society, as regards its spiritual affairs, to be in the hands of a theological power, since theologians were then the only general metaphysicians. By contrast, once our knowledge in all its parts is founded exclusively on observation, the direction of spiritual affairs must be entrusted to positive scientific capacity, since it is obviously far superior to theology and metaphysics.

The introduction of the positive sciences into Europe by the Arabs created the germ of this important revolution, which is today wholly complete as regards our particular knowledge, and as regards the critical part of our general doctrines.

The Arabs had scarcely begun to establish schools for teaching the sciences of observation in the parts of Europe they had conquered, when a general fervour directed all the most eminent minds towards this new light. Similar schools soon arose throughout western Europe; observatories, dissecting theatres, natural history collections were instituted in Italy, in France, in England, in Germany. Already in the thirteenth century Roger Bacon was doing brilliant work in the physical sciences. The superiority of the positive over the conjectural, of physics over metaphysics, was so clearly felt from the beginning, even by the spiritual power, that several eminent members of the clergy, among them two popes more or less in the same period, went to complete their education at Cordova, where they studied the sciences of observation under Arab professors.

Thus, summing up our foregoing observations, we can lay down the factual rule that at the moment when the feudal and theological system was definitively organized, the elements of a new social system began to form. A positive temporal capacity – that is, industrial capacity – came into being alongside the temporal power that had attained its fullest development; and a positive spiritual capacity – that is, scientific capacity – arose behind the spiritual power, at the moment when the latter was beginning to develop its activity to the full.[a]

---

[a] The division of society, and of everything relating to society, into temporal and spiritual, must continue in the new system as in the old. This division, which did not exist among the Romans, is the most important innovation in social organiz-

Before passing to the examination of subsequent events, let us consider this notable difference between the two systems, which is to be seen from the birth of the new system, and which I have tried to express by the contrast between the words power and capacity. I do not say: a new power arises alongside each of the old powers, but: a *capacity* arises alongside a *power*. In other words, the action of principles came into being then and is today substituting itself for the action of men; reason is to replace will.

Because in the old system temporal power was military, it demanded by its nature the highest degree of passive obedience on the part of the nation. By contrast, in industrial capacity, considered as destined to direct the temporal affairs of society, arbitrary will has no place and can have no place, since, on the one hand, in the plan it can form to work for general prosperity everything is capable of rational assessment; and on the other the execution of this plan needs only to a very limited extent to resort to commands.

In the same way the spiritual power, being by nature conjectural, necessarily had to require the highest degree of trust and mental submission. That was an indispensable condition for its existence and its action. By contrast, positive spiritual capacity, conceived as directing the spiritual affairs of society, demands neither blind belief nor even trust, at least on the part of all those who are capable of understanding logical demonstration; as for the rest, experience has given sufficient proof that their faith in the demonstrations unanimously agreed among positive scientists can never be prejudicial to them, and that this kind of faith is in short not capable of being abused.

Thus we can, if we wish, consider positive scientific capacity as giving rise to a power, insofar as it creates strength; but it is the power of demonstration instead of the power of revelation.

This is therefore our point of departure:

In the eleventh century, the temporal power and the spiritual power were definitively constituted, and at the same time two positive capacities began to form behind these two powers, and to prepare the way for their decay and their replacement. In short, one

---

ation made by the moderns. This is what originally created the possibility of making politics into a science, by allowing us to make theory distinct from practice. But in the new system this division is no longer between two powers, but between two capacities.

system was established, and another was born. Since that period, these two systems have always coexisted, colliding with each other sometimes silently and sometimes openly, in such a way that the first has increasingly lost its strength, whereas the second has increasingly grown in strength.

The examination of the past is therefore divided, from this moment, into two contemporaneous series: the first consisting of observations on the decay of the old system, and the second of the building of the new one. This is also the division which we are going to follow in all that remains to be said.

First series

In the era we have just settled on for the origin of our observations, the balance of forces between the two coexisting systems (one of which was entering maturity, whereas the other was only just born) was too unequal for it to be possible for any direct and palpable struggle to arise between them for long. Besides, history shows us that the struggle began to exist openly only in the sixteenth century. The four or five hundred years which had gone before formed the period of splendour of the feudal and theological system. But all this splendour rested on a minefield.

If historians had better analysed and more closely examined the Middle Ages, they would not have spoken to us solely of the visible aspect of this period; they would have noticed the gradual preparation of all the great events which unfolded later, and they would not have presented the explosions of the sixteenth century and the following centuries as sudden and unforeseen. However that may be, it was incontestably only in the sixteenth century that the open struggle began between the two systems. That is where we shall take it up.

Luther's and his fellow reformers' attack on pontifical authority constituted a *de facto* overthrow of the spiritual power as a European power; and that was its true political character. At the same time it sapped the roots of the influence which theological authority still retained by destroying the principle of blind belief, replacing this principle with critical enquiry, which, at first confined within quite narrow limits, would inevitably expand continuously and in the end embrace an unlimited field.

This dual change occurred as completely in the countries that remained Catholic, and above all in France, as in those which embraced Protestantism.

There was nevertheless this difference, which it is essential to note, that in countries which remained Catholic the spiritual power, realizing that it was destroyed as a distinctive and independent power, in general put itself at the service and commands of the royal power, offering it the support of those same doctrines by which it had formerly dominated it.

This change in the role of the clergy had the effect of prolonging the duration of its political influence a little beyond its natural life-span; but for royalty it had the major disadvantage of binding its lot more intimately to that of doctrines which had lost all their credit with the educated class.

The implementation of the reformation (because of the wars it brought about) required the whole of the sixteenth century and the beginning of the seventeenth. The attack on temporal power took place immediately afterwards, in France and in England.

In both countries, this attack was carried out by the communes and had at its head one of the two branches of the temporal power. In this regard there was just one difference between the two nations. With the English it was feudalism that was united with the communes against royal authority, whereas in France it was royalty that put itself at their head against feudal power. *two sides of same coin*

This combination of the communes with one half of the temporal power against the other half had arisen in both countries immediately after the enfranchisement of the communes, and perhaps it contributed not a little to bringing it about. The effects of this combination had since manifested themselves, well before the seventeenth century, in unequivocal results which had laid the foundations for the important events that have come to fruition in this century.

In France, Cardinal Richelieu worked directly to overturn feudal power, and after him Louis XIV completed this enterprise. He reduced the nobility to the most complete political nullity, and the most absolute insignificance, and he left it no other role to play than that of guard of honour to royalty. It is essential to observe that Richelieu and Louis XIV both strongly encouraged the fine arts, the sciences and the industrial arts; they sought to raise the political status of scientists, artists and artisans, at the same time as they lowered that of nobles. This intention was principally manifested by the minister Colbert, who was an artisan. But we shall again come across this fact in our second series, and it is enough to point it out here.

The result of the struggle was, in England, the revolution of 1688, which limited royal power as much as was possible without overturning the old system. Thus in each of these two countries the attack on the temporal power enfeebled, as far as could be, a different part of this power. In such a way that, in both, the two peoples had brought about the complete overthrow of this power, up to the point beyond which this overthrow would become impracticable without departing from the old social system. For this total outcome to occur, in both cases, it was sufficient for each of the two nations to adopt the modification accomplished by the other. That is what has just taken place in France, by the way in which the French have adopted the English constitution.[2]

The coalition of the communes with a part of the temporal power to attack the other part, as well as the very active protection accorded by the temporal power of several countries against the spiritual power (at the time of the reformation), make it impossible to grasp the true nature of these attacks without a very detailed examination.

From this has sprung a very widespread error which it is important to notice and to destroy. Instead of seeing in these events the struggle of the communes, under the leadership of certain parts of the feudal and theological system, against the other elements of this system, people have seen only the quarrel of kings with popes, and between royal and feudal authorities: the communes have been regarded only as instruments employed by the different powers, and almost never from any other point of view.

Before setting out the factors by means of which we can rectify the error we have just pointed out, it is pertinent to recall that, whatever line one might take on this subject, our present series will not be affected in the least; it will remain no less true, since its essential goal is to record the continual decadence of the old system.

---

[2] Comte is here referring to the institution of constitutional monarchy in France under the terms of Louis XVIII's Charter of 1814.

In spite of that, it is far from being a matter of indifference whether or not we understand the real influence that artisans, artists and scientists (who, considered collectively, form the communes) have exerted to bring about this decadence.

We can lay down the principle that any schism between the elements of a system is an evident sign of decadence. Thus, once the first great act of division between the temporal power and the spiritual power was seen, one could have predicted the more or less imminent fall of each.

Divisions of this kind broke out very early in the old system; they manifested themselves even before it had been completely organized; but they became continuous almost immediately after its definitive constitution. If we are prepared to reflect about it, we shall recognize that they were inevitable in that system.

Powers are necessarily rivals and jealous of each other, even when their most evident common interest prescribes the closest union between them. Indeed, because these powers are not capable of being clearly defined, it is natural that each of them should claim exclusive domination. There can exist true combination, solid combination, only between positive capacities. Combination then becomes possible, and so to speak necessary, because each of these capacities tends of itself to confine itself within its natural role, which is always circumscribed as closely as possible. The claim to universality, which could alone disturb this natural arrangement, is revealed to all eyes as absurd, and consequently could never obtain a large enough number of supporters to become dangerous.

The communes, obviously too weak at the origin of their political existence, were forced to place themselves alongside leaders of the enemy camp in order to fight against the old system. They sought to profit from the divisions which had formed there, and their prudence was such that in fact they always profited from them. Their plan was quite simple: it consisted in constantly lending their support to the power which, in each era and in each country, was the most liberal, that is the most in conformity with their interests. This was the plan they constantly followed, by a wonderful kind of instinct, in all the partial crises which preceded the two great struggles of the sixteenth and seventeenth centuries. Thus their conduct, in these latter eras, was not in the least accidental; it derived from habits contracted over a long period.

That is what explains why in England the communes placed themselves alongside the lords against kings, whereas in France they united with royalty against feudalism. In more distant times, the communes, in France and in England, had in the same way embraced the cause of the spiritual power, because it was then the more liberal. Thus, in reality, it was not at all the communes who were instruments in the hands of the old powers; it is rather these powers themselves which ought to be considered as having served as instruments for the communes, even though they were moved by their own impetus. In fact, the attack on the old system occurred both through and for the communes.

Furthermore, in the two struggles of the sixteenth and seventeenth centuries, the communes exerted an influence that was wholly direct and purely derived from themselves. The two elements of the new system, industrial capacity and scientific capacity, each put in their share in this influence. Although they always acted concurrently, yet it was the second (scientific capacity) which particularly attached itself to the spiritual power, as the first (industrial capacity) did to the temporal power, just as the nature of things demanded. Each capacity fought hand to hand with the corresponding power, and (what deserves to be noticed) in the arguments then employed by the scientific capacity to overturn theological doctrines it was on theology itself that it at first saw itself as obliged to take its stand, or at least it believed itself forced to adjust its stance to fit the theological style. This is what is chiefly to be observed in the works of Chancellor Bacon. This fact, in the spiritual struggle, corresponds to that of the coalition of the communes with half of the military power in the temporal struggle.

We do not need to demonstrate the fundamental influence which the progress of the sciences of observation exerted on Luther's reformation, because no one today casts any doubt on it: it is enough for us to note it. As for the influence, less strong and less direct, of the progress of the manufacturing arts on this same reformation, the best historians who have dealt with this period have brought out a striking example, by pointing out the incontestable influence exerted here by the great boost given to commerce, and consequently to industry, by the discovery of America and of the route to India by the Cape of Good Hope, which was itself a consequence of the progress of the industrial arts combined with that of the sciences of observation.

Two other first-order discoveries, one in the arts, the other in the sciences, the one made around the end of the fifteenth century, the other about a century afterwards, helped ensure and hasten the decadence of the old system and helped give the struggle undertaken by the elements of the new system a course which was at once more direct, surer, calmer and more rapid.

The first was that of printing, which if it did not contribute to bringing the reformation about, at least served to disseminate it much more rapidly and more completely than would have happened otherwise. But that was not its most essential effect as far as the decadence of the old system is concerned.

We shall not repeat the very well-known arguments which show what an immense change this discovery introduced into the social order, by creating the sovereignty of public opinion. We shall consider it from the only perspective that concerns us here.

From this point of view, we can say: (i) that it assured the new system of the means to take the most direct and the most complete initiative to prepare the replacement of the old, without being obliged to continue to place itself under the protection of one or other of the powers to be extinguished; (ii) it largely eradicated the violent character that the struggle had had up to then, because it changed the attack into critique.

The second discovery of which I wish to speak is that of the true theory of astronomy, which Copernicus happened upon and Galileo proved and established.

The best minds do not ordinarily appreciate the true worth of the influence, which in reality was very powerful, exercised by the intellectual change which this theory brought about in relation to the radical destruction of the theological system. This influence is such that it alone would have sufficed to bring about the annihilation of this system. We shall content ourselves with indicating it by means of the following consideration, which each person can fully develop.

The entire theological system is founded on the supposition that the earth is made for man, and the whole universe for the earth: remove this supposition, and all supernatural doctrines collapse.

Theological supposition

collapses w/out it

And since Galileo demonstrated to us that our planet is one of the smallest, that it is in no way different from the others, that with the rest it turns about the sun; the hypothesis that the whole of nature is made for man clashes so openly with common sense, it is in such opposition with the facts, that it cannot avoid appearing absurd and being soon overturned, taking with it the beliefs of which it was the basis. In short, theological doctrines are absolutely incompatible with full and entire belief in modern astronomical theory, even in minds in which this conviction does not rest on knowledge of the demonstrations that establish it.

If we weigh this reflection sufficiently, we shall agree that the inquisition was doing its proper job in policing the spiritual power when it tried to stifle Galileo's theory at birth.

If we sum up everything we have said up to now, it follows that by the end of the seventeenth century there had been two partial attacks on the old system: one in the sixteenth century, against the spiritual power, the other in the seventeenth, against the temporal power.

At first sight, this dual attack might have seemed sufficient; but it was a long way from being so, for the system had been attacked in its elements and not as a whole: it had been beaten in detail, but it had still to be beaten as a system. Moreover, each particular struggle having taken place under the direction of a branch of the old powers, it had not had a clear enough character, it had not asserted itself firmly enough as a clash between one system and the elements of another. That was a second reason, distinct from the previous one, for the insufficiency of the first two conflicts.

Thus anyone who, at the end of the seventeenth century, properly understood the true state of things, could have predicted with complete assurance that the two partial attacks carried out up to then were only preparatory, and that in the following century the attack would be directed in a general way against the whole of the system, and that in the end it would be decisive in bringing about its fall. Such events were the inevitable consequence of all that had occurred since the eleventh century, and the immediate consequence of the two centuries which had just finished.

It would be superfluous here to go into any detail on events so near to us, which are present in everyone's memory. The eighteenth century was in fact what it had to be, the consequence, the complement, and the epitome of the two previous centuries.

As for the spiritual power, the principle of freedom of thought in religious matters (laid down by Luther, but initially in a very limited way) was extended to its furthest limit. The boldest application of this right went side by side with attempts made to establish it in all its latitude. Theological beliefs, subjected to examination, were entirely overturned, no doubt too imprudently, too precipitately, and too carelessly, with too absolute a neglect of the past and with views on the future that were too confused and too uncertain. But the fact is that they were overturned, and in such a way that they could not be restored, since criticism was pushed to the point of covering them with ridicule in the eyes of the least educated men. It is a fact that cannot be denied, and we do not judge this criticism, we observe it.

As for the temporal power, if we examine what happened in this respect in France – for that is where the whole of the eighteenth century should chiefly be observed – we shall see that feudalism, having lost in the previous century all its political power, in this lost all its civil esteem.

Royalty, which under Louis XIV had achieved the full and entire possession of the temporal power by means of the support that the communes had lent it, ceased to combine with them. This was a great mistake on its part.

Louis XIV committed a great error in joining with the nobility, which in the end resigned itself to adopting, in return for money and honours, a subordinate and insignificant political standing, appearing to have forgotten that it had marched hand in hand with royal authority.

If Louis XIV had not committed this major error; if he had abandoned to its destiny a power that had become obsolete, a power whose lot was irrevocably settled in the decrees of the human mind, and which he himself had effectively helped to destroy; if he had in short continued simply to follow the direction set out by the communes, he would no doubt have avoided all the misfortunes that later befell Louis XVI.

That was in fact what originally discredited royalty in the eyes of the communes, and which alienated them from it. The shame which later rebounded on royal power from the morals of the regent and the debauchery of Louis XV brought this discredit to its height. At the same time, as the philosophers had subjected the temporal power to the same scrutiny as the spiritual power, it did not hold out any better, not least because since the reformation it had largely been founded on the same doctrines.

Thus the eighteenth century brought criticism of the two powers to its furthest limits; and it completed the ruin of the old system in its elements and as a whole. A more detailed examination of the way in which this overthrow was conducted would be out of place here.

I shall merely indicate the influence which the immense and ever-growing progress made by the sciences of observation since Galileo was inevitably to exert on the destruction of theological doctrines. The discovery by Newton of a general physical law, the analysis undertaken by Franklin of the chief meteorological phenomenon,[3] as well as the invention of the means of subjecting it to the power of man, and – in short – all the remarkable discoveries made in such great numbers in that century in astronomy, in physics, in chemistry and in physiology, contributed more to the radical and irrevocable destruction of the theological system than all the writings of Voltaire and his co-workers, in spite of their prodigious influence. This has been inadequately appreciated both by the supporters of the old system and by its opponents.

The outbreak of the French Revolution was prepared or, properly speaking, made inescapably necessary by this state of things; from its origin it took a wrong path and royalty was overthrown.

Royalty did not take long to reconstitute itself, because as it was in France the head and the heart of the old system, it can only be extinguished along with that system; and because a system can be extinguished only when another already exists fully formed and is ready to replace it immediately.

The final result of all this great commotion was the abolition of privileges, the proclamation of the principle of unlimited freedom of conscience, and finally the establishment of the English constitution, bestowed by royal power itself.

The abolition of privileges only completed the ruin of feudalism, and completely reduced the temporal power to royal power alone.

---

[3] The reference here is to Franklin's identification of lightning with electricity, and his invention of the lightning conductor.

The proclamation of the principle of unlimited freedom of conscience totally and irrevocably annihilated the spiritual power.[b]

Finally, the establishment of the English constitution must be
considered from two different and in some ways opposed points of
view.

On the one hand, it continued the demolition of the old system,
by limiting royal power (which is today the only real relic of that
system) as far as was possible without abandoning that system.

On the other hand, by the establishment of a chamber representing public opinion, it instituted the true means of transition,
the means which allows us to arrive peacefully – without effort and
promptly – at the system which must follow, as soon as it is formed
and capable of taking effect.

Having arrived at the last term of the first series of observations,
I am going to sum up in a few words the consequences of this
survey.

My point of departure was this:

In the eleventh century, the feudal and theological system was
definitively constituted, as regards the temporal power and as
regards the spiritual power.

In the same era, the elements of a new social system came into
being, namely industrial capacity, or artisans (born of the enfranchisement of the communes) behind the temporal or military power;
and scientific capacity (born of the introduction of the sciences of
observation into Europe by the Arabs) behind the spiritual power.

These two systems coexisted for four or five hundred years without clashing openly, their forces being so unequal: the conflict was
prepared silently during this time.

---

[b] This proclamation made it impossible to establish any theological authority, political or simply moral; for once beliefs have been left to the arbitrary will of each
individual there will perhaps be no two professions of faith that are completely
identical, and each person's might vary from morning to evening, according to the
variations that might be inspired in him by the perpetually changing state of his
moral and physical affections as well as by the equally changeable social circumstances in which he successively finds himself.

In short it is clear that unlimited freedom of conscience and absolute theological
indifference amount to exactly the same thing in terms of their political consequences. In both cases, supernatural beliefs can no longer serve as the basis for
morality. This is a fact that, far from needing to be hidden, cannot be too often
repeated, since it proves the necessity of constituting morality on other principles,
on positive principles (that is, ones deduced from observation), and morality is the
basis, or rather the general bond, of social organization.

also review

From the beginning of the sixteenth century, there were three principal attacks by the elements of the new system against the old; two partial and one general: each of them occupied about a century.

The sixteenth century saw the attack on the spiritual power; the seventeenth century that on the temporal power; and finally the general and decisive attack on the old system took place during the eighteenth century; it ensured the fall of the theologico-military regime.

This is, without any exaggeration, the true state of the old system at present.

OMG harsh

On the one hand, no more doctrine: all the beliefs that served as its basis are extinguished or ready to be extinguished; thus the spiritual power can no longer exert any influence except on the most backward class of society.

On the other hand, the temporal power is reduced simply to one only of its two branches, and this branch, royal power, is reduced to the smallest dimensions it can have without dropping, as an inert mass, the whole of that old system that is suspended from it.

Finally, the old system today has no strength other than what is logically necessary to maintain order until the establishment of the new one; and it is highly doubtful whether it can continue to maintain it if this process is too long delayed.

I leave readers to judge, according to this exposition, whether the organization of the new system is an urgent matter, and whether artists, scientists and artisans are not committing a great mistake in slacking off in this respect.

This is in reality the present state of society, from the perspective of the old system. We shall soon know, through an examination of the second series of observations, if it is not more satisfying from the perspective of the new.

Second series

Just as the course of civilization seemed stormy to us in the preceding series, so we shall find it calm in the one we are about to examine. So far we have considered only the successive disorganization of the old social system. But at the same time as this decadence was occurring, society was little by little organizing itself in all its parts in accordance with a new system, which is today sufficiently developed to be capable of replacing the old, which has reached the stage of extreme obsolescence. It is this gradual development of the new system which it remains for us to observe and explain.

Let us first of all restate the point of departure.

We have seen that in the eleventh century, at the very moment when the old system was successfully constituting itself, the elements of a new social organization had come into being. These elements were, in the temporal domain, industrial capacity (born of the enfranchisement of the communes), and, in the spiritual domain, scientific capacity (the result of the introduction of the positive sciences into Europe by the Arabs).

If some man of genius had at that time been able to observe this state of things with the necessary knowledge, he would have infallibly foreseen, at its origin, the whole of the great revolution that has occurred since; he could have recognized that the two elements that had just been created inevitably tended to overturn the two powers whose combination formed the system then in force.

[margin note: possible to find guiding thread]

He would equally have foreseen that these two elements developed more and more at the expense of the two powers, in such a way as gradually to constitute a system which was in the end to substitute itself for the old one.

Let us begin by concentrating on clearly stating this fundamental insight which will show us that the germ of this second series existed fully in the first term of the series. We shall then examine the way in which the organization of the new system has actually operated.

This dual tendency of the new system (equally necessary from both points of view) to destroy the old system and to replace it resulted directly from the two following causes:

In the first place, by the very nature of things, industrial capacity and scientific capacity are antagonists of military power and theological power respectively.

[margin note: naturally against]

In the second place, from the way in which these two capacities had just been constituted, they were established outside the old system, being possessed by classes that were distinct and independent, in this respect, from the temporal power and the spiritual power.

It was this last circumstance which stamped the two capacities with the fundamental and indelible character of opposition to the old system, at the same time as it guaranteed them the future possibility of realizing their complete development.

So little attention has up to now been paid to this essential observation, that we must now develop it at some length.

In the state of society that today still exists in Russia, where all industrial activities are directed in this last resort by men of the feudal class, industrial capacity does not at all appear to be by nature opposed to military power or to correspond necessarily to a distinct social system. It has not yet acquired its own distinctive character. Artisans are only passive instruments in the hands of military men. It is the same for scientific capacity when the cultivation of the sciences is still in the hands of the theological power, which was the case at the origin of civilization in the old theocracies of the Orient, and which has continued to the present in China. Scientific capacity is then in reality only an instrument of domination for the priesthood.

That was precisely the state of things in Europe up to the historic period we took as our point of departure.

Before the enfranchisement of the communes, the small amount of agricultural, commercial and manufacturing industry which already existed was in its entirety, if not controlled by, at least absolutely dependent upon the temporal power.

In the same way, before the introduction of the positive sciences into Europe by the Arabs, the small amount of extant knowledge was wholly in the hands of the spiritual power.

Let us note that this state of things, as long as it survived, ensured that the life of the old system was indestructible, not only because the two elements which could lead to a new system were absolutely at the mercy of the two old powers; but also because, for this very reason, the two capacities were for ever arrested in their development.

When the sciences and the arts are considered exclusively as instruments, they can never rise above a very low level, as we can see in China and in India.

By contrast, once the communes were enfranchised, and once the positive sciences were exclusively cultivated by men of a secular outlook – which occurred soon after their introduction into Europe – the face of things was totally altered.

These two great events first of all allowed the arts and sciences to move freely towards their fullest development; they left no other limits on the course of the two positive capacities than the life-span of the human race.

In the second place, from this moment, industrial capacity and scientific capacity, freed for ever from the old system, solidly established themselves outside it, and acquired their own characteristic and independent existence. And they could not cease to be instruments for the old system without becoming its enemies: this is a case of the adage, *qui non est mecum, contra me est.*[4]

[margin handwritten: separate from old enemies]

This fundamental revolution therefore created two new forces in society, the forces of industry and science, which from their origin, and by virtue of this same origin, have been for ever stamped with the dual character of being antagonists of the old political order, and elements of a new order.

The contempt and hatred that feudalism and theology have constantly displayed since that time, the first for the industrial arts, the other for the sciences of observation, have only had the effect of reinforcing this opposition and making it more clear-cut.

Thus the change that occurred in the eleventh century contained at one and the same time the principle of the destruction of the old system and the germ of a new system.

[margin handwritten: germ of new system]

All that has occurred since that time has been the simple consequence and development of this dual original state of society. In the previous series we have considered this development from the first point of view. We are now going to concern ourselves exclusively with following it and studying it from the second perspective.

It would certainly be absurd to think that the successive organization of the new system was conducted by scientists, artists and artisans in accordance with a premeditated plan, followed unwaveringly from the eleventh century to the present. At no time has the progress of civilization obeyed so systematic a course, conceived in advance by a man of genius, and adopted by the masses.[*c*] That is

---

[4] Luke xi.23: 'he that is not with me is against me'.

[*c*] The great error of the legislators and philosophers of antiquity consisted precisely in seeking to subject the course of civilization to their systematic views, whereas their plans ought on the contrary to have been subordinated to it. This error, however, was very pardonable and very natural on their part; for at that time men were still too close to the origin of civilization to be able to observe that civilization follows a course, or to be able to recognize the course it follows; still less to have been able to see that this course is beyond our control.

Obviously we could arrive at this truth only *a posteriori* and not *a priori*. In other words, politics could become a science only by being based on observations, and observations could only exist after a very prolonged period of civilization. A

even completely impossible in the nature of things; for the superior law of the progress of the human mind leads and dominates everything; for it, men are only instruments. Although this force derives from us, it is not any more in our power to remove ourselves from its influence or to control its action, than it is to change at will the original impetus which makes our planet revolve around the sun.

Secondary effects alone are subject to our control. All we can do is obey this law (our true providence) intelligently, understanding the course it prescribes to us, instead of being pushed about by it blindly; and it is worth saying in passing that that is precisely what constitutes the great philosophical progress reserved for our age. But in spite of that, when we see in the political order a series of events which are connected in the same way as if the men who were their agents had acted in accordance with a plan, may we not employ this assumption so as better to bring out this connectedness?[d] This is to follow – but departing much less from reality – the usage of the natural sciences; where, to present a group of phenomena more clearly, we attribute systematic intentions and designs even to unorganized matter. Besides, an inevitable necessity which connects a series of events, and a preconceived plan which directs them, are very similar in their consequences, and we shall see that the course followed by the new system had been necessitated by the situation of its elements at their origin.

The following may be regarded as the plan which the communes followed from the time of their enfranchisement to prepare, little by little, the organization of society on foundations that were characteristic of them:

system of social order would have to be established, it would have to be accepted by a very large population and be composed of several great nations, and this system would have to have endured for a prolonged period before a theory could be founded on this great experience.

[d] I shall moreover allow myself to note that, if it is true that a science becomes positive only in founding itself exclusively on observed facts whose accuracy is generally recognized, it is equally incontestable (according to the history of the human mind in all positive directions) that any branch whatever of our knowledge can become a science only at the time when, by means of hypothesis, we have connected all the facts which serve as its basis.

Thus when politics has become a science, it is certain that hypotheses will be employed in it, in the same way as in other sciences, and that they will be employed in the spirit I have just indicated.

To concern themselves solely with acting on nature, to modify it as much as possible in the manner that is most advantageous to the human race; to seek to act upon men only to lead them to co-operate with this general action on things.

This is, in brief, the simple course which scientists and artisans have invariably followed since the origin, by setting themselves a single goal: the former to study nature in order to understand it, the latter to apply this understanding to the satisfaction of the needs and desires of man.

[margin note: ONE GOAL! 2 Pts]

This course was so sensible that a better one could not have been chosen if it had been possible for scientists and artisans to act in accordance with preconceived views freely discussed from the outset.

In the end this plan has been found so perfect that all that remains for us to do today is to apply it (without changing anything) to the direction of the whole of society, in the same way as our fathers gradually succeeded in bringing into conformity with it all parts of social action considered in isolation.

It is easy to explain why this plan had to be followed without ever having been formulated, or even felt by anyone. Having given this explanation, we shall sketch the reasons for the success it obtained.

The communes, by the very fact of their enfranchisement, found themselves rid of the individual dependence that previously weighed on each of their members; but they remained subject to collective dependence imposed on the mass of artisans and scientists by the mass of military men and theologians.

This dependence was so great at the origin, and the communes were so weak, that they could obviously not conceive the idea of removing themselves from it. This obstacle, which at first sight would appear to have been necessarily harmful to them, was precisely what ensured the success of their efforts: it prevented them from going astray, and forced them by invincible necessity to follow the course which was basically the best. Not being able to contemplate sharing authority, or even removing themselves from collective despotism, the communes tended only to profit from the degree of individual liberty they had obtained to develop industrial capacity and scientific capacity to the utmost.

[margin note: course of history]

improve mankind

Scientists and artisans sought only to act upon nature; the former to penetrate to a knowledge of its laws by means of observations and experiments, the latter to apply this knowledge to the production of necessary, useful or agreeable objects. In doing that they were all only following the natural tendency that leads us towards the improvement of our lot; for by the very fact of their political inferiority, acting upon nature was the only way open to the communes to improve their social condition. We can thus see quite clearly what force obliged the communes to follow without realizing it the plan I have just indicated.

To see how far this plan was in conformity with their true interests, let us first make an assumption: let us accept that the state of things was not, at the beginning, as I have just described it; let us imagine that the communes, immediately after their enfranchisement, had obtained a full and complete share in the exercise of the supreme political power then existing. What would they have done with this power? What would have happened? Here, probably, is the answer.

This participation in authority would have made them lose sight of their true object, which was the development of industrial capacity and scientific capacity. This development would at least have been far slower, and consequently the communes would have remained much longer in subordination to military power and theological power. For it was only by a great development of the strength of their common interest, combined with the power of proof, that they could hope to struggle with any marked degree of success against physical force combined with the force of superstition. Thus we can see that the communes have until quite recent times shown little eagerness, in France and in England, to enjoy the share of legislative authority which had been bestowed upon them in these two countries by one of the branches of the temporal power during the disputes between royalty and feudalism.[e]

---

[e] The coalition of the communes with one half of the temporal power against the other half, in France and in England, was really very useful to artisans and scientists; but this is not the point of view we are examining here. It is in relation to the destruction of the old system that this coalition must be considered, and not relative to the organization of the new one. This is how I considered it in my first series of observations.

As for the fact that the communes showed little eagerness to enjoy the share of legislative authority which had been procured for them by their allies in the old system, this was very visible in England, where nevertheless the communes worked

Let us now examine directly the advantages of the course followed by the communes.

Without concerning themselves with the way in which the military and the theologians directed the overall shape of society, and abstracting, so to speak, from the old system, the communes organized all private work (arrangement of which was left at their free disposal) with the simple goal of acting on nature. This sensible line of conduct ensured not only that they did not displease, but that they were agreeable to the existing powers, who would give them all encouragement compatible with the exercise of authority. There was still more: they were certain gradually to succeed – by the exercise of greater action upon nature, and by the wealth as well as the esteem they derived from it – in steadily redeeming themselves from the major part of the authority that weighed upon them.

Finally, they would also count on the fact that, by the steady increase of industrial capacity and scientific capacity, they would acquire a progressively growing strength which would gradually allow them to deal as equals with their rulers, and later even to gain the upper hand over them, which is what has actually become possible today.

how to succeed ✗ ✗

Those who derive all their happiness from the exercise of arbitrary authority solely for the pleasure of exercising it are fortunately rare anomalies in human nature. If the majority of men desire power when it is within their reach, it is not at all as a goal but as a means. It is less through love of ruling[f] than because they find it

power = usually a means (not goal)

much more steadily for this kind of political progress than elsewhere. We know that before the era when they began to obtain a deliberative voice in voting taxes, they considered it a very onerous obligation to send deputies to parliament, because the military men called them there only to let them know what the communes could pay, in order to know how far they could pillage them.

[f] This love of ruling, which is certainly an indestructible element in man, has, however, been to a large extent quashed by the progress of civilization; or, at least, its disadvantages have almost disappeared in the new system. In fact the development of action upon nature has changed the direction of this sentiment, by transferring it onto things. The desire to command men has gradually been transformed into the desire to make or unmake nature at will.

From this moment the need to rule, which is innate in all men, has ceased to be harmful, or at least we can glimpse the time when it will cease to be harmful, and when it will become useful. It is thus that civilization has improved the moral side of man, not only in relation to the intellect, but also as regards the passions. Although, in accordance with the laws of human organization, this second order of vital functions is not perfectible by itself, it is through the influence which the first order exercises over it.

convenient – because of their laziness or their incapacity – to make others work to procure them their pleasures, instead of participating in this work.

In the last analysis, the chief desire of almost all individuals is not to act on man, but on nature. There is no one, as it were, who would not eagerly renounce the most absolute authority, when the exercise of that authority would exclude the enjoyment of the advantages of civilization, which are the result of action exerted upon things. The English nabob, who has made his fortune in Bengal and who exercises the most unlimited power over thousands of Indians, longs for the moment when he can return to Europe in order to enjoy the amenities of life, even though he knows that in England the least arbitrary act towards the lowest sailor would involve him in risks and dangers. We can therefore be certain of success with the majority of men when we suggest that they should sacrifice a part of their right to command in return for a certain amount of power over nature.

The success of the political plan followed by the communes since their enfranchisement was therefore founded upon a law derived from human organization.

We are now in the position of having explained by means of the foregoing the cause of all important progress which the elements of the new social system have so far achieved in their gradual organization. This progress stemmed essentially from the consistency with which the communes followed the plan – so simple and so perfect – that we have just set out. Events independent of this plan accelerated its success; but it is always to the plan that this success must in the last analysis be traced back. It therefore only remains for us to recapitulate this progress.

To avoid any confusion in this exposition of the development of the new system in its temporal and spiritual aspects, we must first distinguish the progress made by the mass of the communes from that made by their temporal leaders and their spiritual leaders. Besides, we shall consider the civil progress of the new system separately from the political progress. We understand by civil progress of the new system, its distinctive development, considered in abstraction from any relationship with the old system; and by political progress, the influence which the old system allowed it to assume in the formation of the general political plan, as well as in the share of legislative authority which the new system has obtained.

Let us first consider the civil and political progress of the new system in the temporal sphere; and in the first place the civil progress.

This is not the place to retrace, even in outline, the truly immense progress made by the industrial arts since the enfranchisement of the communes: let us restrict ourselves to considering it as it relates to the organization of the new system.

Since that time, industrial capacity has developed in ways that the most active imagination could not accurately picture. All the arts known up to then have been prodigiously improved, and an incomparably greater host of new arts have been created. Agriculture has multiplied its production to an enormous extent. Commercial relations have been incalculably improved, and at the same time they have grown considerably, especially since the discovery of the New World. In short, the power of the human race over nature has increased to an inestimable extent; or, rather, it was then that it was really created.

[margin note: improve-ments! — art — agriculture — comm. relations]

As a result of this increased power, a much greater part of the human race in civilized countries was securely and abundantly provided with the necessities of life, even though the population grew considerably; and the use of objects of comfort and convenience has grown proportionately.

Such were the chief consequences of this progress for the temporal organization of the new system.

The communes progressively acquired a preponderant influence and esteem. Everything in society fell under their control; all real strength came into their hands; even military strength was subordinated to them after the invention of gunpowder.

On the one hand, the discovery of gunpowder eliminated the physical superiority which arms gave to the military over artisans, and it ensured the latter of the means to protect themselves against violence without needing to receive a military education. On the other hand, it made the whole system of war dependent upon the industrial arts and the sciences of observation.

At the same time, since war has thus become more and more costly as well, it can no longer be waged without loans, for which military power is heavily dependent upon the communes. In short, things have steadily reached the point where war could not take place if industrial capacity and scientific capacity were to refuse their co-operation.

The political progress of the new system, in the temporal domain, has been the direct and necessary consequence of its civil progress. As the communes acquired more wealth, more esteem and more civil importance, they also gained in influence over the general direction of society, and in direct political authority.

It is chiefly in England that the course followed by the communes is to be observed in this respect, because it is there that it has been most manifest.[g]

The communes having begun, in the parliament of England, by obtaining a sort of consultative voice in voting taxes, they gradually succeeded in obtaining a deliberative voice, and at last it subsequently occurred that voting taxation was specially accorded to them. This exclusive right was laid down as a fundamental principle, and irrevocably, as a result of the revolution of 1688.

At the same time, the influence of the communes on the formation of the plan of general politics was ever greater. In the same period, it reached the point, in England, when the old system admitted the principle that social prosperity is based on industry, and that consequently the political plan must be conceived in the interest of the communes. From this dual point of view, the modification of the old system in favour of the new was pushed as far as it can be as long as society in its overall shape remains subject to the old system.

This step taken by the communes was certainly most essential, but it is also most essential not to exaggerate its importance; it is most essential not to see in a simple modification a total change of system.

[g] Almost immediately after their enfranchisement, the communes were called – in France as in England – to participate in the formation of estates-general; but in France this had almost no consequences.

I shall seize this opportunity to say that I did not think I should take into consideration the attempts made soon after their enfranchisement in almost all points in civilized Europe – and especially in Italy and Germany – to organize industrial societies. These attempts, which were only the dawn of the new system, left no durable trace; they did not and could not have an organic character.

In such a rapid exposition, they would have cast confusion over our ideas rather than illuminating them.

In principle, to accord to the communes the exclusive right to vote taxes should have been to invest them with supreme political power. But in reality this right has up to now been of very little use to the communes, because in fact it has not been exercised by them. The so-called House of *Commons* has essentially been only a sort of appendix to royalty and feudalism; it has been a mere instrument for the old system. In the same way, the axiom accepted by the temporal power in England that the political plan must be conceived in the interest of industry has been of only very modest benefit to the communes up to the present. The reason is that, since it was for the old system to form this plan, and since that system must necessarily retain the same function until the new one was definitively organized, it could offer the communes, to contribute to their happiness, only its own means of action, that is force and cunning. It is in this way that, since the famous Navigation Act, the temporal power has conducted systematic wars, and thought up machiavellian plans, with the intention of serving the interests of the communes.

The establishment of the parliamentary regime in England must therefore be considered only as having modified the old system as much as possible, and constituted the means of passing to the new system. It is simply from this point of view that it was of any use to the communes; for if it is considered in itself, in an absolute sense, its consequences were at the very least as harmful as they were advantageous.

France, by her recent adoption of the English constitution, has put herself on a level with England, from the dual perspective which we have just examined. But as this change took place at a much more advanced period of civilization, it was much more complete. Feudalism having been overturned before the parliamentary regime was established, the modification of the old system was far greater than in England. The principle which considers the interest of the communes as the goal and the regulator of political combinations assumed a much broader, more general and more preponderant character.

Finally, by the fact that this was implemented in France at a time when the need for a complete change of political system was profoundly felt, the transitional character attached to the parliamentary regime became much more pronounced.

Let us now observe the civil and political progress of the new system in its spiritual dimension.

Before the introduction of the positive sciences into Europe, all our particular knowledge, as well as our general knowledge, was wholly theological and metaphysical. The little reasoning about nature that then took place was solely founded upon religious beliefs. But since that historic period, the natural sciences have begun to be based more and more upon observations and experiments. Nevertheless, they remained mingled with superstition and metaphysics, up to quite recent times. Only around the end of the sixteenth century and in the first years of the seventeenth did they succeed in freeing themselves wholly from theological beliefs. The period when they began to become truly positive is to be traced back to Bacon, who gave the first signal for this great revolution; to Galileo, his contemporary, who gave its first example; and finally to Descartes, who irrevocably destroyed the mental yoke of authority in scientific matters. It was then that natural philosophy came into being and that scientific capacity assumed its true character, that of the spiritual element of a new social system.

From that time, the sciences successively became positive in the natural order they had to follow, that is according to the closeness of their relations with man. It is thus that astronomy first of all, then physics, later chemistry, and finally today physiology have been constituted as positive sciences. This revolution is therefore fully carried out in all our particular knowledge, and it is nowadays clearly occurring in philosophy, morals and politics, over which the influence of theological doctrines and metaphysics has already been destroyed in the eyes of all educated men, though they are not founded on observation. That is the only thing which is missing in the spiritual development of the new social system.

As the sciences have become positive, and as – in consequence – they have made ever-increasing progress, a larger and larger mass of scientific ideas has entered our common education, at the same time as religious doctrines gradually lost their influence. Special schools have been set up for the sciences, in which the influence of theology and metaphysics is, so to speak, null and void. Finally the state of minds has changed so much in this respect that today each individual's system of ideas, from the least educated to the most enlightened citizen, is derived almost wholly from the positive sciences, and the old beliefs in comparison occupy only a very small place, even in the classes among whom these beliefs have retained most power.

One can say without exaggeration that the only influence religious doctrines have on our minds is that which stems from the fact that morality has remained attached to them. This influence will necessarily remain until the time when morality has undergone the revolution that has already occurred in all our particular branches of knowledge as they became positive. From that moment, the power of theological beliefs will evaporate for ever; for it is most evident that this state of things in which all parts of our system of ideas have become positive, whilst the ideas destined to serve as a general bond remain superstitious, could only be transitory; otherwise there would be an implied contradiction in the general course of things.

The political progress of the new system, in its spiritual dimension as in the temporal, has been the inevitable consequence of its civil progress.

Since the establishment of the first schools for the teaching of the sciences of observation, which occurred in the thirteenth century, royal power in France and feudalism in England have constantly and increasingly encouraged the sciences and raised the political standing of scientists.

In France, royalty increasingly acquired the habit of consulting them on matters within their competence, and of seeking their approval, which was implicitly to recognize the superiority of positive scientific ideas over theological and metaphysical ideas.

Gradually, what our kings had at first considered only as a praiseworthy thing to do, they came to look upon as a duty, and they recognized the obligation to encourage the sciences and to submit to the decisions of scientists. The establishment of the Academy of Sciences, instituted under Louis XIV by his minister Colbert, is a solemn declaration of this principle. At the same time, this measure was a first step towards the political organization of the spiritual element of the new system.

The number of academies has multiplied prodigiously since that time, on all points of the territory of Europe, and through the influence of scientific capacity on our minds. This capacity has been constituted in a regular and legal manner. Its political authority has increased to an analogous degree; it has exerted a direct and

ever-growing influence on the direction of national education. If we
consider in this respect the legal powers with which the first class
of the Institute[5] is nowadays invested, we shall agree that they are
about as extensive as they can be as long as the body which exercises
them is not entrusted with the teaching of morality.[h] And this is
what can only take place at a time when morality has become a
positive science. Thus in this respect, as in all the others we have
so far considered, the old system has given way to the new, and has
cleared its path as far as possible. We can go further only by
organizing the new system.

It is essential to observe that at the same time that the power
of science has been constituted and increasingly extended in each
European nation considered in isolation, the scientific forces of the
different countries have also co-operated. In this respect the sense
of nationality has been totally set aside, and scientists from all parts
of Europe have formed an indissoluble league, which has always
tended to Europeanize any scientific progress made in any particular
place. This holy alliance, against which the old system has no means
of resistance, is in a stronger position to bring about the organization of the new system than the coalition of all the bayonets in
Europe could be to prevent it or even to slow it down.

The same co-operation has indeed taken place, up to a certain
point, among the industrial capacities of the different European
nations, but this has been only to a far smaller degree. The feeling
of national rivalry, the inspiration of a fierce and absurd nationalism,
created by the old system and carefully sustained by it, have
retained up to the present a great influence as far as the temporal

---

[5] The first class of the Institut de France was the Académie des Sciences. It had
the right to make recommendations for appointments to university chairs in the
sciences, and this seems to be one of the powers to which Comte refers.

[h] It is clear, in principle, that the supreme direction of national education and the
teaching of morality must be in the same hands: to separate them would be absurd.
Thus, as long as morality continues to be based solely on religious beliefs, it is
inevitable that the general direction of education will belong in the last analysis to
a theological body, or at least to the theological spirit.
  The men who today rise up so brusquely against the Jesuits, against the
Missionaries and other religious corporations, ought therefore to realize that the
only way to eliminate the remaining influence of these societies is to found morality
upon observation of the facts. Until this sort of task has been accomplished, all
these protests will be more or less useless, because they largely occur at the wrong
time.

domain is concerned. This is why the league of the different European nations to organize the new system can only begin with the spiritual domain. The coalition of temporal capacities can only come about after and as a result of this first coalition.

Finally, it is important to observe that as the two elements of the new system have each separately made national progress and European progress towards their final political organization, co-operation between these two elements, and consequently the formation of the system, has also occurred more and more. An intermediate class between scientists, artists and artisans – the class of engineers – has come into being; and we could regard the co-operation of the two capacities as having begun from this moment. It became greater and greater, to the point where today, in the common opinion of scientists as in that of artisans (though to a lesser degree in the latter), the true destiny of the sciences and the arts is to co-operate to modify nature to the advantage of man, the former by studying it in order to understand it, the latter by applying this understanding.

Numerous public and private establishments, principally in France and in England, have brought this principle to life by organizing the beginnings of co-operation. Among them are, in France, the Conservatoire des Arts et Métiers and the different schools connected with it, the Société d'Encouragement pour l'Industrie, the Ecole des Ponts et Chaussées, etc.

Thus not only has each of the two elements of the new system tended in turn towards its complete organization and in the end prevailed over the corresponding element in the old system, but their co-operation has made ever-increasing progress, which has prepared them to co-ordinate their activities to govern society.

In all the preceding, we have considered only the civil and political progress made by the temporal and spiritual leaders of the new system. It remains for us to observe the steps taken by the mass of members of the communes towards the new social organization.

These steps have been of two kinds: the first have consisted in the capacity acquired by the mass of members of the communes, in the temporal and spiritual domains, to live under the new regime; the others relate to the gradual co-ordination of the mass under the new temporal and spiritual leaders.

A population must have acquired a certain degree of temporal and spiritual capacity if it is to be able to live under a system of social order in which it is not subjected, in the temporal domain, to the rule of physical force, and in the spiritual domain to that of blind beliefs. A man who in the temporal domain has not contracted certain habits of order, economy and love of work, and who in the spiritual domain does not possess a certain degree of education and foresight, is not in a state to be emancipated: he indispensably needs to be led to the edge. It is the same with a people: as long as it has not fulfilled these conditions, it cannot be governed other than in an arbitrary manner. It is thus, for example, that the serfs of Russia, who eat seed corn out of pressing need, are still incapable even of enjoying individual liberty. To try to emancipate them before they have contracted better habits would be truly absurd, and could not succeed. Whereas in France, where the entire mass of the nation is able to endure hunger in the presence of seed corn without touching it, the people no longer needs to be governed (that is, commanded). It is enough, for the maintenance of order, that affairs of common interest should be administered.

In the same way, in the spiritual domain, a people who, for example, had sufficient belief in wizards to let themselves be guided by them in important matters, would need to be governed arbitrarily in matters of the mind by more enlightened men. They could not be left to themselves without harm to their own interests. But it is obvious that as soon as the mass of a people are in a state to act, in the ordinary business of life, in accordance with their own knowledge, and consequently have satisfied the two conditions we laid down, they do not in the least need to be governed: they can act by themselves, without any threat to order. We can even add that any act of command, exerted over them at a time when it has become useless, tends to disturb order rather than helping to maintain it.

Since the enfranchisement of the communes, the mass of the French population have gradually contracted the habits and acquired sufficient knowledge to live under the new system. The abolition of slavery in itself made all individuals proprietors: since then there have been no more real proletarians, in the strict meaning of the word. It is even relevant to observe that industrial property, which was born out of the enfranchisement, by its nature demands a much greater capacity than territorial property, as it has existed since then. For the latter, when it exists separately from cultivation of the land, demands no other ability than that of enjoying one's income with sufficient moderation so as not to eat into one's capital. It is the farmer who needs capacity, not the owner of the land.

Having become proprietors, the people gradually contracted all the habits of love of order and of work, all those habits of foresight and respect for property;[i] and at the same time it quite widely acquired – in France, in England, and in the north of Germany – the first stages of education.

No doubt much remains to be done in these two respects, and especially in the second. But progress has been great enough for the people no longer to need to be governed by force and by beliefs. They have acquired the necessary capacity to become associates, by living under the new system, in which the action of government is to be reduced to what is essential to institute a proper co-ordination of work contributing to the general action of men upon nature, which is the ultimate goal of the system.

In reality, peace is today essentially maintained only by new habits; the military apparatus of the temporal power contributes to it only incidentally,[j] in the same way as the infernal apparatus of the spiritual power.

Let us now examine in what way the population has been organized step by step by the new temporal and spiritual leaders.

Before the enfranchisement of the communes, the mass of the people were in the position of having the military as their sole and permanent leaders in the temporal domain. Since enfranchisement, by contrast, the people have gradually detached themselves from these leaders, and have at the same time organized themselves under the direction of industrial leaders. They contracted towards them habits of subordination and discipline which, though not strictly necessary, were wholly sufficient to maintain order in work and smooth harmony in society.

---

[i] When, in the frightful famine of 1794, at the moment when the lowest class of the people were all-powerful, we see that same class dying of hunger in their thousands without an instant's disturbance to order in this respect, we can rightly say that the French people have learnt how to respect property.

[j] The action of the old system is still indispensable for the maintenance of order; but not in the sense we have just considered. Rather, its importance lies only in preventing schemers and men of ambition from disturbing tranquillity by contending for a power which will excite their desires until it is extinguished by the definitive organization of the new system. But it is not the people who thus aim at power, it is the idle and parasitic class of society, that is to say today the old feudalism, and the feudalism of Bonaparte.

The moment of the complete separation of the people from the military leaders can be traced to the origin of the institution of permanent and paid armies under Charles VII. In the time that passed from enfranchisement to the birth of this institution, the people were more or less equally co-ordinated under the two kinds of leaders. For all the usual peaceful work, they were under the direction of industrial leaders; but for military work and exercises they were, in general, under the command of military leaders.

Once permanent and paid armies were established, because the profession of soldier had come to belong to a particular and separate section of the population, the mass of the people no longer had any connection with military leaders and were now organized only industrially. Someone who became a soldier no longer regarded himself and was no longer regarded as belonging to the people. He passed from the ranks of the new system into those of the old; having belonged to the commune, he became feudal, and that was that: it was he who denatured himself, and not the system to which he previously belonged.

Thus this institution of permanent armies, which today has become through the progress of civilization so onerous and so useless, was an indispensable intermediary for the realization of the organization of the new system.

If we consider the state of the people nowadays, we shall see that in the temporal sphere they are actually no longer in direct and continuous relations with anyone but the industrial leaders. If you follow in your mind the daily relations of any worker, whether in agriculture or in manufacturing or in commerce, you will find that he is habitually in contact with – and subordination to – only the agricultural, manufacturing or commercial leaders, and not at all, for example, with the great lord who is proprietor of the land, or the idle capitalist to whom the factory or the firm belong, in whole or in part. His relations with society's military leaders all fall within the general relations of the new system with the old; he has none of any other kind.

This is the place to comment, in relation to the people, on the fundamental difference that exists – to their advantage – between their present co-ordination *vis-à-vis* their industrial leaders, and their former subordination to military leaders. This difference brings out one of the most important and most fortunate contrasts between the old system and the new.

In the old system, the people were *regimented* under their leaders; in the new, they are *co-ordinated* with them. The military leaders *commanded* whereas the industrial leaders *direct*. In the first case the people were *subjects*, in the second they are *partners*. This is actually the admirable character of industrial combinations, that those who participate in them are, in reality, all collaborators, all associates, from the simplest labourer to the richest manufacturer and the most enlightened engineer. *[work together]*

In a society which includes men who bring neither capacity nor any other kind of stake, there are necessarily masters and slaves; otherwise the workers would not be dupes enough to agree to such an arrangement if they could get out of it. We cannot even conceive such a society beginning other than through force. But in a co-operative arrangement where all bring a capacity and a stake, there is a real association, and there exists no inequality other than that of capacities and that of stakes, which are both necessary (that is inevitable), and it would be absurd, ridiculous and harmful to seek to eliminate it. *[→ should stay this way]* *[inequality of capacities ONLY]*

Each person obtains a degree of importance and profits proportionate to his capacity and his stake: this constitutes the highest degree of equality which is possible and desirable. This is the fundamental character of industrial societies, and that is what the people have gained by organizing themselves in relation to the leaders of arts and manufactures. Their new leaders exercise no command over them other than that which is strictly necessary to maintain good order at work; that is, very little. Industrial capacity is by nature just as reluctant to exercise arbitrary power as to endure it. Besides, let us not forget that in a society of workers, everything naturally tends towards order; disorder in the last analysis always comes from layabouts. *[little control over people → bare min.]* *[ORDER → reason!]*

Let us finally observe that the progress of industry, the sciences and the fine arts, by multiplying the means of subsistence, by diminishing the number of the idle, by enlightening minds and by polishing manners, tends increasingly to eliminate the three greatest causes of disorder: poverty, idleness and ignorance.

We have observations to make for the spiritual domain that are analogous to those which have just been made for the temporal.

Before the introduction of the positive sciences into Europe, or – to be more accurate – before the sciences had passed from the hands of the clergy into those of laymen (an event which followed the first very closely), the mass of the people were organized spiritually by their relations with their theological leaders. The people believed them at their word; they consulted them on everything, and blindly relied on their decisions; the doctrines it suited the theological leaders to establish became those of the people. In short, the people habitually had an absolute trust in and a completely unlimited mental subordination towards the theological leaders. But, from the moment that the positive sciences had reached a certain level of development, this trust and this respect were gradually withdrawn from the clergy and steadily transferred to the scientists.

This change was powerfully supported by the analogous change that had already occurred in the temporal sphere. The people, organized industrially, soon noticed that their ordinary manufacturing work had no connection with theological ideas, and that they could derive from the theologians no real knowledge about the objects of their daily occupations. Everywhere where they could be in contact with scientists, whether directly or indirectly, they lost the habit of consulting priests, and took to getting into contact with those who possessed positive knowledge. No doubt this relationship is still far from being as close as it could and should be, and that stems chiefly not from the people's lack of desire for instruction, but from their lack of means of instruction and from the lack of care we take to enable them to acquire the knowledge which would be useful to them. The people are, on the contrary, eager for instruction: much more so than the idle folk in our salons, because their work brings its necessity home to them at every moment. Wherever they found the opportunity to study, they have studied. But although the influence of scientific capacity on the people is still very weak, in comparison with what it might be, it is no less true that it is much greater than we usually imagine. Salient and incontestable facts prove that the people today place the same degree of confidence in the unanimous opinion of scientists that in the Middle Ages they placed in the decisions of the spiritual power.

Thus, for example, for about a century, the people have unanimously ceased to believe that the earth does not move. They have accepted the modern theory of astronomy, and attach as much certainty to it as they ever attached to the old religious beliefs. What is the cause of this revolution in popular opinions? Is it because the people have read the proofs that establish the theory of the movement of the earth? Certainly not, for these proofs are understood by perhaps only three thousand individuals in the whole of the French population. The people's confidence obviously stems from the unanimity they have recognized in the opinions of scientists on this point of doctrine.

If we likewise take all the discoveries in the sciences of observation that have today been popularized, we can see that they all became so in the same way. It is in this way that the people have in turn accepted the circulation of the blood, the identity between lightning and electricity, etc., etc. Moreover, in the sciences, all those who are not capable of understanding proofs belong to 'the people'. The same confidence which has led society people to accept the analysis of air and water, the law of universal gravitation, the decomposition of light, and so many other discoveries in astronomy, physics, chemistry and physiology will also ensure their acceptance by the people a little later.

It is therefore proved, by means of the most palpable facts, that the people are today spiritually trusting and subordinate towards their scientific leaders, just as they are temporally towards their industrial leaders, and I consequently have the right to conclude that trust is organized in the new system as well as subordination.

We must also observe here that the confidence of the people in their new spiritual leaders is of a wholly different nature from that which they had in the old system for their theological leaders. That consisted in a totally blind mental submission, which demanded in each individual an absolute abnegation of his own reason. The confidence in the opinions of scientists has a quite different character. It is assent given to propositions about things that are capable of verification, propositions accepted unanimously by men who have acquired and proved the necessary capacity to pass judgement.

In truth, the fact is accepted without proofs; but is accepted in this way only by those whose reason is judged incapable of following the demonstrations that establish these truths. This confidence always implicitly embraces the express reservation of the right of contradiction in the event that new demonstrations are produced that prove that it is ill-founded, or in the event that the believer acquires sufficient knowledge to combat received opinions. The people are therefore far from thereby renouncing the free exercise of their reason.

This confidence of the people in the opinions of scientists is of absolutely the same kind as, though much more extensive than, that of scientists in each other.

Mathematicians daily take physiologists' word on trust, and vice versa; each for their respective classes.

Within the same science, is it not an everyday occurrence for scientists provisionally to believe each other at their word, before they are able to understand and judge the demonstrations? What, for example, would we think of a mathematician who refused to accept a proposition on Lagrange's authority before he was able to test it himself?

This belief has no drawback in the sciences, because it is never other than provisional. The confidence of the people in scientists has precisely the same character; except that here the 'provisional' extends indefinitely, though it is always looked upon as provisional. Thus, this confidence is not at all humiliating for the people, and it could never have any of the damaging consequences for their interests that mental submission to theologians had.

The fear of one day seeing the establishment of a despotism founded on the sciences is a chimera as ridiculous as it is absurd: it could only arise in minds that are absolutely alien to all positive ideas.

According to what we have said, as the people are today organized temporally and spiritually in relation to the new system, the most difficult part of the establishment of this system is fully executed. This great change has simplified as much as possible the work to be done for this definitive establishment, by reducing all that remains to be done for that purpose to relations between the leaders of the new system and the leaders of the old.

The people have been eliminated from the question.

It is for the people that the question will be resolved, but they will remain external and passive.

The only danger to be feared, the only precaution to be taken, is not to let ourselves be sidetracked from our goal by the intrigues of ambitious men who tended to dispute among themselves for the obsolete power of the old system.

These are, in summary, the principal parts of the picture which is presented to us by the course of civilization since the eleventh century, considered from the point of view of the gradual development of the new social system. Let us now try to sum up as briefly as possible the results of this great organic series.

Résumé of the second series

We started with this fundamental fact:

The enfranchisement of the communes and the introduction of the positive sciences into Europe formed, in the eleventh century, the two elements of a new social system: industrial capacity and scientific capacity.

We next observed:

1 That the two elementary capacities of the new social system were established on bases quite different from the powers on which the old system rested.

2 That these two capacities were formed outside the old system, and in such a way as to make them as independent of it as possible.

3 That the communes, or the two capacities united, from the beginning took the wise course of not presuming to share the authority of the old system, and simply sought to profit from the degree of independence they enjoyed to come to exercise as much power over nature as possible.

4 That this plan, consistently followed, had the dual effect that it had to have. On the one hand, the elements of the new system developed fully and freely; whence it resulted that their civil strength became preponderant. On the other hand, they gradually obtained a greater degree of freedom which they always used in the same way; and finally they found themselves quite naturally invested with a share in legislative authority, at which they had not directly aimed.

5 That all the temporal and spiritual forces of society have passed into the hands of the communes; that military force itself has been subordinated to their influence.

6 That the communes have obtained as much ascendancy over the political plan formed by the old system as is possible as long as this plan is not formed by them. The temporal power has accepted in principle that the whole social organization should be conceived in the interest of the communes.

7   That the temporal power has established the parliamentary regime, which, by according the exclusive right to vote taxes to the communes (at least in principle), has invested them with all the legislative authority it could cede to them without destroying itself.

8   That this authority is more than sufficient for the communes today to be able to proceed directly and legally to the final organization of the new system.

9   That at the same time as this progress has been made by the temporal and spiritual leaders of the new system, the mass of the communes have detached themselves wholly from their military and theological leaders, and have organized themselves, from the temporal and from the spiritual point of view, in relationship with the leaders of the two positive capacities.

That the old system has thus ceded to the new everything it could abandon without annihilating itself, and that it has smoothed the path to the definitive constitution of the new system.

This, then, is the present state of the new system, presented as the result of all that has occurred since the eleventh century: all society's forces belong to it. All the doctrines necessary for its organization exist in their elements, which are the sciences of observation. In short, society is organized in all its parts to act upon nature. It only remains to organize the whole in the same way. The means which the communes needed for that exist.

General résumé of the two series

When the old social system was definitively formed (in the eleventh century), the elements of the system which was to succeed it came into being.

Since that time, the new system has been simultaneously and uninterruptedly exercising two lines of action of different kinds: on the one hand it has tended to destroy the old system, on the other hand to replace it.

For the first line of action, the communes at first combined with one of the powers of the old system against the other, profiting from the divisions that had arisen between them. Having defeated the power they had fought, they formed a new alliance with one section of the power with which they had been in league, against another section of that same power.

For the second line of action, they kept themselves on the outside of the old system, and they limited themselves to acting upon nature.

These processes of overthrow and organization were always co-ordinated in such a way that the new system in turn took possession of all the posts occupied by the old, as they were abandoned.

During the era when it was at full strength, the old system governed at the same time the general action of society and all particular social action, whether in the spiritual or the temporal domain. All private action and all particular knowledge first freed themselves, little by little, from the bonds of the old system, and they co-ordinated themselves in relation to the new. The new system was organized in all the details of society.

The old system, having absolutely lost all its influence over details, in turn lost, in the temporal and the spiritual domains, the major part of its control over general social action.

It remains in control of the formation of the general political plan; it could not be otherwise prior to the total organization of the new system. But it has been accepted, as a fundamental principle, that this plan must be conceived in the interest of the communes.

The temporal power has been reduced to the smallest dimensions possible prior to the entire extinction of the old system and its replacement by the new. The spiritual power has been completely overthrown as a political power. It no longer has any influence other than that derived from the fact that the teaching of morality is still in its hands, as it is still based on its doctrines.

The new system, having obtained the exclusive direction of all the details of society, has successively gained, in the direction of the whole, everything that the old system has lost.

In the temporal sphere, it has been recognized that the communes had the right to modify at will the general political plan, and the legal exercise of this right has been regularly constituted. This at the same time established the means of transition. In the spiritual sphere, scientific capacity has obtained as much influence over national education as is possible as long as the teaching of morality has not yet passed into its hands.

The strength of these two systems, in respect of the power that they exercise over the direction of the overall shape of society, is today more or less the same; if there is a difference, it is to the advantage of the new rather than the old.

Thus the present state of society is the coexistence of a system in its declining years and an adult system; one of which has lost all its influence over the details, and half of what it possessed over the overall shape, whilst the other dominates all the parts and a half of the whole.

The new system therefore has only one final step to climb to reach its complete organization and succeed in replacing the old. It only remains to complete its progress in the temporal and the spiritual sphere. In the temporal, by taking possession of the lower house;[6] in the spiritual, by establishing morality on principles exclusively deduced from observation. And everything is ready for that: the means exist, it is only necessary to use them.

[6] The French is 'la Chambre des communes'.

Essay 3
Plan of the Scientific Work Necessary for the Reorganization of Society[1]

Foreword

This work will consist of an undetermined number of volumes, forming a sequence of distinct but interrelated works, which will all have as their direct goal, either to establish that politics must today rise to the rank of the sciences of observation, or to apply this fundamental principle to the spiritual reorganization of society.

The first two volumes, which may be regarded as a sort of philosophical prospectus for the work as a whole, will contain both the exposition of the plan of scientific work on politics, divided into three great series, and a first attempt to execute this plan.

The first volume is, consequently, composed of two parts: one relates to the plan of the first series of works; the other, which will be published shortly afterwards, concerns its execution.

The goal of the first part is, properly, to establish on the one hand the spirit which should reign in politics, considered as a positive science; and on the other hand to demonstrate the necessity and the possibility of such a change. The object of the second is to outline the work which is needed to imprint this character on politics, by presenting a first scientific overview of the laws which have guided the general course of civilization, and in turn a first glimpse

---

[1] This is the essay Comte referred to as his 'opuscule fondamental'. Details of publication are given in the Notes on text and translation above.

of the social system which the natural development of the human race must bring to dominance today. In short, the first part considers method in social physics, and the second considers its application.

The same division will be observed in the following volume in relation to the other two series of works.

Although I am the pupil of M. Saint-Simon, and am pleased to declare it, I have been led to adopt a general title distinct from that of my master's works. This is to characterize the spirit of my work with all appropriate precision. But this distinction does not at all influence the identical goal of the two kinds of work, which should be viewed as forming one single body of doctrine, tending, by two different routes, to the establishment of one and the same political system.

I have completely adopted this philosophical idea put forward by M. Saint-Simon, that the present-day reorganization of society must give rise to two kinds of spiritual work, of opposite kinds but of equal importance. One class, which demands the employment of the scientific capacity, have as their object the recasting of general doctrines; the others, which are to bring into play the literary capacity and that of the arts, consist in the renewal of social sentiments.

M. Saint-Simon's career has been employed in discovering the chief ideas necessary to allow the effective cultivation of these two branches of the great philosophical operation reserved for the nineteenth century. Having long reflected upon M. Saint-Simon's seminal ideas, I have devoted myself exclusively to systematizing, developing and perfecting such of the insights of this philosopher as relate to the scientific mission. This work has had as its result the formation of the system of positive politics, which I am today starting to submit to the judgement of thinkers.

I thought I should make public the foregoing declaration, so that if my works should seem to merit any approval it should revert to the founder of the philosophical school to which I have the honour of belonging.

No doubt it is superfluous here to justify the uprightness of my political intentions, and to set about proving the utility of the views I expound: the public and statesmen will judge these two points by reading this work. To them belongs the task of determining, on mature examination, whether these ideas tend to cast new elements of discord into society; or whether they bring special and indispensable means of support to the efforts of governments to re-establish order in Europe.

Introduction

A social system which is dying, a new system whose time has come and which is in the process of taking definitive shape, this is the fundamental character which the general course of civilization has assigned to the present age. In conformity with this state of things, two different kinds of movement are today stirring society: one of disorganization, the other of reorganization. By the first, considered in isolation, society is drawn towards a profound moral and political anarchy which seems to threaten it with imminent and inevitable dissolution. By the second, it is led towards the definitive social state of the human race, the one which best suits its nature, that in which all its means of prosperity are to receive their fullest development and their most direct application. It is the coexistence of these two opposed tendencies that constitutes the great crisis experienced by the most civilized nations. If we are to understand it, we must consider it in this dual aspect.

From the moment that this crisis began to manifest itself up to the present, the tendency towards the disorganization of the old system has been dominant; or rather it alone has asserted itself clearly. It was in the nature of things that the crisis should begin thus, and it was useful too, so that the old system could be sufficiently modified to allow us to proceed directly to the formation of the new.

But today, now that this condition is fully satisfied, and the feudal and theological system is as attenuated as is possible until the new system starts to establish itself, the predominance that the critical tendency still retains is the greatest obstacle to the progress of civilization, and even to the destruction of the old system. It is the primary cause of the terrible and constantly recurring upheavals which accompany the crisis.

The only way to put an end to this tempestuous situation, to stop the anarchy which is daily invading society, in short to reduce the crisis to a simple moral movement, is to induce the civilized nations to abandon the critical direction for the organic direction, to turn all their efforts towards the formation of the new social system, the final object of the crisis, and the goal for which everything that has occurred hitherto is just the preparation.[2]

This is the primary need of the present age. This is also in outline the general aim of my work, and the special aim of this essay, whose object is to bring into play the forces which are to lead society on the road to the new system.

A brief examination of the causes which have hitherto prevented society and which still prevent it from openly taking the organic direction, must naturally precede the exposition of the means to be employed to make it enter on that path.

The numerous and unremitting efforts which peoples and kings have made to reorganize society prove that the need for this reorganization is generally felt. But on both sides it is felt only in a vague and imperfect manner. These two sorts of endeavours, though opposed, are equally pernicious in different respects. They have not hitherto had and they could never have a truly organic result. Far from tending to bring the crisis to an end, they simply contribute to its prolongation. This is the real cause which, in spite of so much effort, keeps society moving in the critical direction and so leaves it prey to revolutions.

To establish this fundamental assertion it is sufficient to take an overview of the attempts at reorganization undertaken by kings and by peoples.

The error committed by kings is the easier to grasp. For them, the reorganization of society is the re-establishment, pure and simple, of the feudal and theological system in all its fullness. In their eyes there is no other way to put a stop to the anarchy which results from that system's decline.

It would be unphilosophical to see this opinion as principally[3] dictated by the private interest of rulers. However chimerical it may be, it must have presented itself naturally to minds which are in good faith seeking a remedy for the present crisis, and which feel,

---

[2] The antithetical pairing of 'organic' and 'critical', which is fundamental to Comte's argument, was derived from Saint-Simon, who contrasted stable or organic periods, in which society possessed an *organizing principle*, with critical periods which, lacking such a principle, were transitional.

[3] 1822: 'uniquely'.

in its full extent, the need for a reorganization, but which have not considered the general course of civilization. Contemplating the present state of things in only one of its aspects, they do not perceive the tendency of society towards the establishment of a new system, more perfect and no less solid than the old one. In short, it is natural that this should properly be the rulers' way of looking at things; for, from their vantage-point, the anarchic state of society must seem more conspicuous, and consequently they must feel with more force the need to remedy it.[4]

This is not the place to insist on the manifest absurdity of such an opinion. It is today universally recognized by the mass of enlightened men. No doubt kings, in seeking to reconstruct the old system, do not understand the nature of the present crisis, and are far from having gauged the full extent of their undertaking.

The fall of the feudal and theological system does not stem, as they think, from recent, isolated and so to speak accidental causes. Instead of being the effect of the crisis, it is on the contrary its source. The decline of this system has taken effect gradually over the preceding centuries, by a succession of modifications, to which, independent of any human will, all classes of society have contributed, and of which kings themselves have often been the primary agents or the most ardent promoters. It has been, in short, the necessary consequence of the course of civilization.

To re-establish the old system, it would therefore not be sufficient to turn society back to the age when the present crisis began to make itself felt. For, supposing it could be achieved, which is absolutely impossible, we should simply have put the social body back into the situation which made the crisis necessary. In going back through the centuries, one would therefore have to make good in turn all the losses which the old system sustained over six hundred years, in comparison with which those brought about in the last thirty years are of no importance.

The only way of effecting this would be to annihilate one by one all the developments of civilization which induced these losses.

Thus, for example, it would be vain to assume the destruction of the philosophy of the eighteenth century, the direct cause of the

---

[4] Sentence added in 1824.

fall of the old system, in its spiritual aspect, if we did not also assume the abolition of the reformation of the sixteenth, of which the philosophy of the last century was only the consequence and the development. But as Luther's reformation was, in its turn, only the necessary result of the progress of the sciences of observation introduced into Europe by the Arabs, we should still have done nothing to ensure the re-establishment of the old system, if we did not also succeed in stifling the positive sciences.

In the same way, from the temporal point of view, we should be led nearer and nearer to putting the industrial classes back into a state of serfdom, since in the last analysis the enfranchisement of the communes was the first and general cause of the decay of the feudal system. In short, to sum up such an undertaking, after overcoming so many difficulties, of which the least, considered in isolation, is beyond all human powers, we should still have obtained nothing but the adjournment of the final fall of the old system, by forcing society to recommence the destruction of that system. This is because we should not have extinguished the principle of progressive civilization, inherent in the nature of the human race.

It is obvious that no one person could have conceived a project so monstrous in its extent as in its absurdity. In spite of ourselves, we each belong to our time. Intellects which think they are struggling most against the course of civilization unknowingly obey its irresistible influence, and themselves contribute to it.

Accordingly kings, in planning to reconstruct the feudal and theological system, fall into perpetual contradictions as they contribute through their own actions either to making the disorganization of that system more complete or to accelerating the formation of the system that is to replace it. A host of facts of this kind present themselves to the observer.

To indicate here only the most striking, we see kings who consider it a matter of honour to encourage the advancement and diffusion of the sciences and the arts, and to stimulate the development of industry; we see them create for this purpose numerous and useful institutions, even though in the last analysis it is to the progress of the sciences, the arts and industry that the decay of the old system is to be traced.

Again, it was in the same way that by means of the treaty of the Holy Alliance[5] the kings, as far as it was in their power to do so, have degraded the theological power, the principal base of the old system, by forming a supreme European council in which this power does not even have a consultative voice.

Finally, the way in which opinions are today divided on the subject of the struggle undertaken by the Greeks offers a still more palpable example of this spirit of inconsistency.[6] In this case[a] we can see men who claim to be restoring to theological ideas their ancient influence themselves involuntarily testifying to the decay of those ideas in their own minds; for they do not fear to make a pronouncement in favour of Mohammedism, which would have brought down upon them the accusation of sacrilege in the times of splendour of the old system.

In pursuing the line of thought just indicated, everyone will easily be able to add to it new instances which multiply daily. Kings cannot take, so to speak, a single action or a single measure tending to the re-establishment of the old system, which is not immediately followed by an act pointing in the opposite direction; and often the same decree contains both the one and the other.

It is this radical incoherence which is best suited to bring out into the open the absurdity of a plan which is not understood even by those who follow its implementation most ardently. It shows clearly how complete and irrevocable is the ruin of the old system. It is pointless here to enter into greater detail on this subject.

The manner in which the peoples have hitherto conceived the reorganization of society is no less pernicious than that of kings,

---

[5] The Holy Alliance was formed in September 1818 by the Tsar of Russia, the Emperor of Austria and the King of Prussia. They agreed that their political transactions would be governed by Christian principles with a view to the maintenance of peace.

[6] Comte's point here is that exponents of the Holy Alliance, which sought to make Christian principles the foundation of international order, found themselves propping up the Islamic Ottoman Empire in defiance of the claims of Christian subject peoples.

---

[a] To realize the full import of this fact, one must remember that the Pope himself pronounced in this sense by categorically [1822: 'openly'] refusing the young men of the Roman nobility permission to go to aid of the Greeks.

even though in different respects. But their error is more excusable, since they go astray in the search for the new system towards which the course of civilization leads them, but whose nature has not yet been determined clearly enough, whereas the kings pursue an undertaking which even a moderately careful study of the past could have shown conclusively to be absurd. In short, the kings are in contradiction with facts, and the peoples are in contradiction with principles, which are always much more difficult to keep in sight. But the error of the peoples is much more important to uproot than that of the kings, because the former alone forms an essential obstacle to the course of civilization, and because it alone gives the kings' error some foundation.

The dominant opinion in the mind of the peoples on the way in which society should be reorganized has as its distinctive character-istic a profound ignorance of the fundamental conditions which any social system must fulfil in order to have true solidity. It amounts to presenting as organic principles the critical principles which have served to destroy the feudal and theological system; or, in other words, taking simple modifications of that system as the bases of the system to be established.

If indeed we examine attentively the doctrines which are today gaining ground among the peoples, in the speeches of their ablest supporters, and in the writings which present their most methodical exposition; and if, after considering them in themselves, we observe historically the way in which they were successively formed, we shall find them to be conceived in a purely critical spirit, which could not serve as the basis for reorganization.[b]

Government, which in any regular state of things is at the head of society, the guide and the agent of general action, is systemati-cally divested by these doctrines of any principle of activity. Deprived of any significant participation in the collective life of the social body, it is reduced to a wholly negative role. It is even argued that any action of the social body upon its members must be strictly limited to the maintenance of public tranquillity; yet in no active society has this been other than a subordinate object, and its import-

---

[b] A discussion of this importance can perhaps only be sketched in this piece. It will be more fully developed in a special work which will be published later [1822: 'soon']. [Footnote deleted in 1854]

ance has been sharply diminished by the development of civilization, which has made it very easy to maintain order.

Government is no longer conceived as the head of society, destined to bind together all individual activities and direct them
towards a common goal. It is represented as a natural enemy,
encamped in the midst of the social system, against which society
must fortify itself by the guarantees it has won, keeping itself in a
permanent state of defiance and defensive hostility which is ready
to explode at the first sign of attack.

If we move from the overall picture to the details, the same spirit
presents itself still more clearly. It is enough here to show its main
lines in the spiritual and temporal spheres.

In the spiritual sphere, this doctrine takes as its principle the
dogma of unlimited freedom of conscience. Examined in the sense
in which it was originally conceived, that is to say, as having a
critical object, this dogma is nothing other than the expression of a
great general fact, the decline of theological beliefs.

The result of that decline, this principle has, by a necessary reaction, made a powerful contribution to its acceleration and diffusion;
but by the nature of things its influence has been limited to that. It
is in line with the progress of the human mind, so long as it is
viewed as no more than a means of struggle against the theological
system. It is out of line and loses all its worth as soon as it comes
to be seen as a basis for the great social reorganization reserved for
the present era; it then even becomes as harmful as it was formerly
useful, for it becomes an obstacle to this reorganization.

In proclaiming the sovereignty of each individual mind, this principle in fact tends essentially to prevent the uniform establishment
of any system of general ideas; yet without them there can be no
society. For, whatever level of education the mass of men may
reach, it is evident that most of the general ideas destined to become
commonplace will only be able to find acceptance on trust, and not
by means of proof. Thus such a dogma is, by its nature, applicable
only to ideas which are to disappear, because then they become
matters of indifference; and in practice it has only ever been applied
to them, at the moment when they begin to go into decline, and to
hasten their fall.

To apply it to the new system as to the old, and, still more,
to see in it an organic principle is to fall into the strangest

contradiction; and if such an error were capable of lasting, the reorganization of society would be forever impossible.

There is no freedom of conscience in astronomy, in physics, in chemistry, in physiology, in the sense that we would each find it absurd not to take on trust the principles established in these sciences by competent men. If it is different in politics, it is because the old principles having collapsed, and the new ones not having been formed yet, in the interval there are properly speaking no established principles. But to convert this transient fact into an absolute and eternal dogma, and to make it into a fundamental maxim, is obviously to proclaim that society must always[7] remain without general doctrines. It must be admitted that such a dogma indeed merits the reproaches of anarchy which are addressed to it by the best defenders[8] of the theological system.

The dogma of the sovereignty of the people is, in the temporal sphere, the one which corresponds to the dogma which has just been examined, and of which it is only the political application. It was created to combat the principle of divine right, the general political basis of the old system, shortly after the dogma of freedom of conscience was formed to destroy the theological ideas on which this principle was founded.

What has been said about one is therefore applicable to the other. The anti-feudal dogma, like the anti-theological dogma, has achieved its critical purpose, the natural end of its career. The first can no more be the political basis of social reorganization, than the second can be its moral basis. Both of them being born to destroy, they are equally incapable of constructing.

One of these doctrines, though people wish to find in it an organic principle, presents nothing other than individual infallibility substituted for papal[9] infallibility; the other in the same way simply replaces the arbitrary will of kings with the arbitrary will of peoples, or rather with that of individuals. The latter tends to the general dismemberment of the political body, by leading us to confer power on the least civilized classes; whilst the former tends to the complete isolation of minds, by investing the least enlightened men with

---

[7] 1822: for ever.
[8] 1822: the most capable champions.
[9] 1822: sacerdotal.

absolute control over the system of general ideas determined by superior minds to serve as a guide for society.

The analysis just sketched for the two fundamental dogmas can easily be applied to each of the more special ideas that constitute the doctrine of the peoples. We shall always get a similar result. It will be seen that all of them, like the two principal ones, are none other than the dogmatic enunciation of a corresponding historical fact, relative to the decay of the feudal and theological system. It will likewise be recognized that all of them have a purely critical purpose, which alone constitutes their worth and which makes them absolutely inapplicable to the reorganization of society.

Thus a close examination of the doctrine of the peoples confirms what a philosophical survey should have led us to expect, that weapons of war cannot, by a strange metamorphosis, suddenly become building instruments. This doctrine, purely critical in its overall shape and in its details, has been of the greatest importance in contributing to the natural course of civilization, as long as the main action was to be the struggle against the old system. But conceived as capable of presiding over social reorganization, it is absolutely inadequate. It necessarily places society in a state of constituted anarchy, in the temporal and in the spiritual domains.

Without doubt it was in conformity with human weakness that the peoples should begin by adopting as organic the critical principles with which they had been familiarized by continual application. But the prolongation of such an error is nonetheless the greatest obstacle to the reorganization of society.

Now that we have considered separately the two different ways in which peoples and kings conceive this reorganization, if we go on to compare them with each other, we can see that each of them, by dint of its own peculiar vices, is equally powerless to launch society in a truly organic direction, and thus to prevent in the future the return of the storms which have hitherto always accompanied the great crisis characterizing the present age. Both are anarchical in the same degree, one by its innermost nature, the other by its necessary consequences.

The only difference which exists between them in this respect is that, in the opinion of kings, government intentionally sets itself up in direct and continuous opposition to society; whereas, in the opinion of peoples, it is society which systematically establishes itself in a permanent state of hostility towards government.

These two opposed and equally pernicious opinions tend, in the nature of things, to reinforce each other, and, in consequence, indefinitely to sustain the source of revolutions.

On the one hand, the kings' attempts to reconstruct the feudal and theological system necessarily provoke in the peoples an explosion of the critical doctrine's principles with all their formidable energy. It is even obvious that, had it not been for these attempts, the doctrine would already have lost the greater part of its vigour: it would no longer have any object once the kings' solemn adherence to its fundamental principle (the dogma of freedom of conscience) and to its main consequences had by implication formally declared the irrevocable ruin of the old system. But the efforts to revive divine right awaken the sovereignty of the people and give it new life.

On the other hand, owing to the fact that the old system is more than sufficiently modified to allow us to work directly towards the formation of the new one, the predominance which the peoples still accord to critical principles naturally impels the kings to try to re-establish the old system so as to avert a crisis which, as it currently appears, seems to lead to nothing but the dissolution of the social order. This prolongation of the reign of the critical doctrine, in an era when society needs an organic doctrine, is the very thing which alone gives some force to the opinion of kings. For though this opinion is not in practice any more truly organic than that of peoples, because of the absolute impossibility of realizing it; in theory at least it is so. Because society absolutely must have a system of some kind, the kings' opinion has a relationship, though an imperfect one, with the needs of society.

If we add to this accurate picture the influence of the various factions, to whose projects such a state of things offers so vast and so favourable a field of activity; if we examine their efforts to prevent the question from becoming clarified, to divert kings and peoples from understanding one another and recognizing their mutual errors, we shall have a clear idea of the sad situation in which society finds itself today.

All the considerations set out above prove that the means of finally escaping from this deplorable vicious circle, this inexhaust-

ible source of revolutions, does not consist in the triumph of the
opinion of kings, nor in that of the opinion of peoples, as they exist
today. There is no other means of escape than the formation and
general adoption, by peoples and by kings, of the organic doctrine
which can alone lead kings away from their reactionary course, and
peoples from their critical course.

This doctrine alone can terminate the crisis, by leading society
as a whole on the road to the new system, whose establishment
has been prepared by the course of civilization since its origin,
and which it today calls to replace the feudal and theological
system.

By the unanimous adoption of this doctrine, the reasonable
elements in the present opinions of peoples and kings will be satisfied; the pernicious and discordant elements they contain will be
pruned. With the dissipation of the kings' justifiable alarm about
the dissolution of society, they will no longer have any legitimate
motive for opposing the blossoming of the human spirit. The
peoples, turning all their desires towards the formation of the new
system, will no longer be inflamed by the feudal and theological
system, and will leave it to pass away peacefully in accordance with
the natural course of things.[10]

Having established the necessity of adopting a new and truly
organic doctrine, if we come to examine the timeliness of its establishment, the following considerations will suffice to demonstrate
that the moment has at last arrived when we can set to work at once
on this great operation.

Observing accurately the present state of the most advanced
nations, it is impossible not to be struck by this singular and almost
self-contradictory fact. Although there exist no political ideas other
than those founded on the reactionary doctrine or on the critical
doctrine, yet neither of them today any longer possesses a true predominance, whether among kings or among peoples; neither exerts
an influence powerful enough to direct society. These two doctrines
which, from a theoretical point of view, sustain one another, as we
have established above, are nevertheless no longer employed in
doing anything but restricting or rather cancelling out one another
in the general conduct of affairs.

[10] The following section did not appear in the 1822 text, but was added in 1824.

The great political movement produced thirty years ago by the implementation of critical ideas deprived them of their chief influence. On the one hand, by delivering the final blow to the old system, it closed their natural career; it almost completely destroyed the general motive which won them popular favour. On the other hand, the application of new opinions to the reorganization of society brought their anarchical character quite out into the open. Since this decisive experience, there is no longer any true critical passion among the peoples. Consequently, and whatever may be the appearance, there can no longer be any true reactionary passion among kings, since they positively recognize the decay of the feudal and theological system and the necessity of abandoning it.

Any real action, in one or the other of these directions, is now exerted both outside the sphere of government and outside the sphere of society. Kings and peoples both in practice use the reactionary opinion or the critical opinion in an essentially passive way; that is, as a defensive weapon. They each even employ each in turn, and almost to the same degree, with this sole natural difference that, as a means of reasoning, the peoples still remain attached to the critical doctrine, because they feel more completely the need to abandon the old system; and the kings remain attached to the reactionary doctrine, because they feel more deeply the necessity of some kind of social order.

This observation can easily be verified and illuminated by the single fact of the existence of and credit enjoyed by a sort of hybrid opinion, which is only a mixture of reactionary ideas and critical ideas.[11] It is obvious that this opinion, which was without influence at the origin of the crisis, has today become dominant, as much among the ruled as among the rulers. The two active parties recognize its dominance in the least equivocal way, by the strict obligation they are each now under to adopt its language.

The success of such an opinion testifies clearly to two facts which are most essential to a precise understanding of the present era. It proves, first, that the inadequacy of the critical doctrine to meet the great current needs of society is felt as deeply and as universally as the incompatibility of the theological and feudal system with the

---

[11] The reference here is to the doctrine of spiritualism or eclecticism, whose chief exponent was Victor Cousin.

present state of civilization. Secondly, it guarantees that neither the
critical opinion nor the reactionary opinion can any longer attain
real ascendancy. For when one of them seems on the point of
acquiring primacy, the general disposition of minds immediately
becomes favourable to the other; until the latter, deceived by this
apparent approval, has recovered enough strength to give rise to the
same alarms and, in consequence, experience in its turn the same
disappointment.' These successive oscillations occur sometimes in
one direction, sometimes in the other, according to whether the
natural course of events specially manifests the absurdity of the old
system or the danger of anarchy. This is, at the moment, the mechanism of practical politics, and it will inevitably remain so as long
as there are no fixed ideas on the way to reorganize society; as long
as no opinion has been produced which is capable of fulfilling at
the same time these two great conditions which our age prescribes
and which up to the present have seemed contradictory, the abandonment of the old system, and the establishment of a regular and
stable order.

This reciprocal cancellation of the two opposed doctrines, which
can be observed even in men's opinions, is above all incontestable
in their actions. If indeed we examine all the events of any importance that have taken place for ten years, whether with a critical
tendency or with a reactionary tendency, we shall find that they

---

' The merit of the intermediate, or rather self-contradictory, opinion consists precisely in serving as the organ for this tendency. It is moreover obvious that, by its
nature, it suffers from a lack of constructive power, since it has no distinctive
character of its own, and is only composed of opposite maxims, which mutually
cancel each other out. It can achieve nothing, as experience has sufficiently confirmed, but to make the course of affairs oscillate between the critical tendency
and the reactionary tendency, without ever stamping any determinate character on
it. This indecision is certainly essential in the present political situation, and until
the establishment of a truly organic doctrine, to prevent the violent disorder to
which society would be exposed by the preponderance of the reactionary party or
the critical party. In this sense, all sensible men must rush to assist it. But while
such a policy makes the revolutionary era less stormy, it is no less incontestable
that it tends directly to prolong its life, for an opinion which elevates inconsistency
into a system, and which leads us carefully to prevent the total extinction of the
two extreme doctrines so that we can always play one off against the other, necessarily hinders the social body from ever achieving a fixed state. In short, this policy
is reasonable and useful today, as a simple expedient; but it becomes absurd and
dangerous if we wish to consider it as definitive.

These are the reasons for which I have not mentioned this point of view in the
above examination of existing opinions on social reorganization.

have never led to the achievement of any real progress in the corresponding system, and that their result has always been simply to prevent the dominance of the opposite system.

To sum up, then, not only can neither the opinion of kings nor the opinion of peoples satisfy in the least the fundamental need for reorganization that characterizes the present era; which establishes the necessity of a new general doctrine; but the triumph of either the one opinion or the other is today equally impossible; and in truth neither the one nor the other can any longer have any real influence: whence it follows that men's minds are sufficiently prepared to receive the organic doctrine.[12]

Society's destination, once it has arrived at its maturity, is not to inhabit for ever and ever the old and dilapidated hut which it built in its infancy, as kings think; neither is it to live eternally without shelter after having left the hut, as the peoples think; but, with the help of the experience it has acquired, to build itself, with all the materials it has amassed, the edifice which is most appropriate to its needs and to its pleasures. That is the great and noble enterprise reserved for the present generation.

General exposé

The spirit in which the reorganization of society has been conceived up to the present by peoples and by kings having been shown to be pernicious, we must necessarily conclude that both have set about forming a plan of reorganization in the wrong way. This is the only possible explanation of a fact of this kind; but it is important to demonstrate this assertion in a direct, specific and precise manner.

The inadequacy of the opinion of kings and of that of peoples has proved the need for a new and truly organic doctrine, which is alone capable of putting an end to the terrible crisis which torments society. In the same way, by examining the methods which have led to imperfect results on both sides, we shall discover which course will have to be adopted for the formation and establishment of the new doctrine, and which are the social forces called to direct this great work.

---

[12] End of the section added in 1824.

The general defect of the course followed by peoples and by kings in the search for a plan of reorganization lies in the fact that both have hitherto had a radically false idea of the nature of the task, and, consequently, have entrusted this important mission to men who are necessarily unqualified for it. That is the primary cause of the fundamental aberrations noted in the previous chapter.

Although this cause has affected kings as much as peoples, it is nevertheless pointless to consider it specifically with reference to the former. For kings have invented nothing, and have limited themselves to reproducing for the new social state the doctrine of the old, and this is in itself sufficient testimony to their power-lessness to conceive a true reorganization. On the other hand, for the same reason, their course, although as absurd in its principle as that of peoples, naturally had to be more methodical, being prede-termined in the closest detail. The peoples alone have produced a sort of new doctrine, and so it is their way of proceeding which we must principally examine in order to discover there the source of this doctrine's defects. Besides, it will be easy for anyone later to apply to the kings, with appropriate modifications, the general observations made with reference to the peoples.

The multiplicity of the so-called constitutions to which the peoples have given birth since the beginning of the crisis, and the excessive minuteness of the drafting which is to be found more or less in all of them, would alone be sufficient to show beyond a shadow of doubt to any mind capable of judging how far the nature and difficulty of the formation of a plan of reorganization have been misunderstood up to now. When society has been truly reorganized, it will be a matter of deep astonishment to our descendants that in a space of thirty years we produced ten constitutions, each in its turn proclaimed to be eternal and irrevocable, several of them con-taining more than two hundred very detailed articles, not counting the organic laws annexed to them. Such verbiage would be the shame of the human mind in politics, were it not, in the natural progress of ideas, an inevitable transition towards the true and final doctrine.

Society does not progress like that, nor can it do so. The conceit of building, in one go, in a few months or even in a few years, the whole economy of a social system in its complete and definitive development, is an extravagant chimera, which is absolutely incompatible with the weakness of the human mind.

Let us indeed observe the way in which the mind proceeds in analogous but far simpler cases. When a science of any kind is reconstituted according to a new theory, which is already sufficiently advanced, the general principle is produced, is discussed, and is established first of all; it is then, by a long chain of operations, that we succeed in co-ordinating all the parts of the science into a system which no one at the outset could have been in a position to conceive, not even the inventor of the principle. Thus, for example, after Newton had discovered the law of universal gravitation, almost a century of very difficult work was needed on the part of all the geometers in Europe, to give physical astronomy a constitution compatible with that law. It is the same in the arts. To cite just a single example, when the elastic force of steam was conceived as a new motive power applicable to machines, in this case too nearly a century was needed to develop the series of industrial reforms which were the most direct consequences of this discovery. If that is evidently the natural and invariable course of the human mind in revolutions which, in spite of their importance and their difficulty, are yet only particular ones, how frivolous must seem the presumptuous course which has been followed up to the present in the most general revolution, and the most important and most difficult of all: that which has as its object the complete recasting of the social system!

If we move from these indirect but decisive comparisons to direct comparisons, the result will be the same. Let us examine the foundation of the feudal and theological system, a revolution of just the same kind as that of the present era. Far from the constitution of that system having been produced at one go, it took its distinctive and definitive form only in the eleventh century, that is to say more than five centuries after the general triumph of the Christian doctrine in western Europe, and the definitive settlement of the northern peoples in the western empire. It would be impossible to conceive of any man of genius in the fifth century being in a position to trace in any detail the plan of this constitution, even though the fundamental principle, of which it was only the necessary development, was already solidly established, both in the temporal and in the spiritual domains. No doubt, because of the progress of knowledge and because of the more natural and simpler character of the system which is to be established today, the total organization of this system must take place much more rapidly. But as the course of society, though varying in speed, is necessarily always essentially the same, depending as it does on the permanent nature of the human constitution, this great experience proves just as conclusively that it is absurd to seek to improvise in the smallest details the total plan of social reorganization.

If we needed confirmation for this conclusion, we could get it by observing the way in which the critical doctrine adopted by the peoples has itself evolved. This doctrine is obviously just the general development and complete application of the right of private judgement laid down as a principle by Protestantism. It took almost two centuries, after the establishment of this principle, for all its important consequences to be deduced and the theory to be formed. It is undeniable that the resistance put up by the feudal and theological system had a lot of influence on the slowness of this process; but it is not less evident that that could not have been the only cause, and that this slowness stemmed in large part from the very nature of the operation. And what is true of a purely critical doctrine must be true, *a fortiori*, of the genuinely organic doctrine.

We must therefore conclude from this first class of considerations that the peoples have not up to now understood the great work of social reorganization.

In seeking to specify in what respects the nature of this work has been misunderstood, we find that it is in having regarded as purely practical an enterprise which is essentially theoretical.

The formation of any sort of plan of social organization is necessarily composed of two series of operations, totally distinct in their object, as well as in the kind of capacity they demand. One, theoretical or spiritual, has as its goal the development of the seminal idea of the plan, that is of the new principle according to which social relations must be co-ordinated, and the formation of the system of general ideas intended to serve as a guide for society. The other, practical or temporal, determines the mode of distribution of power and the system of administrative institutions which are in closest conformity with the spirit of the system as settled by the theoretical operations. The second series being founded on the first, of which it is only the consequence and the realization, it is with the first that the general work must begin. The first series is the soul, the most important and the most difficult part, even though only preliminary.

It is through not having adopted this fundamental division, or in other words through having fixed their attention exclusively on the practical part, that the peoples have naturally been led into conceiving social reorganization according to the pernicious doctrine examined in the last chapter. All their errors are the consequence of this great original deviation. We can easily establish this connection.

In the first place, a result of this offence against the natural law of the human mind is that the peoples, while believing themselves to be constructing a new social system, have remained enclosed in the old system. That was inevitable, since the aim and the spirit of the new system were not determined. It will always be so until this indispensable condition has first been fulfilled.

Any system of society, whether made for a handful of men or for several millions, has as its final object to direct all individual powers towards a general goal [of activity].[13] For society only exists where a general and combined action is exerted. On any other assumption, there is only an agglomeration of a certain number of individuals on the same soil. That is what distinguishes human society from that of other gregarious animals.

It follows from this consideration that the clear and precise determination of the goal of our activity is the first and most important condition of a true social order,[14] since it fixes the direction in which the whole system is to be conceived.

On the other hand, there are only two possible goals of activity for a society, however numerous it may be, as for an isolated individual. These are conquest, or violent action on the rest of the human race, and production, or action on nature to modify it to the

[13] Cf. Mill to d'Eichthal, 8 October 1829:

> To begin with the first and fundamental principle of the whole system, that government and the social union exist for the purpose of concentrating and directing all the forces of society to some one end. . . . What a foundation for a system of political science this is! . . . The united forces of society never were, nor can be, directed to one single end, nor is there, so far as I can perceive, any reason for desiring that they should.
> *The Early Letters of John Stuart Mill* (*Collected Works of John Stuart Mill* vol. XII) (1963), p. 36.

[14] 1822: 'true contract of association'. Laffitte says, wrongly, that the change to 'true social order' was made in 1854.

advantage of man. Any society which is not clearly organized for one or other of these ends is just a hybrid association devoid of character. The military goal was that of the old system, the industrial goal is that of the new.

The first step to be taken in social reorganization was therefore to proclaim this new goal. Since we have not done so, we have not yet abandoned the old system, even when we thought we had diverged most markedly from it. Now, it is clear that this strange lacuna in our so-called constitutions stemmed from our attempt to organize the details before the framework of the system had been conceived. In other words, it resulted from our having gone straight to the regulatory part of reorganization, without having determined the theoretical part, or even thought of instituting it.

As a necessary consequence of this primary error, we mistook simple modifications for a total change of the old system. The substance remained essentially intact; all the alterations were concerned only with the form. We occupied ourselves in dividing up the old powers, and in setting up their different branches against each other. The discussions directed towards this object were regarded and are still regarded as the sublime element in politics, whereas they form only a very subordinate detail. The direction of society, the nature of the powers were conceived as the same as ever.

It is, besides, essential to notice another consequence of the original deviation: that discussions on the division of powers, the only ones with which we have occupied ourselves, have been as superficial as can be. For we have lost sight of the great division between the spiritual power and the temporal power, the principal improvement which the old system introduced into general politics. Our attention was directed wholly towards the practical part of social reconstruction, and so we were led naturally to this monstrosity of a constitution without spiritual power, which, if it were capable of lasting, would be a truly immense regression towards barbarism. Everything touched only the temporal sphere. We only saw the division into legislative power and executive power, which is obviously only a subdivision.

It was to provide some intellectual guidance in the modification of the feudal and theological system that the peoples were necessarily induced to conceive as organic the critical principles which had served in the struggle against the old system, from the time when its decay had become perceptible, and which by that very fact were destined to modify it. We must not forget to note in this connection that, at the same time as ignoring the division of the general work of reorganization into a theoretical series and a practical series, the peoples involuntarily testified to the necessity of this law, dictated by the imperious nature of things, by themselves obeying it in their attempts to modify the old system.

This is the necessary chain of consequences derived from the fundamental error of considering the essentially theoretical work of social reorganization as if it were purely practical. It is thus that the peoples gradually came to view as a truly new social system, the outcome of the progress of civilization, what is merely the old system stripped by the critical doctrine of everything that gave it vigour, and reduced to the miserable state of a fleshless skeleton. That is the true ancestry of the fundamental errors pointed out in the last chapter.

As the need for a true reorganization is always making itself felt, and will inevitably do so until it has been satisfied, the peoples' minds get restless, and exhaust themselves in the search for new combinations. But confined by an inflexible destiny to the narrow circle where their pernicious course originally placed them, and which civilization in vain urges them to leave, they believe they have found the completion of their efforts in new modifications of the old system, that is in still more thorough applications of the critical doctrine. Thus from modification to modification, that is to say by destroying more and more the feudal and theological system, without ever replacing it, the peoples march onwards towards total anarchy, the only natural outcome of such a course.

This conclusion obviously proves the urgent and inevitable need to adopt the course which the nature of the human mind so clearly dictates for the great work of social reorganization. This is the only means of escaping the disastrous consequences with which the peoples are threatened as a result of following a different course.

As this assertion is fundamental, since it determines the true direction of the great political works that have to be undertaken today, it would be impossible to cast too much light upon it. It is therefore useful to recall in brief the direct philosophical consider-ations on which it is founded, although one could regard it as suf-ficiently demonstrated by the examination which has just been sketched of the pernicious course followed by the peoples up to the present.

It is dishonourable to human reason that we are obliged to prove methodically, with regard to the most general and most difficult undertaking, the necessity of a division which is today universally recognized as indispensable in the least complicated cases. We admit as an elementary truth that the operation of any sort of manufacture, the construction of a road, of a bridge, the navigation of a vessel, etc., must be directed by preliminary theoretical knowledge, and yet we want the reorganization of society to be a purely operational matter which can be entrusted to merely practical men!

Any complete human operation, from the simplest to the most complicated, whether executed by just one individual or by many, is inevitably composed of two parts, or, in other words, gives rise to two sorts of consideration: the one theoretical, the other practical; one a matter of conception, the other of execution. The first, as a matter of strict necessity, precedes the second, which it is meant to direct. In other words, there is never action without preliminary speculation. This analytical process can be observed even in operations which seem to be matters of pure routine; the difference is only in whether the theory is well- or ill-conceived. The man who, whatever the subject may be, claims not to allow his mind to be directed by theories, restricts himself, as we have seen, to refusing to allow the theoretical progress made by his contemporaries and to sticking with superannuated theories long after they have been replaced. Thus, for example, those who proudly affect not to believe in medicine ordinarily hand themselves over with an eager stupidity to the crudest charlatanism.

In the infancy of the human mind, theoretical works and practical works are executed by the same individual for all operations; which does not prevent, even then, the existence of a very real, if less salient, distinction between them. Soon these two orders of works begin to separate, demanding as they do different and in a sense opposite capacities and cultures. As the collective and individual intelligence of the human race develops, this division becomes more and more pronounced and becomes more and more generalized, and it comes to be the source of further progress. From a philosophical point of view one can truly measure the degree of civilization of a people by how far the division of theory and practice is pushed, together with the degree of harmony that exists between them. For the great instrument of civilization is the separation of works[15] and the combination of effort.

By the definitive establishment of Christianity, the division of theory and practice was constituted in a regular and complete manner for the general acts of society, as it already was for all private operations. It was invigorated and consolidated by the creation of a spiritual power, distinct and independent of the temporal power, whose relations with the latter were the natural ones of a theoretical authority with a practical authority, modified according to the special character of the old system. This great and fine conception was the principal cause of the admirable strength and solidity which distinguished the feudal and theological system in the times of its splendour. The inevitable fall of this system momentarily caused us to lose sight of this important division. The superficial and critical philosophy of the last century underestimated its value. But it is evident that it must be treasured, with all the other conquests made by the human mind under the influence of the old system, and which could not perish with it. This division – between spiritual and temporal powers of a different kind – must figure in the forefront of the system to be established today. There is no doubt that society must be organized no less completely in the nineteenth century than it was in the eleventh.[d]

If the necessity of the division between theoretical and practical works must be recognized in the case of day-to-day and commonplace political operations, how much more indispensable is this division, principally founded on the weakness of the human mind, in the vast operation of the total reorganization of society? It is the first condition for treating this great question in the only way which is commensurate with its importance.

What philosophical observation indicates is confirmed by direct experience. No important innovation has ever been introduced into the social order, unless the works relative to its conception have preceded those whose immediate object is to put it into operation,

---

[15] Some translators give 'division of labour' here; but Comte says 'séparation des travaux' and not 'division du travail'.

[d] This great question of the division of the spiritual and temporal powers will later be the subject of a separate work. [Footnote added in 1824.]

and have served at once as their guide and support. History presents us with two decisive experiences in this respect.

The first relates to the formation of the theological and feudal system, an event which today must be an inexhaustible source of instruction for us. The framework of institutions by means of which this system was fully constituted in the eleventh century had evidently been prepared by the theoretical works carried out in previous centuries on the spirit of this system, and which date from the elaboration of Christianity by the school of Alexandria.[16] The establishment of the pontifical power, as the supreme European authority, was the necessary consequence of this prior development of Christian doctrine. The general institution of feudalism, founded on reciprocal relations of obedience and protection between the weak and the strong, was likewise only the application of this doctrine to the regulation of social relations in the state of civilization of that time. Who cannot see that neither the one institution nor the other could have come into being without the preliminary development of Christian theory?

The second experience, still more palpable because it is almost under our noses, is concerned with the very course of the modifications introduced by the peoples to the old system since the beginning of the present crisis. It is clear that they were entirely founded on the development and systematic arrangement given to the critical principles by the philosophy of the eighteenth century. Being critical, these works belonged to an inferior kind of theory; but their theoretical character was so obvious, they were so distinct from subsequent practical works, that not one of the men who contributed to them imagined at all clearly or extensively the modifications they were to produce in the next generation. This thought must have struck anyone who has attentively compared their works with the practical modifications which succeeded them; and yet go through the writings and speeches of the ablest of the men who took the lead in drawing up our so-called constitutions, and eliminate the ideas borrowed from the philosophers of the eighteenth century, and you will see how little remains.

---

[16] The Catechetical School of Alexandria played an important role in the exposition of Christian doctrine from the end of the second century, notably under Clement and Origen.

If the question which occupies us is to be examined from an historical point of view, it can easily be determined by the following considerations, which we shall simply point to here before developing them more fully in the second part of this volume.

Society is today disorganized, both from a spiritual point of view and from a temporal point of view. Spiritual anarchy preceded and engendered temporal anarchy. Even today the social malaise depends much more on the first cause than on the second. On the other hand, a careful study of the course of civilization proves that the spiritual reorganization of society is now more fully prepared than its temporal reorganization. Thus the first series of direct efforts to close the revolutionary era must have the object of reorganizing the spiritual power; whereas, up to the present, attention has been directed only at the recasting of the temporal power.[17]

From all the preceding considerations we must obviously deduce the absolute necessity of separating the theoretical works of social reorganization prescribed at the present time from the practical works; the necessity, that is, of conceiving and executing those which relate to the spirit of the new social order, to the system of general ideas which must correspond to it, in isolation from those whose object is the system of social relations and the administrative form which must result from it. Nothing essential and durable can be done for the practical part, until the theoretical part is established or, at least, very advanced. To proceed otherwise would be to build without foundations, to give the form priority over the substance; in short, it would be to prolong the fundamental error committed by the peoples, which has just been presented as the primary source of all their aberrations, the obstacle which must be destroyed before all else if their desire to see society reorganized in a manner commensurate with the present state of knowledge is at last to be realized.

Having established the nature of the preliminary works which have to be executed in order that the organization of the new social system may be founded on solid bases, we can easily determine which are the social forces destined to fulfil this important mission. This is what remains to be specified, before we explain the plan of works to be carried out.

---

[17] This paragraph and the preceding one were added in 1824.

Since it has now been demonstrated that the way in which the peoples have hitherto proceeded to the formation of the plan of reorganization is radically flawed, it would no doubt be superfluous to dwell on showing that the men to whom this great task was entrusted were absolutely unqualified. It is in fact clear that the one is the inevitable consequence of the other. As the peoples misunderstood the nature of the task, they could hardly avoid going astray in the choice of the men called upon to undertake it. Just because these men were suited to the task as the peoples conceived it, they are for that reason incapable of directing it in the way in which it ought to be conceived. The incapacity of these delegates, or rather their incompetence, was therefore only to be expected, for no-one is suited to two things which are absolutely opposed.

It is principally the class of legists which has provided the men called upon to direct the work on the so-called constitutions which the peoples have been drawing up for thirty years. The nature of things necessarily invested them with this function, in the form in which it has hitherto been conceived.

For, because up to now the peoples have just been engaged in modifying the old system, and because the critical principles intended to direct these modifications were fully established, eloquence had to be the faculty specially brought into play in this work, and it is above all by legists that this faculty is habitually cultivated. Although it is only a subordinate faculty, since it simply sets itself to ensuring the triumph of a given opinion without participating in its formation and its examination, it is for that very reason eminently suited to the work of dissemination. The principles of critical doctrine were not elaborated by the legists but by the metaphysicians, who, besides, form the class in the spiritual domain which corresponds to that of the legists in the temporal domain. But it is by the legists that these principles have been propagated. It is they who have chiefly occupied the political scene for the whole duration of the immediate struggle against the feudal and theological system. To them therefore it must naturally belong to direct the modifications to be introduced into this system in accordance with the critical doctrine, which they alone were truly used to handling.

Obviously it could not be the same for the truly organic works whose necessity has just been demonstrated. Here it is no longer eloquence, that is to say the faculty of persuasion, that has to be brought specially into operation, but reasoning, that is to say the faculty of analysis and co-ordination. For the very reason that the legists are generally the men who are most capable in the first respect, they are the most incapable in the second respect. Because they make a living out of seeking means of persuading people of an opinion, whatever it may be, the more skill they acquire in this sort of work through practice the less suited they become to co-ordinate a theory according to its true principles.

So we are not concerned here with a vain question of self-esteem; rather, all is reducible to the necessary and exclusive relation that exists between each kind of ability and each kind of work. The legists directed the formation of the plan of reorganization when it was conceived in an absolutely pernicious spirit. They did what they had to do. Called upon to modify, to criticize, they modified, criticized. It would be unjust to reproach them for the defects of a direction they did not choose, and which it was not their job to rectify. Their influence was useful, and even indispensable, as long as this direction itself was. But at the same time we must recognize that this influence has to stop if a wholly opposite direction is to prevail. It is no doubt quite absurd to purport to undertake the reorganization of society, while conceiving it as a purely practical matter, and before any of the necessary theoretical works have been executed. But a still greater absurdity would be the strange hope of seeing a true reorganization carried out by an assembly of orators, unacquainted with any positive theoretical idea, and chosen, without any determinate condition as to capacity, by men who for the most part are still more unqualified.*

---

* We are very far from concluding, from the preceding considerations, that the class of legists must no longer have any political role today. We just wanted to establish that their activity must change in character.

   According to the process of reasoning we have just expounded, the present state of society demands that the supreme direction of minds ceases to belong to legists; but they are nonetheless called upon, by their nature, to provide backing, in very important respects, for the new general direction which others will impart. For a start, by virtue of their powers of persuasion, and of the fact that they are more accustomed than any other class to look at things from a political point of view, they need to make a potent contribution to the adoption of the organic doctrine. Secondly, legists, and especially those among them who have made a special study of positive law, alone possess the aptitude to make regulations, which is one of the major aptitudes necessary in the formation of the new social system, and which will be brought into play just as soon as the purely spiritual part of the general work of reorganization is complete, or even sufficiently advanced. [Footnote added in 1824.]

The nature of the works to be carried out itself indicates, in the clearest possible way, to which class the task of undertaking them belongs. These works being theoretical, it is clear that men who make a living out of methodically forming logical theoretical combinations, that is the scientists engaged in the study of the sciences of observation, are the only ones whose type of ability and intellectual culture satisfies the necessary conditions. It would obviously be monstrous if, when society's most urgent requirement gives rise to a general work of the first order of importance and difficulty, this work was not directed by the greatest existing intellectual forces; by those whose method is universally recognized as the best. No doubt there are in other sections of society men with a theoretical capacity equal or even superior to that of the majority of scientists, for the actual classification of individuals is far from being in total conformity with the natural or physiological classification. But in such an essential task we have to consider classes and not individuals. Besides, even as regards individuals, the education, that is the system of intellectual habits[18] which results from the study of the sciences of observation, is the only one capable of properly developing their natural theoretical capacity. In short, whenever, in any particular direction, society needs theoretical works, it is acknowledged that it must appeal to the corresponding class of scientists: it is therefore the whole class of scientists which is called upon to direct the general theoretical works whose necessity has just been noted.*ᶠ*

---

[18] 'the system of intellectual habits' was added in 1824.

ᶠ In conformity with ordinary usage we here include among the scientists men who, without devoting their lives to the special cultivation of any science of observation, possess an aptitude for science, and have made a sufficiently close study of the general shape of positive knowledge to be penetrated by its spirit, and to have become familiar with the principal laws of natural phenomena. It is, no doubt, for this class of scientists, still too few in number, that the essential role in the formation of the new social doctrine is reserved. The other scientists are too absorbed by their particular occupations, and even still too affected by certain pernicious intellectual habits, which today result from this specialization, to play a truly active role in the establishment of political science. But they will nevertheless fulfil a very important though passive function in this great act of foundation, that of natural judges of the works. The results obtained by the men who trace the new philosophical direction will have worth and influence only insofar as they are adopted by specialists ['les savants spéciaux'], as having the same character as their usual works. We thought it necessary to give this explanation, to forestall an objection which will come naturally to most readers' minds. But in any case it is obvious

Furthermore, the nature of things, when properly examined, should stop us going astray here; for it absolutely prohibits freedom of choice by showing, from several distinct points of view, the class of scientists to be the only one suited to carry out the theoretical work of social reorganization.

In the system to be constituted, spiritual power will be in the hands of the scientists, and temporal power will belong to the heads of industrial works. These two powers must naturally therefore proceed, in the formation of this system, as they will proceed in its daily application once it is established, allowing only for the greater importance of the work to be carried out today. There is, in this work, a spiritual part which has to be dealt with first, and a temporal part which will be dealt with in its turn. Thus it is for the scientists to undertake the first series of works, and for the most important industrialists to organize the administrative system according to the bases laid down by that first series. This is the simple course indicated by the nature of things, which teaches that the very classes which form the elements of the powers of a new system and which must one day be placed at its head, can alone constitute it, because they alone are capable of grasping its spirit properly, and because they alone are pushed in this direction by the combined impetus of their habits and their interests.

Another consideration makes the need to entrust the theoretical work of social reorganization to the positive scientists even more palpable.

It has been observed in the previous chapter that the critical doctrine has produced in the majority of minds, and tends more and more to strengthen, the habit of setting oneself up as supreme judge of general political ideas. This anarchic state of the intellect, erected as a fundamental principle, is an obvious obstacle to the reorganization of society. Thinkers who are genuinely competent to form the true organic doctrine destined to terminate the present crisis would therefore labour in vain if their previous situation did not already give them the acknowledged power to speak with authority. In the absence of this condition their work, subject to the

that this distinction between the section of the scientific class which must be active and the section which must be simply passive in the elaboration of the organic doctrine is quite secondary, and that it in no way affects the fundamental assertion established in the text. [Footnote added in 1824]

arbitrary and conceited control of the politics of whim, could never be uniformly adopted. And if we take a glance at society, we will soon recognize that this spiritual influence is today to be found exclusively in the hands of the scientists. They alone exercise an uncontested authority in matters of theory. Thus, independently of the fact that they are alone competent to form the new organic doctrine, they are exclusively invested with the necessary moral force to secure its acceptance. The obstacles which that task faces from the critical prejudice that conceives moral sovereignty as an innate right in each individual would be insurmountable by anyone other than them. The only lever capable of dislodging this prejudice is found in their hands. This is the habit which society has gradually acquired, since the foundation of the positive sciences, of submitting itself to the decisions of scientists for all particular theoretical ideas, a habit which the scientists will easily extend to general theoretical ideas, when they are entrusted with their co-ordination.

Thus scientists today possess, to the exclusion of any other class, the two fundamental elements of moral government, capacity and theoretical authority.

One last essential character, not less peculiar to the scientific force than the preceding ones, is still worth mentioning.

The present crisis is evidently common to all the peoples of western Europe, though they do not all participate in it to the same degree. Nevertheless, it is treated by each of them as if it were simply national. But it is obvious that a European crisis needs European treatment.

This isolation of the peoples is a necessary consequence of the fall of the theological and feudal system, a process which dissolved the spiritual bonds which that system had established among the peoples of Europe, and which there were vain attempts to replace with a state of reciprocal hostility, disguised under the name of the European balance of power. The critical doctrine is incapable of re-establishing the harmony which it destroyed in its old fundamental principle; and, on the contrary, it makes it still more remote. First, by its nature, it tends to isolation; and, secondly, the peoples could not completely agree on the very principles of this doctrine, because they each want to modify the old system to different degrees in accordance with the doctrine.

The true organic doctrine can alone produce this union, so imperiously demanded by the state of European civilization. It must necessarily bring it about by presenting all the peoples of western Europe with the system of social organization to which they are all now summoned, and which each of them will enjoy in its entirety at a time nearer or further away according to its particular state of knowledge. It should be observed, besides, that this union will be more perfect than that produced by the old system, for there union existed only in the spiritual domain; whereas today it must equally come about in the temporal domain, so that these peoples are called upon to form a true general society, complete and permanent. And, indeed, if this were the place to undertake such an analysis, it would be easy to show that each of the peoples of western Europe is placed, by the particular variation of its state of civilization, in the most favourable position to treat this or that part of the general system; whence results the immediate utility of their co-operation. And it follows from this that these peoples must also work in common for the establishment of the new system.

In considering the new organic doctrine from this point of view, it is clear that the force destined to form it and to establish it, because it has to meet the condition of instituting the combination of the different civilized peoples, must be a European force. And that too is the special property, no less exclusive than those enumerated above, of the scientific force. It is noticeable that scientists alone form a true coalition, compact and active, all of whose members understand each other and correspond easily and continuously, from one end of Europe to the other. That stems from the fact that they alone today have ideas in common, a uniform language, a general and permanent goal for their activity. No other class possesses this powerful advantage, because no other fulfils these conditions in their entirety. Even the industrialists, so pre-eminently directed towards union by the nature of their work and by their habits, still allow themselves to be too dominated by the hostile moods of a savage patriotism for it to be possible at this time to establish a truly European combination among them. That can only be produced by the action of scientists.

It is doubtless superfluous to demonstrate that the current contacts between scientists will acquire a much increased intensity when they direct their general forces towards the formation of the new social doctrine. This consequence is obvious, since the force of a social bond is necessarily in proportion to the importance of the goal of the association.

To appreciate properly, in its full extent, the value of this European force peculiar to scientists, we need to compare the conduct of kings, from the point of view which concerns us, with that of peoples.

We observed above that kings, while navigating according to a plan whose principle is absurd, proceed to carry it out much more methodically than peoples do, because the line they follow is wholly described in the past in the smallest detail. Thus from the point of view we are considering, kings combine their efforts across the whole of Europe, whereas the peoples are isolated from one another. For this reason alone, the kings have an advantage relative to the peoples, against which the latter have nothing to fight with, which makes it an extremely important factor.

The leaders of opinion among the peoples have no course open to them other than to cry out against such a positional advantage, which does not exist any the less for that. They proclaim, as a general rule, that the different states have no right to intervene in each other's social reforms. And this principle, which is nothing other than the application of the critical doctrine to foreign relations, is absolutely false like all the other dogmas which compose it; like them, it is only the pernicious generalization of a transient state of affairs, the dissolution of the bonds which existed, under the influence of the old system, between the European nations. It is clear that the peoples of western Europe, having a common and interconnected civilization, whether it is considered in its development over time or in its present state, form a great nation, whose members have reciprocal rights which, though doubtless less extensive, are of the same kind as those of the different sections of a single state.

Moreover, we can see that this critical idea, even if it were true, does not attain its goal, but rather the opposite, since it tends to prevent the peoples from uniting. As one force can only be contained by another, the peoples will obviously, from a European point of view, be in a state of inferiority in relation to the kings, so long as the force of scientists – the only European force – does not preside over the great work of social reorganization. It alone, perhaps, can be the peoples' real equivalent of the holy alliance, allowing for the necessary superiority of a spiritual coalition over a purely temporal coalition.

Thus, in the last analysis, the necessity of entrusting to the scientists the preliminary theoretical works acknowledged to be indispensable for the reorganization of society is founded on four distinct considerations, any one of which would be sufficient to achieve it: (1) the scientists, by their type of intellectual capacity and culture, are alone competent to carry out these works; (2) they are destined for this function by the nature of things, being the spiritual power of the system to be organized; (3) they alone possess the moral authority necessary today to bring about the acceptance of the new organic doctrine, when it is formed; (4) finally, of all the existing social forces, that of the scientists is the only one that is European. Such a collection of proofs must doubtless place the great theoretical mission of the scientists beyond the reach of any uncertainty and any dispute.

It follows from all that has been said so far that the fundamental errors committed by the peoples in their manner of conceiving the reorganization of society have as their primary cause the pernicious course according to which they have embarked on this reorganization; that the flaw of this course consists in the fact that social reorganization has been viewed as a purely practical operation, whereas it is essentially theoretical; that the nature of things and the most compelling historical experiences prove the absolute necessity of dividing the total work of reorganization into two series, one theoretical and the other practical, of which the first must be carried out beforehand and is meant to serve as the basis for the second; that the preliminary execution of the theoretical works demands the activation of a new social force, distinct from those which have hitherto occupied the scene, which are absolutely incompetent; and finally that, for several decisive reasons, this new force has to be that of the scientists devoted to the study of the sciences of observation.

These ideas can be considered as a whole as having the object of gradually raising the minds of reflective men to the elevated point of view from which one can embrace, at a single glance, both the vices of the course hitherto followed in the reorganization of society, and the character of the course which must be adopted today. In the last resort everything can be reduced to establishing in politics, by the combined force of European scientists, a positive theory distinct from practice, and having as its object the conception of the new social system corresponding to the present state of knowledge. When we think about it, we can see that this conclusion can be summed up in this single idea: *the scientists must today raise politics to the rank of the sciences of observation.*

This is the culminating and definitive point of view we must adopt. From this point of view, it is easy to compress into a series of very simple considerations the substance of everything that has been said since the beginning of this work. It remains for us to make this important generalization, which alone can provide us with the means of advance, permitting the acceleration of the progress of thought.

By the very nature of the human mind, each branch of our knowledge is necessarily liable in its course to pass in its turn through three different theoretical states: the theological or fictional state; the metaphysical or abstract state; the scientific or positive state.

In the first, supernatural ideas serve to link the small number of isolated ideas which then constitute science. In other words, observed facts are *explained*, that is, *seen a priori*, in the light of invented facts. This state is necessarily that of any science at its cradle. However imperfect it may be, it is at that time the only way of connecting facts. It consequently provides the only instrument by means of which one can reason from the facts, by supporting the activity of the mind, which needs above all some kind of rallying point. In a word, it is indispensable if we are to be allowed to go further.

The second state is simply destined to serve as a means of transition from the first towards the third. Its character is illegitimate, for it connects facts in the light of ideas which are no longer wholly supernatural, and which are not entirely natural. In a word, these ideas are personified abstractions, in which the mind can see, according to taste, either the mystical name of a supernatural cause or the abstract enunciation of a simple series of phenomena, depending on whether the mind is closer to the theological state or the scientific state. This metaphysical state assumes that facts, having become more numerous, have at the same time drawn closer together when viewed in the light of more extended analogies.

The third state is the definitive mode of any science; the first two being destined only to prepare the way for it gradually. In this stage, facts are connected according to ideas or general laws of a wholly positive kind, suggested or confirmed by the facts themselves, which are often only simple facts sufficiently general to become principles. We still try to reduce them to the smallest number possible, but without dreaming up any hypothesis that is not of a kind that can be verified one day by observation; and we view them, in all cases, as nothing but a means of general expression for phenomena.

Men familiar with the course of the sciences can easily verify the accuracy of this general historical summary in relation to the four fundamental sciences which are today positive: astronomy, physics, chemistry and physiology, as well as for their ancillary sciences. Even those who have only considered the sciences in their present state can carry out this verification for physiology, which, although it has at last become as positive as the three others, still exists under the three forms in the different classes of mind which are unequally contemporary. This fact is manifest above all in the case of that part of this science which considers phenomena specifically called *moral*,[19] conceived by some as the result of a continuing supernatural influence, by others as the incomprehensible effects of the activity of an abstract being, and by others, finally, as stemming from organic conditions susceptible to demonstration, and beyond which one cannot go further back.

If we consider politics as a science, and apply to it the preceding observations, we find that it has already passed through the first two states, and that it is now ready to reach the third.

The doctrine of kings represents the theological state of politics. It is indeed on theological ideas that it is founded in the last analysis. It shows social relations as based on the supernatural idea of divine right. It explains the successive political transformations of the human race by reference to an immediate supernatural direction, exercised continuously from the first man to the present. It is

[19] i.e. psychological phenomena.

exclusively in this way that politics was conceived, until the old system began to decline.

The doctrine of the peoples expresses the metaphysical state of politics. It is founded in its entirety on the abstract and metaphysical assumption of an original social contract, prior to all development of the human faculties by civilization. The means of reasoning it habitually employs are rights, viewed as natural and common to all men to the same degree, which it guarantees by this contract. This is the doctrine, originally critical, drawn, at its origin, from theology, to fight against the old system, and which was then viewed as organic. It was principally Rousseau who summed it up in a systematic form, in a work which served and which still serves as a basis for popular reflections on social organization.[20]

Finally, the scientific doctrine of politics considers the social state in which the human race has always been found by observers as the necessary consequence of its organization. It conceives the object of this social state to be determined by the rung which man occupies in the system of nature, as it is fixed by the facts and without being viewed as susceptible to explanation. Indeed it sees resulting from this fundamental relation the constant tendency of man to act on nature, to modify it to his advantage. It next considers the social order as having as its final object to develop collectively this natural tendency, to regularize it and to channel it so that the amount of useful action can be maximized. Once that has been done, it tries to connect the fundamental laws of human organization, by direct observation of the collective development of the species, with the course it has followed and the intermediate states through which it has been forced to pass before arriving at this definitive state. By taking its directions from this series of observations, it views the improvements reserved for each era as dictated, without any need for further speculation, by the point of this development which the human race has reached. Next, for each level of civilization, it conceives political combinations as having exclusively the object of facilitating the steps to be taken after they have been accurately determined.

This is the spirit of the positive doctrine which we need to establish today, setting ourselves the goal of applying it to the present

---

[20] *Du contrat social*, 1762.

state of the civilized human race, and considering previous states only in so far as they need to be observed to establish the fundamental laws of the science.

It is easy to explain at the same time why politics did not become a positive science sooner, and why it is called to become one today.

Two fundamental conditions, distinct though inseparable, were indispensable.

In the first place, it was necessary for all the individual sciences to become positive in succession; for the whole could not be positive when all the elements were not. This condition is now satisfied.

The sciences have become positive, one after the other, in the order in which it was natural for this revolution to operate. This order is that of the greater or lesser degree of complication of their phenomena, or, in other words, of their more or less close connection with man. Thus astronomical phenomena first, as the simplest, and then successively the physical, the chemical and the physiological were reduced to positive theories; the last-named in a very recent period. The same reform could only be carried out last of all for political phenomena, which are the most complicated, since they depend on all the others. But it is obviously just as necessary that it should be carried out now, as it was impossible for it to occur sooner.

In the second place, it was necessary for the preparatory social system, in which action upon nature was only the indirect goal of society, to have arrived at its last stage.

On the one hand, in fact, the theory could not have been established until then because it would have been too far ahead of practice. Being intended to direct it, it could not get so far ahead of it as to lose it from sight. On the other hand, it could not have had an adequate experimental basis any sooner. A system of social order had to be established, accepted by a numerous population and composed of several large nations; and this system had to have lasted for an extended period, so that a theory could be founded on this vast experience.

This second condition is today satisfied as well as the first. The theological system, destined to prepare the human mind for the scientific system, has reached the end of its career. That is incontestable, since the metaphysical system, whose exclusive object is to overturn the theological system, has generally achieved preponderance among the peoples. Scientific politics must therefore be founded as a matter of course, since, given the absolute impossibility of doing without a theory, if this did not happen we should have to suppose that theological politics could be reconstituted; metaphysical politics not being, properly speaking, a true theory, but a critical doctrine appropriate only for a transition.

In summary, there has therefore never been a moral revolution at once more inevitable, more mature and more urgent than that which is now to elevate politics to the rank of the sciences of observation in the hands of the combined scientists of Europe. This revolution alone can introduce into the great current crisis a truly dominant force, which is alone capable of regulating and preserving society from the terrible and anarchical explosions with which it is threatened, by placing it on the true path to an improved social system, which the state of its knowledge imperiously demands.

To activate as promptly as possible the scientific forces destined to fulfil this salutary mission, it was necessary to present the general prospectus of the theoretical works to be executed in order to reorganize society by raising politics to the rank of the sciences of observation. We were so bold as to conceive this plan, and we solemnly offer it to the scientists of Europe.

Profoundly convinced that, when this discussion is under way, our plan, whether accepted or rejected, will necessarily lead to the formation of the final plan, we are not afraid to summon all the scientists in Europe, in the name of society – which is threatened by a long and terrible agony from which their intervention can alone preserve it – publicly and freely to voice their reasoned opinion in respect of the general chart of organic works which we submit to them.

This prospectus is composed of three series of works.

The first has as its object the formation of the system of historical observations on the general course of the human mind, destined to be the positive basis of politics, in such a way as wholly to deprive it of its theological and metaphysical character and stamp it with a scientific character.

The second works towards the foundation of the complete system of positive education which is appropriate to regenerated society, constituted so as to act upon nature; or, in other words, it aims to improve this action insofar as it depends upon the faculties of the agent.

Finally, the third consists in the general exposition of the collective action which, in the present state of their knowledge of all kinds, civilized men can exercise upon nature in order to modify it to their advantage, by directing all their forces towards this aim, and viewing social combinations as simple means to attain it.

First series of works

The fundamental condition to be met if we are to treat politics in a positive manner consists in the accurate determination of the limits within which, in the nature of things, combinations in society are confined. In other words, in politics, following the example of the other sciences, the role of observation and that of imagination must be made quite distinct, and the second should be subordinated to the first.

To present this capital idea in its fullest significance, we must compare the general spirit of positive politics with that of theological politics and that of metaphysical politics. To simplify this parallel we can consider the last two together; which should not alter the results, since, according to the last chapter, the second is at bottom only a nuance of the first. Its only essential difference is that it is less pronounced.

The theological state and the metaphysical state of any science have as a common characteristic the predominance of imagination over observation. The only difference that exists between them from this point of view is that in the first imagination is exercised on supernatural beings and in the second on personified abstractions.

The necessary and constant consequence of such a state of the human mind is to persuade man that, from all points of view, he is the centre of the system of nature, and, consequently, that he is endowed with an unlimited power of action over phenomena. This conviction evidently results directly from the supremacy exercised by the imagination, which combines with the organic propensity by virtue of which man is in general led to form exaggerated ideas of his importance and his power. Such an illusion forms the most perceptible characteristic feature of this infancy of human reason.

Considered from the philosophical point of view, the revolutions which have brought the different sciences to the positive state have had the general effect of reversing this primitive order of our ideas.

The fundamental character of these revolutions has been to transfer to observation the predominance up to then exercised by imagination. As a result, the consequences too have been reversed. Man has been displaced from the centre of nature and placed in the rank he actually occupies in it. In the same way, his sphere of action has been confined within its true limits: to modify, to a greater or lesser extent, a certain number of phenomena he is destined to observe, by bringing some to bear on others.

It is enough to mention the foregoing historical insight for it to be immediately verified, in relation to the sciences which are today positive, by all those who have clear notions about them.

Thus in astronomy man began by viewing celestial phenomena, if not as subject to his influence, at least as having direct and intimate relations with all the details of his existence; all the authority of the strongest and most numerous proofs was needed before he resigned himself to occupying only a subordinate and imperceptible place in the general system of the universe. Likewise, in chemistry, we first thought we could modify at whim the innermost nature of bodies, before we confined ourselves to observing the effects of the reciprocal action of the different earthly substances. Similarly, in medicine, it was after he had long aspired to rectify at will the disorders of his structure, and even indefinitely to resist the causes of his destruction, that man finally recognized that his action was in vain when he did not work with that of the structure, and all the more so when he worked against it.

No more than the other sciences has politics escaped from this law founded on the nature of things. The state it has always been in up to now, and which it is still in, corresponds with a perfect analogy to astrology in relation to astronomy, alchemy in relation to chemistry, and the search for the universal panacea in relation to medicine.

First, it is evident from the previous chapter that theological politics and metaphysical politics, viewed in their way of proceeding, agree in giving the upper hand to imagination over observation. No doubt we could not claim that hitherto observation has not been employed in theoretical politics; but it has been employed only in a subordinate manner, on the orders of the imagination, as it was, for example, in chemistry in the age of alchemy.

In politics, this preponderance of imagination necessarily had to have consequences analogous to those described above for the other sciences. That can easily be verified[21] by direct observations of the spirit common to theological politics and metaphysical politics, considered from a theoretical point of view.

Up to the present, man has believed in the unlimited power of his political combinations for the improvement of the social order. In other words, the human race has hitherto been viewed in politics as lacking any impetus peculiar to it, always able to receive passively the impetus, whatever it may be, which the legislator, armed with sufficient authority, might want to give it.

By a necessary consequence, the absolute has always reigned, and still reigns, in theoretical politics, whether theological or metaphysical. The common goal they set themselves is to establish, each in its own way, the eternal type of the most perfect social order, without having in mind any particular state of civilization. Both claim exclusively to have found a system of institutions which attains this goal. The only thing which distinguishes them in this respect is that the first categorically forbids any important modification of the plan it has sketched, whereas the second permits scrutiny, provided it is directed by same goal. With that difference, their character is equally absolute.

This absolute character is still more perceptible in their applications to practical politics. Each of them sees, in its system of institutions, a sort of universal panacea applicable, with infallible certainty, to all political evils, of whatever kind they may be, and whatever the present degree of civilization of the people for whom the remedy is intended. In the same way too, both judge the regimes of the different peoples in the different ages of civilizations uniquely according to their greater or lesser conformity with or difference from the invariable standard of perfection which they have set up. Thus, to cite a recent and palpable example, the supporters of theological politics and those of metaphysical politics in turn, and with very little interval between them, have proclaimed the social organ-

---

[21] 1854: 'But it is easy to verify this similarity of effects, independently of a similarity of cause'.

ization of Spain to be superior to that of the most advanced European nations, without either group taking any account of the present inferiority of the Spaniards in terms of civilization in relation to the French and the English, above whom they have been placed as far as the political regime is concerned. Such judgements, which could easily be multiplied, show clearly to what extent it is in the spirit of theological politics and metaphysical politics totally to disregard the state of civilization.

To complete our characterization of them, it is important to note in this regard that in general they agree, for different reasons, in identifying the perfection of the social organization with a very imperfect state of civilization. We can even see that the most consistent supporters of metaphysical politics, like Rousseau, who co-ordinated it,[22] have been led so far as to view the social state as the degeneration of a state of nature invented by their imagination, which is only the metaphysical analogue of the theological idea relating to the degradation of the human race by original sin.

This accurate summary confirms that in politics the predominance of the imagination over observation has produced results that are very similar to those it had engendered in the other sciences before they became positive. The absolute search for the best possible government, regardless of the state of civilization, is obviously entirely of the same kind as the search for a general treatment applicable to all illnesses and to all constitutions.

In seeking to reduce the general spirit of theological and metaphysical politics to its simplest expression, we can see, from what has gone before, that it boils down to two essential considerations. In relation to the manner of proceeding, it consists in the predominance of imagination over observation. In relation to the general ideas destined to direct the works, it consists, on the one hand, in envisaging social organization in an abstract manner, that is to say independently of the state of civilization; and, on the other hand, in viewing the march of civilization as being subject to no law.

If we turn this spirit on its head, we must necessarily find the spirit of positive politics, since the same opposition is to be observed, in accordance with what has been established above, between the conjectural state and the positive state of all the other

---

[22] 1854: (summed it up in a systematic form).

sciences. By this intellectual operation we are doing nothing but extending to the future the analogy observed in the past. In carrying out the operation we are led to the following results.

In the first place, in order to render political science positive, we have to introduce into it, as in the other sciences, the predominance of observation over imagination. In the second place, for this fundamental condition to be fulfilled, we must, on the one hand, conceive social organization to be intimately tied to the state of civilization and determined by it; on the other hand we must consider the course of civilization to be subject to an invariable law founded on the nature of things. Politics could not become positive, or, what amounts to the same thing, observation could not take the upper hand over imagination, so long as these last two conditions are not fulfilled. But it is clear, conversely, that if they are fulfilled, if the theory of politics is wholly established in this spirit, imagination will find itself in fact subordinated to observation, and politics will be positive. Thus in the last analysis everything reduces to these two conditions.

These are therefore the two capital ideas which must govern the positive works on theoretical politics. Given their extreme importance, it is essential to consider them in greater detail. It is not here a matter of establishing their proof, which will be precisely the result of the works to be carried out.[23] It is simply a question of presenting a sufficiently complete survey of them so that minds capable of judging can do a sort of preliminary verification by comparing them with facts that are generally known; a verification which is sufficient to convince them of the possibility of treating politics in the manner of the sciences of observation. Our principal goal will be attained if we have given birth to this conviction.

Civilization consists, properly speaking, in the development of the human mind, on the one hand, and, on the other hand, in the development of man's action on nature which is its consequence. In other words, the elements of which the idea of civilization are composed are: the sciences, the arts and industry; this last expression being taken in the widest sense, the one we have always given it.

When we consider civilization from this precise and elementary point of view, it is easy to see that the state of social organization is

[23] 1822: 'and of which it would be rash to presume to give even a brief outline in this prospectus'.

essentially dependent upon that of civilization, and that the former must be regarded as a consequence of the latter, whereas the politics of imagination views them as isolated and even wholly independent.

The state of civilization necessarily determines that of social organization, whether in the spiritual or the temporal dimension, from the two most important points of view. First, it determines its nature, for it fixes the goal of activity for society; furthermore, it prescribes its essential form, for it creates and develops the temporal and spiritual social forces which are destined to direct this general activity. It is indeed clear that the collective activity of the social body, being only the sum of the individual activities of all its members, directed towards a common goal, could not be different in nature from its elements, which are obviously determined by the more or less advanced state of the sciences, the arts and industry. It is still more palpable that it would be impossible to conceive the prolonged existence of a political system which does not confer supreme power on the preponderant social forces, whose nature is invariably prescribed[24] by the state of civilization. What reasoning indicates, experience confirms.

All the varieties of social organization that have existed up to now have simply been more or less extensive modifications of a single system, the military and theological system. The original formation of this system was an obvious and necessary consequence of the imperfect state of civilization at that time. Industry being in its infancy, society naturally had to take war as the goal of its activity, especially when we think that such a state of things made the means of war easy to come by, at the same time as imposing the law of war by the most energetic incentives that act on man, the need to exercise his faculties and the need to live. In the same way, it is clear that the theological state in which all the particular theories were then to be found necessarily stamped the same character on the general ideas destined to serve as a social bond. The third element of civilization, the arts, was then predominant; and indeed it was that which was principally responsible for putting this first organization on a regular footing. If the arts had not developed, it would be impossible to imagine how society could have been organized.

[24] 1822: 'whose nature is invariably still prescribed'.

If we next observe the successive modifications which this original system has undergone up to our day, and which metaphysicians have taken as so many different systems, the same result will be found. In all of these modifications we shall see inevitable effects of the ever-growing expansion of the scientific element and the industrial element, which were almost non-existent at the beginning. It is thus that the passage from polytheism to theism, and, later, the Protestant reformation, were chiefly produced by the continuous, though slow, progress of positive knowledge, or, in other words, by the influence exerted on the old general ideas by the particular ideas which had gradually ceased to be of the same kind. In the same way, from a temporal point of view, the passage from the Roman state to the feudal state – and, still more clearly, the decline of the latter due to the enfranchisement of the communes and its consequences – must be essentially attributed to the progressively increasing importance of the industrial element. In a word, all the general facts testify to the close dependence of social organization on civilization.

The best minds, those who are closest to the positive state of politics, are today beginning to glimpse this fundamental principle. They feel that it is absurd to conceive the political system in isolation, to derive all the forces of society from it, whereas on the contrary it receives all its force from society and without it it is null and void. In short, they already concede that the political order is only and can only be the expression of the civil order, which means, in other words, that the preponderant social forces necessarily end up in control. It is just one step from there to recognizing the subordination of the political system to the state of civilization. For, if it is clear that the political order is the expression of the civil order, it is at least as obvious that the civil order itself is only the expression of the state of civilization.

No doubt social organization in turn reacts inevitably on civilization, with more or less energy. But this influence is only secondary, and its very great importance must not lead us to invert the natural order of dependence. The proof that this order is actually as has been indicated can be drawn from this very reaction, looked at in the right way. For it is our constant experience that if social organization is constituted in opposition to the movement of civilization, the latter always in the end prevails over the former.

We have to admit, therefore, as one of the two fundamental ideas which determine the spirit of positive politics, that social organization must not be looked upon, either in the present or in the past, in isolation from the state of civilization, but that it must be looked upon as a necessary derivation from that state. If, for ease of study, we sometimes deem it useful to examine them separately, we must always think of this abstraction as simply provisional; we must never lose sight of the subordination established by the nature of things.

The second fundamental idea consists in the notion that the progress of civilization develops according to a necessary law.

The experience of the past proves most decisively that the progressive development of civilization is subject to a natural and irrevocable course, derived from the laws of human organization, which in turn becomes the supreme law of all political phenomena.

There can obviously be no question here of setting forth in detail the characteristics of this law, and how it is verified by the facts of history, even the most summary ones. That is the object of the second part of this volume. It is now simply a matter of presenting a number of reflections on this fundamental idea.[25]

One primary consideration should make us see the need to posit such a law in order to explain political phenomena.

All men who have any knowledge of the most notable facts of history, whatever their speculative opinions, will agree that, if we consider the whole of the civilized portion of the human race, it has made uninterrupted and ever-growing progress in civilization from the most distant times in history up to our own day. In this statement, the word civilization is understood as it has been explained above, moreover embracing social organization as a consequence.

There can be no reasonable doubt of this great fact for the era which stretches from the eleventh century to the present, that is from the introduction of the sciences of observation into Europe by the Arabs and the enfranchisement of the communes. But it is no less incontestable for the preceding era. Scholars have now come to recognize that learned claims concerning the very advanced scientific knowledge of the ancients are devoid of any real foundation. It

---

[25] Instead of 'That is the object . . .', the 1822 text reads: 'That would be an impossible anticipation of work that is still to be undertaken. It is simply a matter of presenting . . .'.

is proven that the Arabs surpassed them. It was the same, and still more clearly, with industry, at least any demanding true competence and not resulting from purely accidental circumstances. Even when we set aside the fine arts, this exclusion, which can be explained in a wholly natural way, would leave the proposition sufficiently general in scope. Finally, as for social organization, it is as clear as can be that it made progress of the first order in the same period, by the establishment of Christianity and by the formation of the feudal regime, far superior to Greek and Roman organizations.

It is therefore certain that civilization has been continually on an onward course in all its aspects.

On the other hand, without adopting the spirit of denigration of the past, which metaphysics introduced and which is as blind as it is unjust, we cannot stop ourselves from recognizing that because politics has hitherto been in a state of infancy the practical combinations which have guided civilization were not always the best suited to leading it onwards, and indeed often tended of themselves much more to impede than to favour its advance. There have been eras in which all the major political action has been combined to produce deadlock; these are, in general, eras of the decay of systems such as, for example, those of the Emperor Julian, Philip II and the Jesuits, and, lastly, that of Bonaparte. It should be observed furthermore, in accordance with the preceding discussion, that social organization does not at all regulate the advance of civilization; it is, on the contrary, its product.

The frequent healing of illnesses under the influence of obviously defective treatments has disclosed to doctors the powerful influence which any living body exerts spontaneously to counteract the accidental disturbances to its organization. In the same way, the advancement of civilization in the face of unfavourable political combinations clearly proves that civilization is subject to a natural course, independent of and dominating all combinations. If this principle were not admitted, there would be no other line to be taken to explain such a fact, to understand how civilisation has almost always profited from the faults committed instead of being retarded by them, other than to have recourse to an immediate and continuous supernatural control, after the example of theological politics.

Furthermore, it is right to observe on this subject that people have too often regarded as unfavourable to the onward course of civilization causes which were so only in appearance. The reason is above all that even the best minds have not up to now had regard to one of the essential laws of organized bodies, which applies as much to the human race acting collectively as to an isolated individual. This law consists in the necessity of resistance, up to a certain degree, in order for all forces to be fully developed. But this remark in no way affects the foregoing reflection. For, though obstacles may be necessary for forces to be deployed, they do not produce them.

The conclusion deduced from this first consideration would be much strengthened if we took account of the remarkable identity observed in the development of the civilization of different peoples, among whom one might reasonably suppose there was no political communication. This identity could only have been produced by the influence of a natural course of civilization, uniform for all peoples, because it derives from the fundamental laws of human organization, which are common to all. Thus, for example, it is obviously only in this way that we can explain the manners of Greece in the earliest times, as Homer described them, which have been rediscovered in our own times, with a very great degree of similarity, among the savage nations of North America; or feudalism observed among the Malays with the same essential character that it had in Europe in the eleventh century, etc.

A second consideration makes it very easy to see the existence of a natural law which governs the development of civilization.

If we admit, in conformity with the insight presented above, that the state of the social regime is a necessary derivation from that of civilization, then this complicated element can be removed from the observation of the course of progress; and what we see in other elements will be no less applicable to it as a result.

When the question is thus reduced to its simplest terms it is easy to see that civilization is subject to a determined and invariable course.

A superficial philosophy, which would make this world a scene for the staging of miracles, has grossly exaggerated the influence of chance, that is of isolated causes, in human affairs. This exaggeration is manifest above all in the case of the sciences and the arts.

Among other noteworthy causes, everyone knows the singular wonder with which a number of men of intellect were filled when they thought of the law of universal gravitation revealed to Newton by the fall of an apple.

It is today generally recognized, by all men of sense, that chance has only the tiniest of parts in scientific and industrial discoveries; that it plays an essential role only in discoveries of no importance. But this error has been replaced by another which, much less unreasonable in itself, presents the same disadvantages in its effects. The role of chance has been transferred to genius in more or less the same form. This transformation is hardly able to explain any better the acts of the human mind.

Yet the history of human knowledge proves most patently – and the best minds have already recognized it – that in the sciences and the arts all works are interlinked, whether in the same generation or from one generation to another, in such a way that the discoveries of one generation prepare the way for those of the following generation, as their way had been prepared by those of the preceding generation. It has been established that the power of isolated genius is much less than we had supposed it to be. The man who is most illustrious for his great discoveries almost always owes the greater part of his success to his predecessors in the career on which he is proceeding. In short, in the development of the sciences and the arts the human mind follows a determined course, surpassing the greatest intellectual powers, which come to be understood, so to speak, as mere instruments destined to produce the successive discoveries at the appointed time.

If we limit ourselves to considering the sciences, which can be followed more easily from the most distant times, we can see, in effect, that the great historical epochs of each of them – that is to say, its passage through the theological state, the metaphysical state, and finally the positive state – are rigorously determined. These three states necessarily succeed each other in the order founded on the nature of the human mind. The transition from one to the other takes place according to a course whose principal steps are analogous for all the sciences; and no man of genius could overstep even a single essential intermediary. If, from this general division, we pass to the subdivisions of the scientific or definitive state, we again observe the same law. Thus, for example, the great discovery of universal gravitation was prepared by the works of the astronomers and geometers of the sixteenth and seventeenth centuries, principally by those of Kepler and Huygens, without which it would have been impossible, and which could not have failed to produce it sooner or later.

In the light of the preceding, there can be no doubt that the course of civilization, considered in its elements, is subject to a natural and constant law which dominates all particular human differences. As the state of social organization necessarily follows that of civilization, the same conclusion therefore applies to civilization, envisaged at one and the same time in its totality and in its elements.

The two reflections enunciated above are sufficient, not to demonstrate completely the necessary course of civilization, but to make its existence felt, to show the possibility of determining all its attributes with precision by studying it through close observation of the past, and of thus creating positive politics.

It is now a question of determining exactly the practical goal of this science, its general points of contact with the needs of society, and above all with the great reorganization demanded so imperiously by the current state of the social body.

To that end, we must first specify the limits within which all real political action is confined.

The fundamental law which governs the natural course of civilization rigorously prescribes all the successive states through which the human race is bound to pass in its general development. On the other hand, this law is the necessary result of the instinctive tendency of the human race to improve itself. Consequently it is as far above us, in our state of dependence, as the individual instincts whose combination produces this permanent tendency.

As no known phenomenon entitles us to think that human organization is subject to any major change, the course of civilization which derives from it is therefore essentially unalterable as far as the substance is concerned. In more specific terms, none of the intermediate steps it stipulates can be overstepped, and no true retrograde steps can be taken.

The course of civilization is only modifiable, to a greater or lesser extent, in its speed, within certain limits, by several physical and moral causes, which are capable of being estimated. Among these causes are political combinations. This is the only sense in which it is given to man to influence the course of his own civilization.

This action relative to the species is wholly analogous to that which is permitted to us in relation to the individual, an analogy which results from an identity of origin. By appropriate means we can accelerate or delay the development of an individual instinct; but we can neither destroy it nor denature it. The same applies to the instinct of the species, if we make due allowance for the difference in timespan between the life of the species and that of the individual.

It is beyond question, then, that the natural course of civilization determines for each era the improvements which the social state must undergo, whether in its elements or as a whole. They alone can be implemented, and they must necessarily be implemented, with the help of the combinations made by philosophers and by statesmen, or in spite of these combinations.

All men who have exerted a real and lasting influence on the human race, whether in the temporal sphere or in the spiritual, were guided and supported by this fundamental truth, which the ordinary instinct of genius led them to perceive, although it is not yet established on the basis of a methodical proof. They perceived, in each era, what were the changes which were tending to take place, in accordance with the state of civilization, and they proclaimed them, at the same time suggesting corresponding doctrines and institutions to their contemporaries. When their perception was in clear conformity with the true state of things, the changes asserted themselves or became consolidated almost immediately. New social forces, which for a long time had been developing in silence, suddenly began to make their voice heard on the political scene with all the vigour of youth.

Because history has hitherto been written and studied superficially, such coincidences, such striking effects, have not instructed men, as we might naturally have supposed, but have merely astonished them. These ill-understood facts even contribute to the maintenance of the theological and metaphysical belief in the unlimited and creative power of legislators over civilization. They maintain this superstitious idea in minds which might have been disposed to reject it, if it had not seemed to rest on observation. This unfortunate effect results from the fact that behind these great events we see only men, and never the things that impel them with an irresistible force. Instead of recognizing the preponderant influence of civilization, we regard the efforts of these foresighted men as the true causes of the improvements which have taken place, and which would have taken place in any case, a little later, without their intervention. We do not allow ourselves to be troubled by the enormous disproportion between the alleged cause and the effect, a disproportion which makes the explanation much more unintelligible than the fact itself. We stick to what meets the eye, and we neglect the reality, which lies beneath the surface. In short, to use Mme de Staël's ingenious expression, we mistake the actors for the play.[26]

This error is of exactly the same kind as that of the Indians who attributed to Christopher Columbus the eclipse which he predicted.

In general, when man appears to exert a great influence, it is not by his own strength alone, which is very small. It is always external forces that act for him, in accordance with laws on which he can have no impact. His power rests wholly in his intelligence, which puts him in a position to know these laws by observation, to foresee their effects, and consequently to make them work to the goal he sets himself, provided that he employs these forces in a way that is in conformity with their nature. Once the action has occurred, ignorance of natural laws leads the spectator, and sometimes the actor himself, to attribute to man's power what is due only to his foresight.

These general observations apply to philosophical action, in the same way and for the same reasons as to physical, chemical or physiological action. Any political action is followed by a real and lasting effect, when it exerts itself in the same direction as the force of civilization, when it seeks to effect the changes which that force currently commands. In any other circumstance action is to no effect or is at most ephemeral.

The most harmful case is without question that in which the legislator – temporal or spiritual – acts, deliberately or not, in a retrograde sense; for he then sets himself up in opposition to that which alone constitutes his strength. But this course[27] is so far the

---

[26] Madame de Staël, *Considérations sur les principaux événements de la révolution française* (Paris 1818), I, p. 1.

[27] By 'this course' Comte means the irresistible course of civilization, as is clear from the draft version.

precise regulator of political action, that this action is still to no effect, in spite of its progressive tendency, when it favours the onward course but wants to advance further than is provided for. Experience proves, in fact, that the legislator – however much power we may suppose him to be robed in – necessarily fails if he undertakes improvements which, though with the grain of the natural progress of civilization, are too far beyond its present state. Thus, for example, the great attempts of Joseph II to civilize Austria, more than its existing state allowed, were rendered as ineffective as the immense efforts of Bonaparte to turn France backwards towards the feudal regime, even though both men were armed with the most extensive arbitrary powers.

It follows from the considerations indicated above that true politics, positive politics, must no more pretend to govern its phenomena than other sciences govern their respective phenomena. They have renounced this ambitious chimera which characterized their infancy and have restricted themselves to observing and connecting phenomena. Politics must do the same. It must concern itself solely with co-ordinating all particular facts relative to the course of civilization, reducing them to the smallest possible number of general facts; it must connect these general facts in such a way as to bring out the natural law of this course, and it must then assess the influence of the various causes which can modify its pace.

The practical utility of this politics of observation can now be easily determined.

Sound politics cannot have as its object to propel the human race, since this moves by its own momentum, in accordance with a law which is as necessary as that of gravity, though more modifiable. But it has as its goal to facilitate this movement by illuminating it.

There is a very great difference between obeying the course of civilization without realizing it, and obeying it purposefully. The changes it commands take place as much in the first case as in the second, but more slowly, and above all they only take place after producing in society harmful upheavals which are more or less serious according to the nature and importance of these changes. The strains of all kinds that result for the social body can be avoided, in large part, by means based on exact knowledge of the changes which are tending to occur.

These means consist in ensuring that improvements, once fore-seen, occur directly, instead of waiting until they have occurred by the necessity of things and in the face of all the obstacles that ignorance engenders. In other words, the essential goal of practical politics is, properly, to avoid the violent revolutions which arise from poorly understood shackles placed on the course of civilization, and to reduce them as promptly as possible to a simple moral movement, as regular as, though livelier than, that which gently stirs society in ordinary times. To attain this goal, it is obviously indispensable to know as precisely as possible the present tendency of civilization, so as to bring political action into conformity with it.

No doubt it would be chimerical to hope that movements which to a greater or lesser extent compromise the ambitions and interests of whole classes can be effected entirely peacefully. But it is no less certain that hitherto too much importance has been given to this cause in the explanation of turbulent revolutions whose violence has resulted, in large part, from the ignorance of the natural laws which regulate the course of civilization.

It is only too common to see things attributed to egoism which are essentially due to ignorance; and this baneful error contributes to the survival of irritation among men in their private and general relations. But, in the present case, is it not obvious that men who have hitherto been induced to place themselves in *de facto* opposition to the course of civilization would not have tried to do so if this opposition had been solidly demonstrated?

No one is so insane as to set himself up, knowingly, in revolt against the nature of things. No one takes pleasure in undertaking a course of action which he sees clearly must be ephemeral. Thus the proofs of the politics of observation are capable of acting upon the classes whose prejudices and interests would lead them to struggle against the course of civilization.

No doubt we must not exaggerate the influence of intelligence on men's conduct. But certainly the power of proof has a much greater importance than has hitherto been supposed. The history of the human mind proves that this power has often been solely responsible for changes in accomplishing which it has had to struggle against the greatest human forces combined. To cite just the most notable example, it was the power of positive proofs alone that ensured the acceptance of the theory of the earth's movement, which had to overcome not only the resistance of the theological power, still so vigorous at that time, but above all the pride of the human race as a whole, supported by the most plausible grounds a false idea has ever had in its favour. Such decisive experiences should enlighten us about the overwhelming power that results from authentic proofs. It is principally because there have never yet been any such proofs in politics that statesmen have let themselves be carried away into such great practical aberrations. Once proofs appear, aberrations will soon cease.

And besides, if we consider only interests, it is easy to feel that positive politics must provide the means to avoid violent revolutions.

Indeed, if the improvements necessitated by the course of civilization have to combat certain ambitions and certain interests, there exist others which are favourable to them. Furthermore, for the very reason that these improvements have reached maturity, the real forces in their favour are superior to the opposed forces, although appearances do not always indicate this. Even if we doubted, in relation to these opposed forces, whether positive knowledge of the course of civilization could be useful in persuading them to submit to an inevitable law, its importance relative to other forces could clearly not be brought into question. Guided by this knowledge, the ascendant classes, seeing clearly the goal they are called to achieve, will be able to head there directly, instead of wearying themselves with trial and error and detours. They will steadily combine the means to quash all resistance in advance, and to facilitate for their adversaries the transition towards the new order of things. In short, the triumph of civilization will take place both as promptly and as peacefully as the nature of things permits.

To sum up, the course of civilization does not, strictly speaking, follow a straight line. It is composed of a succession of progressive oscillations, more or less extended, faster or slower, above and below a middle line, in much the same way as the mechanism of locomotion. These oscillations can be made shorter or more rapid by political combinations founded on knowledge of the average movement, which always tends to predominate. Such is the permanent practical utility of this knowledge. Obviously its importance is greater the more significant are those same changes necessitated by the course of civilization. This utility is at its height today, since the social reorganization which can alone end the current crisis is the most complete of all the revolutions experienced by the human race.

The fundamental datum of general practical politics, its positive point of departure, is therefore the determination of the tendency of civilization so as to bring political action into conformity with it, and by that means to render as peaceful and as short as possible the inevitable crises to which the human race is subject as it passes in turn through the different stages of civilization.

Good minds which are, however, unfamiliar with the means of proceeding that suit the human mind might recognize the necessity of determining this tendency of civilization, to give a solid and positive basis to political combinations, but might think that to do so it is not necessary to study the general course of civilization from its origin, and that it is enough to consider it in its present state. This idea is natural, in view of the narrow way in which politics has been understood up to now. But it is easy to show its falsehood.

Experience has proved that, as long as the spirit of man remains engaged in a positive direction, there are many advantages and no disadvantages in its rising to the highest possible degree of generality, because it is far easier to descend than to ascend. In the infancy of positive physiology, we had begun by thinking that, in order to understand human organization, it was sufficient to study man alone, which was an error wholly analogous to the one in question here. We have since come to recognize that, in order to form clear and suitably extensive ideas of human organization, it was essential to think of man as a term in the animal series; and even, in a still more general conception, as forming part of the totality of organized bodies. Physiology is definitively constituted only now that the comparison of different classes of living beings is widely established, and now that it is beginning to be employed regularly in the study of man.[28]

In politics, the same is true of the different states of civilization as is true of the different organizations in physiology; except that the reasons which force us to consider the different eras of civilization

---

[28] 1822: Physiology was definitively constituted only when the comparison of different classes of living beings was widely established, and when it began to be employed regularly in the study of man.

are still more direct than those which led physiologists to establish the comparison of all organizations.

Without doubt, a study of the present state of civilization, envisaged in itself, independently of those which preceded it, is capable of providing very useful materials for the formation of positive politics, provided that the facts are observed philosophically. It is even certain that it is through studies of this kind that true statesmen have up to now been able to modify the conjectural doctrines which directed their minds, in such a way as to make them less discordant with the real needs of society. But it remains no less obvious that such a study is totally insufficient to form a truly positive politics. It is impossible to see anything there but materials. In short, observation of the present state of civilization, considered in isolation, can no more determine the current tendency of society than could the study of any other isolated era.

The reason is that, to establish a law, one term is not sufficient, for we need at least three, in order that the relationship, discovered by the comparison of the first two and verified by the third, might help us to find the following term, which is the goal of any law.

When, in tracing an institution and a social idea, or even a system of institutions and an entire doctrine, from their birth up to the present era, we find that, from a certain moment, their influence has always been continually diminishing or continually increasing, we can foresee with complete certainty the lot reserved for them on the basis of this series of observations. In the first case, it will be determined that they go against the grain of the movement of civilization, whence it results that they are destined to disappear. In the second case, by contrast, we shall conclude that they will end up dominant. The era of collapse or that of triumph can even be roughly calculated by the extent and the speed of the variations observed. Such a study is therefore obviously a fertile source of positive instruction.

But what can we learn from the isolated observation of one and the same stage, in which everything is confused, the doctrines, the institutions, the classes which are descending, and the doctrines, the institutions, the classes which are ascending, not counting the ephemeral action that belongs only to the routine of the moment? What human sagacity, faced with such a heterogeneous assemblage, would not be liable to mistake these opposed elements one for the other? How could we discern the realities that make so little noise, in the midst of the phantoms that bustle about on the scene? It is clear that, in such disorder, the observer can only proceed as a blind man; unless he is guided by the past, which alone can teach him to direct his view in such a way as to see things as they are fundamentally.

The chronological order of the epochs is not the philosophical order. Instead of saying: past, present and future, we should say: past, future and present. It is, in effect, only when we have, through the past, conceived the future that we can usefully return to the present – which is only a point – in such a way as to grasp its true character.

These considerations, applicable to any era, are all the more applicable to the present era. Today, three different systems coexist at the heart of society: the theological and feudal system, the scientific and industrial system, and finally the transitory and mongrel system of the metaphysicians and the legists. It is quite beyond the powers of the human mind to establish, in the midst of such confusion, a clear and exact analysis, a real and precise statistic of the social body, without being illuminated by the torch of the past. One could easily demonstrate that excellent minds, whose capacities suggest that they were made to rise to the heights of a truly positive politics, if only their faculties had been better directed, have remained sunk in metaphysics as a result of considering the present state of things in isolation, or even as a result of not having gone back far enough in the series of observations.

Thus we need to study – and study as deeply, as completely as possible – all the states through which civilization has passed from its origin to the present; to co-ordinate them, to determine their causal sequence, to formulate them as general facts capable of becoming principles, by bringing into prominence the natural laws of the development of civilization, the philosophical picture of the future of society, as it is derived from the past, that is to say to determine the general plan of reorganization destined for the present era; and finally to apply these results to the present state of things, in such a way as to determine the direction which must be imparted to political action in order to facilitate the definitive transition towards the new social state. This is the totality of works capable of establishing a positive theory of politics capable of responding to the immense and urgent needs of society.

This is the first series of theoretical investigations which I am bold enough to propose to the combined powers of European scientists.

All the considerations set out so far having adequately indicated the spirit of positive politics, its comparison with theological and metaphysical politics can become more precise.

In comparing them first of all from the most important point of view – in relation to the present needs of society – we can easily understand the superiority of positive politics. This superiority results from the fact that it *discovers* what the others *invent*. Theological and metaphysical politics imagines the system which suits the present state of civilization, in accordance with the absolute condition that it should be the best possible. Positive politics determines it by observation, solely on the basis that it must be the one that the course of civilization tends to produce. In accordance with this different way of proceeding, it would be equally impossible either for the politics of imagination to find the true social reorganization or for the politics of observation not to find it. The one makes the greatest effort to invent the cure, without considering the disease. The other, persuaded that the principal cause of recovery is the vital strength of the patient, limits itself to predicting, by observation, the natural outcome of the crisis, so as to facilitate it by removing the obstacles created by empiricism.

In the second place, scientific politics can alone present men with a theory on which it is possible to agree. This is, in a sense, the most important condition.

Theological politics and metaphysical politics, by seeking the best possible government, draw us into interminable debates, for this question cannot be decided. The political regime must be and is necessarily relative to the state of civilization; the best, for each era, is that which best conforms to that state. There is not, therefore, and there cannot be a political regime absolutely preferable to all the others; there are only states of civilization of which some are more perfected than others. Institutions that are good for one era can be, and even most often are, bad for another, and the other way round. Thus, for example, slavery, which is today a monstrosity, was certainly, at its origin, a very fine institution, since it had as its object to prevent the strong from bleeding the weak; it was an inevitable intermediary in the general development of civilization, as we shall establish more particularly in the second part of this volume.[29] In the same way, but in reverse, freedom, which in a reasonable measure is so useful to an individual and a people who have attained a certain degree of education and contracted certain habits of forethought, because it permits the development of their faculties, is very harmful to those who have not yet fulfilled these two conditions, and who have an essential need – for themselves as much as for others – to be kept in tutelage. It is therefore obvious that we cannot agree on the absolute question of the best possible government. To re-establish harmony there could be no other expedient than to prohibit entirely any discussion of the plan agreed, as did theological politics, more logical than metaphysical politics; because, having lasted, it must have fulfilled the conditions of durability. We know that in the same course of development metaphysics, by giving free rein to the imagination, led people so far as to cast doubt upon, and even formally to deny, the usefulness of the social state for the happiness of man, which clearly shows the impossibility of reaching agreement on such questions.

In scientific politics, on the contrary, the practical goal being to determine the system which the course of civilization, as the past reveals it, tends to produce today, the question is wholly positive, and quite capable of being decided by observation. The freest examination can and must be accorded, without our having any fear of wandering. At the end of a certain time, all competent minds – and in turn all the rest – must finally reach agreement on the natural laws of the course of civilization, and on the system which results from it, whatever their speculative opinions may have been at the outset, in the same way as we have come to reach agreement on the laws of the solar system, on those of human organization, etc.

Finally, positive politics is the only way by which the human race can escape from the state of arbitrariness in which it will remain sunk as long as theological politics and metaphysical politics continue to dominate.

Absoluteness in theory leads necessarily to arbitrariness in practice. As long as the human race is looked upon as if it had no

---

[29] This last clause was added in 1824 and was deleted in 1854.

impulsion of its own, but had to receive it from the legislator, arbitrariness must necessarily exist, in the highest degree and for the most essential of reasons, notwithstanding the most eloquent declamations. It is the nature of things that wills that things should be so. The human race being thus left to the discretion of the legislator, who determines for it the best possible government, arbitrariness can very well be restricted in details, but we should obviously be unable to expel it from the whole. It makes no difference in this respect whether the supreme legislator is one man or many, hereditary or elective. Society as a whole might substitute itself for the legislator, if it were possible, and it would still be the same; except that, arbitrary power being now exercised by the whole of society over itself, the disadvantages would become greater than ever.

In contrast, scientific politics radically excludes arbitrariness, because it removes the absoluteness and the indistinctness which have engendered it and which maintain it. In this politics, the human race is viewed as subject to a natural law of development, which is capable of being determined by observation, and which prescribes as unequivocally as possible the political action that can be exercised in each era. Arbitrariness therefore necessarily ceases. The government of things replaces that of men. It is then that there is really *law* in politics, in the true and philosophic sense attached to this expression by the illustrious Montesquieu. Whatever might be the details of the form of government, arbitrariness cannot reappear, at least as far as the substance is concerned. Everything is determined, in politics, according to a law which is truly sovereign, recognized superior to all human powers, since it derives, in the last analysis, from the nature of our organization, on which we can exert no influence. In short, this law excludes, with the same efficacy, theological arbitrariness, or the divine right of kings, and metaphysical arbitrariness, or the sovereignty of the people.

If some minds could see the supreme rule of such a law as a new form of existing arbitrary government, they should be urged to complain also about the inflexible despotism exercised over the whole of nature by the law of gravitation, and of the despotism – no less real, but still more analogous, being more modifiable – exercised by the laws of human organization, of which that of civilization is only the result.

What we have just said leads us naturally to fix precisely the respective domains of observation and imagination in politics. This demarcation will complete the outline of the general spirit of the new politics.

To this end we need to distinguish two orders of works: the first, which properly constitute political science, are relative to the formation of the system which is appropriate to the present era; the others relate to its propagation.

In the first, it is clear that the imagination must only play a strictly subordinate role, always subject to the command of observation, as in the other sciences. As for the study of the past, it can and must[30] be employed to think up provisional ways of connecting facts, until the definitive relationships spring directly from the facts themselves; which is what we should always have in sight. And this use of imagination must be applied only to secondary facts; otherwise it would obviously be pernicious. In the second place, the determination of the system in accordance with which society is today called to reorganize itself must be derived almost entirely from the observation of the past. This study will determine, not only the overall shape of this system, but also the most important parts, with a degree of precision which will probably astonish the scientists when they get to work. Nevertheless, it is certain that the precision obtained by this method could not entirely descend to the point where the system will be capable of being handed over to the industrialists, so that they can put it into action through their practical combinations, according to the plan indicated[31] in the preceding chapter. Thus, from this second point of view, imagination will still have to fulfil a secondary function in scientific politics; a function which will consist in taking to the necessary degree of precision the sketch of the new system, whose general plan and characteristic features will have been determined by observation.

But there is another kind of operation, equally indispensable for the definitive success of the great enterprise of reorganization, although subordinated to the preceding, and in which imagination finds itself exercised to the full.

---

[30] The words 'and must' were added in 1824.
[31] 1822: 'set out'.

In the determination of the new system, it is necessary to abstract from the advantages or the disadvantages of this system. The main question, the sole question, must be: according to the observation of the past, what is the social system destined by the course of civilization to be established today? To concern ourselves in a significant degree with the goodness of this system would be to confuse things and even to fail in our objective. We must restrict ourselves to understanding the general thesis that, because the positive idea of goodness and that of conformity with the state of civilization meet at their origin, we are certain to have the best system practicable today if we seek the one that is most in conformity with the state of civilization. The idea of goodness not being positive in itself, and becoming so only through its relation with the second idea, it is to the latter alone that we must attach ourselves as the direct goal of our investigations; otherwise politics would not become positive. The indication of the advantages of the new system, of its superiority over its predecessors in this respect, should only be a quite secondary thing, with no influence on the direction of works.

It is undeniable that, by this way of proceeding, we shall be certain to create a truly positive politics, one that is truly in harmony with the great needs of society. But, if it is in such a spirit that the new system must be determined, it is clear that it is not in such a form that it must be presented to society in order to bring about its definitive adoption; for this form is very far from being the one that is best suited to procure this agreement.

For a new social system to be established, it is not enough for it to be conceived properly; it is also necessary for the mass of society to be enthusiastic to constitute it. This condition is not only essential to overcome the more or less powerful resistance which this system will encounter in the decadent classes. It is essential, too, to satisfy that moral need for exhilaration which is inherent in man, when he enters a new course; without this exhilaration, he could neither overcome his natural inertia, nor shake the ever so powerful yoke of old habits; yet this is nevertheless necessary to allow all his faculties full and free development in their new employment. Since this necessity is always to be observed in the least complicated cases, it would be perverse if it did not also occur in the most complete and the most important changes, in those which are to modify human existence most profoundly. Moreover, the whole of history testifies in favour of this truth.

Once it is put thus, it is clear that the way in which the new system can and must become known and presented by scientific politics is not at all capable of directly fulfilling this essential condition.

We shall never arouse the enthusiasm of the mass of men for any system by proving to them that it is the one whose establishment the course of civilization has been preparing since its origin, and which it today calls to direct society. A truth of this kind is within the grasp of too small a number of minds, and even demands of them too long a sequence of intellectual operations, for it ever to be able to enthuse them. It will only produce, in the scientists, that profound and stubborn conviction which is the necessary result of positive demonstrations, and which offers more resistance, but also for that very reason less activity, than the quick and rousing conviction produced by ideas which move passions.

The only means of obtaining this last effect consists in presenting men with a vivid picture of the improvements which the new system, envisaged from all the different points of view and in abstraction from its necessity and its opportuneness, must bring to the human condition. This perspective alone can induce men to bring about in themselves the moral revolution that is necessary for the new system to be established. It alone can stifle the egoism which has become predominant as a result of the dissolution of the old system and which, when ideas have been enlightened by scientific works, will be the only great obstacle to the triumph of the new. It alone, in short, can drag society out of its apathy, and instil it as a whole with this activity which has to become permanent, in a social state which will keep all the faculties of man in a state of continuous action.

This is, then, an order of works in which the imagination must play a preponderant role. Its influence could have no disadvantages, since it will be exercised in the direction established by scientific works, since it will set itself the goal, not of inventing the system to be constituted, but of adopting the one already determined by positive politics. Thus launched, the imagination must be left wholly free to its own devices. The freer and franker its manner, the more complete and salutary will be the indispensable action it must exercise.

Such is the special part reserved for the fine arts in the general enterprise of social reorganization. Thus will all positive forces contribute to this vast enterprise: the scientists, to establish the plan of the new system; the artists, to induce the universal adoption of this plan; the industrialists, to bring the system into immediate operation, by the establishment of the necessary practical institutions. These three great forces will then combine with each other to constitute the new system, as they will do, once it is formed, for its daily implementation.

Thus, in the last analysis, positive politics invests observation with the supremacy that conjectural politics accords to imagination, in the determination of the social system appropriate to the present age. But, at the same time, it entrusts imagination with a new role, far superior, today, to the one which it has in theological and metaphysical politics, where, though sovereign, it has been languishing – ever since the human race has been approaching the positive state – in a range of worn-out ideas and dull images.

Now that we have sketched the general spirit of positive politics, we might usefully cast a quick glance over the major attempts made hitherto with the goal of raising politics to the rank of the sciences of observation. A double advantage will result: to establish, by facts, the maturity of the enterprise, and to enlighten still more the spirit of the new politics, by presenting it from a number of points of view distinct from those so far indicated.

It is to Montesquieu that we should attribute the first direct attempt to treat politics as a science of facts and not of dogmas. This is, obviously, the true goal of the *Esprit des lois*,[32] in the eyes of anyone who has understood that work. The admirable opening, in which the general idea of law is presented, for the first time, in a truly philosophical manner, would alone suffice to establish such a plan. It is clear that Montesquieu essentially set out to gather, as far as possible, under a certain number of major headings, all the political facts known to him, and to bring to the fore the laws connecting them.

[32] Published in 1748.

If it were a matter here of appraising the merit of such work, it would be necessary to judge it in relation to the time when it was executed. We should then see that it establishes in the most categorical manner the philosophical superiority of Montesquieu over all his contemporaries. To have freed himself from the critical spirit, at a time when it exercised, even over the strongest minds, the most despotic rule; to have felt profoundly the emptiness of metaphysical and absolute politics, to have felt the need to escape from it, at the very moment when it was assuming its definitive form in the hands of Rousseau, are decisive proofs of this superiority.

But, in spite of the first-order capacity of which Montesquieu gave proof, and which was to be felt more and more, it is obvious that his accomplishments were far from raising politics to the rank of the positive sciences. They did not at all satisfy the fundamental essential conditions for this goal to be attained, which were expounded above.

Montesquieu did not perceive the great general fact which dominates and is the true regulator of all political phenomena, the natural development of civilization. The result was that his investigations could not be employed in the formation of positive politics, other than as materials, as a collection of observations and insights. For the general ideas which enabled him to connect the facts are not in the least positive.

In spite of Montesquieu's obvious efforts to free himself from metaphysics, he did not succeed, and it was incontestably from metaphysics that he deduced his principal conception. This conception has the double defect of being dogmatic instead of being historical, that is to say, not having regard to the necessary sequence of the different political states; and, secondly, of giving an exaggerated importance to a secondary fact, the form of government. Also, the predominant role Montesquieu made this idea play stemmed purely from imagination, and was in contradiction with the whole body of the best-known observations. In a word, political facts were not truly *connected* by Montesquieu, as they must be in any positive science. They were only *compared*, according to hypothetical views which were most commonly contrary to their real relations.

The only important part of Montesquieu's theoretical accomplishments which is truly in a positive direction is that which has as its object to determine the political influence of local physical circumstances, which act in a continuous manner, and the totality of which can be designated by the word 'climate'. But it is easy to see that, even from this point of view, the ideas Montesquieu produced can only be employed once they have been totally recast, as a consequence of the general vice which characterizes his way of proceeding.

It is, indeed, fully recognized today by all observers that in a number of respects Montesquieu much exaggerated the influence of climates. That was inevitable.

No doubt climate does exercise a very real influence on political phenomena which it is very important[33] to understand. But this influence is only indirect and secondary. It is limited to accelerating or retarding, up to a point, the natural course of civilization, which cannot be diverted by these modifications. This course in fact remains fundamentally the same in all climates, allowing for variations in speed, because it depends upon the most general laws, those of human organization, which are essentially uniform in different localities. Given, then, that the influence of climate on political phenomena has only a modifying influence on the natural course of civilization, which retains its character as a supreme law, it is clear that this influence can be fruitfully studied and properly appreciated only after the determination of this law. If we were to consider the indirect and subordinate cause before the direct and principal cause, such an infringement of the nature of the human mind would have the inevitable result of giving an absolutely false idea of the influence of the first, by confusing it with that of the second. That is what happened to Montesquieu.

The foregoing comment on the influence of climate is obviously applicable to that of all the other causes whatever which can modify the course of civilization in its speed without altering its essence. This influence will only be capable of being determined with precision when the natural laws of civilization have been established, by first abstracting from all these modifications. Astronomers began by studying the laws of planetary movements, abstracting from perturbations. When these laws were discovered, modifications could be determined, and even traced to the principle which had first

---

[33] 1822: 'useful'.

been established only for the principal movement. If they had tried, from the beginning, to take account of these irregularities, it is clear that no exact theory could ever have been formed. It is just the same in the present case.

The inadequacy of Montesquieu's politics can be clearly verified in its applications to the needs of society.

The necessity of a social reorganization in the most civilized countries was as real in Montesquieu's time as it is today. For the feudal and theological system was already destroyed in its fundamental bases. The events which have unfolded since have only made this necessity more tangible and more urgent, by completing the destruction of the old system. Nevertheless, Montesquieu did not give his work the practical goal of conceiving a new social system. As he had not connected political facts in accordance with a theory that was capable of bringing to the fore the need for a new system in the state which society had attained, and at the same time of determining the general character of this system, he had to restrict himself, and did restrict himself – as far as practice was concerned – to suggesting improvements in details, in conformity with experience. These were no more than simple modifications, more or less important, of the theological and feudal system.

By this means Montesquieu no doubt showed a wise reticence, confining his practical ideas within the limits which the facts imposed on him – in the imperfect way he studied them – whereas it would have been so easy for him to invent utopias. But at the same time he decisively witnessed to the inadequacy of a theory which was not capable of meeting the most essential needs of practice.

Thus, in short, Montesquieu felt the necessity of treating politics in the manner of the sciences of observation; but he did not conceive the general work which should stamp it with this character. His investigations were nevertheless of the greatest importance. They furnished the human mind with the means of combining political ideas, by presenting it with a great mass of facts compared in accordance with a theory which, still far removed from the positive state, was nevertheless much closer to it than all those previously produced.

The general conception of the work capable of raising politics to the rank of the sciences of observation was discovered by Condorcet.

He was the first to see clearly that civilization is subjected to a progressive course all of whose steps are rigorously connected to each other according to natural laws, which can be unveiled by philosophical observation of the past. For each era these laws determine in a wholly positive manner the improvements which the social state is called to experience, whether in its parts or in its overall shape. Not only did Condorcet thus conceive the means of giving politics a true positive theory; but he tried to establish this theory by executing the work entitled: *Esquisse d'un tableau historique des progrès de l'esprit humain*,[34] whose title alone and the introduction would suffice to assure its author of the eternal honour of having created this great philosophical idea.

If this essential discovery has hitherto remained completely sterile; if it has as yet caused almost no sensation, if no one has walked in the line indicated by Condorcet; if, in a word, politics has not become positive, this must largely be attributed to the fact that the plan sketched by Condorcet was executed in a spirit absolutely contrary to the goal of this work. He entirely misunderstood its most essential conditions, so that the work needs to be recast in its entirety. This is what it is important to establish.

In the first place, the classification of the periods is, in a work of this kind, the most important part of the plan; or, better, it alone constitutes the plan itself, considered in its greatest generality, for it fixes the principal way in which the observed facts are co-ordinated. And the classification adopted by Condorcet is completely pernicious, in that it does not even satisfy the most palpable of conditions, that of presenting a homogeneous series. We can see that Condorcet did not in the least sense the importance of a philosophical arrangement of the periods of civilization. He did not see that this arrangement must itself be the object of an initial general work, the most difficult of those to which the formation of positive politics must give rise. He believed he would be able to co-ordinate the facts properly by almost randomly taking for the origin of each era a noteworthy event, sometimes industrial, sometimes scientific, sometimes political. By proceeding thus, he did not escape from the circle of the *literati* historians.[35] It was impossible for him to form

[34] Published posthumously in 1795.
[35] The French is 'historiens littérateurs'.

a true theory, that is to establish a real connection between the facts, since those which ought to have served to connect all the others were already isolated from each other.

Naturalists being, of all scientists, those who have to form the most extended and the most difficult classifications, it is in their hands that the general method of classifications has had to make its greatest progress. The fundamental principle of this method has been established since botany and in zoology produced philosophical classifications – ones, that is, founded on real relations, and not on artificial comparisons. It consists in the rule that the order of generality of the different degrees of division should be, as far as possible, exactly in conformity with that of the relations observed between the phenomena to be classed. In this way, the hierarchy of families, genera, etc., is nothing other than the exposition of a co-ordinated series of general facts, arranged into different orders of sequences, becoming more and more specialized. In short, then, classification is the philosophical expression of science, whose progress it follows. To understand classification is to understand science, at least in its most important part.

This principle is applicable to any science at all. Thus, as political science is constituting itself at a time when the principle has been discovered, implemented, and solidly verified, it must profit from this philosophical idea discovered by other sciences, by taking it as its guide in the distribution of the various ages of civilization. The reasons for arranging, in the general history of the human race, the different eras of civilization according to their natural relations are absolutely the same as those of naturalists for arranging animal and plant organizations according to the same law. Only they have still more force.

For, if a right co-ordination of facts is very important in any science, it is everything in political science, which, in the absence of this condition, would completely miss its practical goal. This goal is, as we have seen, to determine, by observation of the past, the social system which the course of civilization is tending to produce today. And this determination can obviously result only from a right co-ordination of the anterior states of civilization, from which will emerge the law of this course. From this it is clear that political facts, however important they may be, have real practical value only through their co-ordination, whereas, in other sciences, the knowledge of the facts in itself most often has an initial value, independent of the way in which they are connected.

Thus the different periods of civilization, instead of being classified unmethodically, according to events of more or less importance, as Condorcet classified them, must be arranged according to the philosophical principle already recognized by all scientists as the one which must govern classifications of any kind. The principal division of periods must present the most general survey of the history of civilization. The secondary divisions, to whatever degree it is judged right to push them, must successively offer more and more precise surveys of this same history. In short, the table of periods must be ordered in such a way as to offer, on its own, an abridged articulation of the overall shape of the work. Otherwise our achievement would have been purely provisional, and however perfectly executed it was, its value would only be in providing materials.

This amounts to saying that such a division could not be invented, and that, even in its highest degree of generality, it can result only from an initial sketch of the picture, from an initial glance over the general history of civilization. No doubt, however important, however indispensable this way of proceeding might be for the formation of positive politics, it would be impracticable, and we should have to resign ourselves to undertaking at first no more than a simply provisional work, if this work were not already sufficiently prepared. But the histories written up to the present day and above all those produced in the last half-century, though far removed from being conceived in the proper spirit, do offer more or less the equivalent of this preliminary collection of materials. We can therefore concern ourselves immediately with a definitive co-ordination.

In the last chapter we presented – though only from the spiritual point of view – a general survey which seems to us to fulfil the conditions set out above for the principal division of the past. It is the result of an initial philosophical study of the overall shape of the history of civilization.

We believe that this history can be divided into three great periods, or states of civilization, the character of each being quite distinct in both temporal and spiritual domains. They embrace civilization considered at the same time in its elements and in its overall shape, which in the light of the views indicated above is obviously an indispensable condition.

The first is the theological and military era.

In this state of society, all theoretical ideas – particular as well as general – are of a purely supernatural order. Imagination straightforwardly and completely dominates observation, and the latter is denied any freedom of investigation.

In the same way, all social relations, whether particular or general, are straightforwardly and completely military. Society takes conquest as the sole and permanent goal of its activity. There is no industry, other than what is essential for the existence of the human race. The pure and simple enslavement of producers is the major institution.

Such is the first great social system produced by the natural course of civilization. It existed in its elements from the first formation of regular and permanent societies. Only after a long sequence of generations was it completely established in its totality.

The second era is the metaphysical and legist era. Its general character is not to have a clearly defined character. It is intermediate and hybrid, and it effects a transition.

From a spiritual point of view, it has already been characterized in the last chapter. Observation is still dominated by imagination, but it is now allowed to modify it within certain limits. These limits are then pushed back step by step until observation at last conquers freedom of investigation on all matters. It obtains it at first on all particular theoretical ideas, and then little by little, by the use it makes of it, it ends up by acquiring it also for general theoretical ideas, which is the natural end of the transition. This period is that of criticism and argument.

From the temporal point of view, industry has expanded further, without yet being predominant. As a consequence society is no longer straightforwardly military, and is not yet straightforwardly industrial, whether in its elements or in its overall shape. Particular social relations are modified. Individual enslavement is no longer direct; the producer, still a slave, begins to obtain some rights from the part of the military. Industry makes more progress. This finally culminates in the total abolition of individual enslavement. After this enfranchisement, producers still remain subject to the arbitrary collective will. However, general social relations soon begin to be modified too. The two goals of activity, conquest and production, are brought face to face. Industry is at first organized and protected as a military means. Later, its importance increases and war ends up being conceived systematically, in its turn, as a means of favouring industry, which is the final state of this intermediate regime.

Finally, the third era is the scientific and industrial era. All particular theoretical ideas have become positive, and general ideas are tending to become so. Observation has come to dominate imagination, as far as the former are concerned, and has dethroned it – without having as of today yet taken its place – as far as the latter are concerned.

In the temporal sphere, industry has become predominant. All particular relations have gradually been established on industrial bases. Society, taken collectively, is tending to organize itself in the same way, by taking production as the sole and permanent goal of its activity.

In short, this last era has already begun to seep in, as regards its elements, and it is ready to begin as regards its overall shape. Its direct point of departure dates from the introduction of the positive sciences into Europe by the Arabs, and the enfranchisement of the communes, that is from about the eleventh century.

To prevent any obscurity in the application of this general survey, we must never lose sight of the fact that civilization had to progress in the spiritual and temporal elements of the social state before progressing in its overall shape. As a consequence, the three great successive eras necessarily began earlier in their elements than in the overall shape, which might occasion some confusion if we did not first of all make ourselves aware of this inevitable difference.

Such are therefore the principal characters of the three eras into which we can divide the whole history of civilization, from the time when the social state began to assume a true consistency to the present. I dare propose to scientists this primary division of the past, which seems to me to fulfil the large conditions of a good classification of the totality of political facts.

If it is adopted, we shall have to find at least one subdivision, so that it might be possible to carry out properly an initial sketch of the great historical picture. The principal division will facilitate the discovery of those which are to follow it, by providing the means to consider phenomena in a way that is at one and the same time general and positive. It is also clear that these various subdivisions, in accordance with the fundamental principle of classifications, will have to be entirely conceived in the same spirit as the principal division, and set out only a simple development of it.

Having examined Condorcet's work in terms of the distribution of periods, we must consider it in terms of the spirit which governed its execution.

Condorcet did not see that the first direct effect of a work aiming at the formation of positive politics must be, as an absolute necessity, irrevocably to sweep away the critical philosophy of the eighteenth century, by turning all the powers of thinkers towards the reorganization of society, the practical goal of such a work. As a consequence he did not sense that the preliminary condition that it is most crucial to fulfil for anyone who wished to execute this important enterprise was to strip oneself, as far as possible, of the critical prejudices introduced into everyone's head by this philosophy. Instead of that, he allowed himself to be blindly dominated by these prejudices; he condemned the past instead of observing it; and as a consequence his work was no more than a long and tiring declamation, from which no positive instruction really resulted.

Admiration and condemnation of phenomena must be banished with an equal severity from all positive science, because every preoccupation of this kind has as its direct and inevitable effect to prevent or to alter the investigation. Astronomers, physicists, chemists and physiologists neither admire nor criticize their respective phenomena: they observe them, even though these phenomena might provide ample matter for considerations of both kinds, as many examples show. Scientists with reason leave such effects to artists, in whose domain they really fall.

In this respect politics must be like the other sciences. Only this reserve is much more necessary, precisely because it is more difficult, and because it alters the investigation more profoundly, given that in this science the phenomena affect the passions much more closely than in any other. Thus, in this respect alone, the critical spirit, by which Condorcet allowed himself to be carried away, is directly contrary to that which should reign in scientific politics, even if all the reproaches he levels at the past were precisely justified. But there is more.

No doubt, following an observation already made in this chapter, the practical combinations of statesmen have not always been conceived properly, and often they have even been led in the opposite direction to that of civilization. If we make this point more precise, we can see that it is limited, for all cases, to the observation that statesmen have sought to prolong, beyond their natural term, doctrines and institutions which were no longer in harmony with the state of civilization; and, of course, such an error will seem very pardonable, if we consider that hitherto there has been no positive means of recognizing it. But to transfer to whole systems of institutions and ideas what is relative only to secondary facts; for example, to depict the feudal and theological system as having never been anything but an obstacle to civilization, whereas its establishment was, on the contrary, the greatest provisional progress for society, and under its happy influence civilization made so many definitive conquests; to represent, over a long sequence of centuries, the classes placed at the head of the general movement as occupied in following a permanent conspiracy against the human race; such a spirit, as absurd in its principle as revolting in its consequences, is an insane result of the philosophy of the last century. It is deplorable that a man such as Condorcet was not able to free himself from its control.

This absurdity, born of the inability to identify the natural sequence of the progress of civilization amidst all its principal parts, obviously makes the explanation of this sequence impossible. What is more, Condorcet's work presents a general and continuous contradiction.

On the one hand, he loudly proclaims that the state of civilization in the eighteenth century is infinitely superior, in a multitude of respects, to what it was at its origin. But this total progress could only be the sum of the partial progress made by civilization in all the preceding intermediate states. And on the other hand, if we examine successively these various states, Condorcet presents them, almost always, as having been times of retrograde movement from the most essential points of view. There is therefore a perpetual miracle, and the progressive course of civilization becomes an effect without a cause.

An absolutely opposite spirit must govern true positive politics.

Institutions and doctrines must be regarded as having been, in all periods, as perfect as the existing state of civilization entailed; which could not have been other, at least after a certain length of time, since they are necessarily determined by it. Further, in the period of their full vigour, they have always had a progressive character, and in no case have they had a retrograde character, for they could not have held out against the course of civilization, from which they borrow all their strength. Only, in their periods of decline, they have ordinarily had a stationary character, which is readily explained, in part by the repugnance for destruction, as natural to political systems as to individuals, and in part by the state of infancy which politics has been in hitherto.

We must consider in the same way the passions developed in the different periods by the ruling classes. In the times of their greatest strength, preponderant social forces are necessarily generous, for they have nothing more to gain and they do not yet fear losses. It is only when their decline manifests itself that they become selfish, because all their efforts have the aim of preserving a power whose bases are destroyed.

These various insights are obviously in conformity with the laws of human nature, and they alone allow us satisfactorily to explain political phenomena. Thus, in the last analysis, instead of seeing the past as a tissue of monstrosities, we must as a general rule come to look upon society as having been most commonly directed as well as the nature of things allowed, from all points of view.

If some particular facts at first seem to contradict this general fact, it is still more philosophical to seek to re-establish the relationship rather than to dispense with it by proclaiming, upon first glance, the reality of this opposition. For it would be deviating from all well-understood scientific discipline to allow the fact that is more important and that has been most often verified to be ruled by a secondary and less frequent fact.

It is nevertheless obvious that we must as far as possible beware of any exaggeration in the application of this general idea, like any other.

No doubt people will find some resemblance between the spirit of positive politics, envisaged from this point of view, and the famous theological and metaphysical dogma of optimism. The analogy is fundamentally a real one. But there is the incommensurable difference between an observed general fact and a hypothetical idea which springs purely from invention. The distance is still more palpable in the consequences.

The theological dogma is metaphysical, in proclaiming absolutely that everything is as good as it can ever be, and tends to make the human race stationary by depriving it of any prospect of real improvement. The positive idea that, over a stretch of time, the social organization is always as perfect as the state of civilization allows in each era, far from arresting the desire for improvements, instead only stamps it with a more efficacious practical impetus by directing towards their true goal – the improvement of civilization – efforts which would have remained without effect if they had been directed immediately onto the social organization. Moreover, as there is nothing mystical or absolute in such an idea, it commits man to re-establish harmony between the political regime and the state of civilization, in the foreseen case where this necessary relation is momentarily disturbed. But it enlightens this operation, by warning us not to mistake effect for cause in this relationship.

It is useful to observe in connection with this analogy that this is not the only time that positive philosophy has, by a suitable transformation, appropriated a general idea originally invented by theological and metaphysical philosophy. True general ideas never lose their value as a mode of reasoning, however pernicious may be their entourage. The ordinary course of the human mind is to appropriate them to its different states, by transforming their character. This is something that can be verified in all the revolutions that have brought the different branches of our knowledge to the positive state.

Thus, for example, the mystical doctrine of the influence of numbers, born of the Pythagorean school, has been boiled down by geometers to the following simple and positive idea: that uncomplicated phenomena are capable of being reduced to mathematical laws. In the same way again, the doctrine of final causes has been converted by physiologists into the principle of conditions of existence. The two positive ideas are no doubt very different from the two theological and metaphysical ideas. But the latter were nonetheless patently the germ of the former. A well-conducted philosophical operation was sufficient to give a positive character to these two hypothetical insights, which were products of genius in the infancy of human reason. Moreover this transformation did not alter – it even increased – their value as a mode of reasoning.

The same comments apply precisely to the two general political ideas, the one positive, the other imaginary, compared above.

Before we leave the examination of Condorcet's work, it is appropriate to infer from it a third point of view from which the spirit of positive politics may be presented.

Condorcet has been much reproached for daring to finish his work with a picture of the future. This bold conception is, on the contrary, the only philosophical perspective of great importance introduced by Condorcet in the execution of his work, and it must be lovingly preserved in the new history of civilization, of which such a picture is obviously the natural conclusion.

What Condorcet could with reason be reproached with was not wanting to determine the future, but determining it wrongly. That stemmed from the fact that his study of the past was absolutely pernicious, for the reasons previously indicated. Because Condorcet co-ordinated the past badly, the future did not result from it. This inadequate observation reduced him to composing the future essentially out of his own imagination; and, as a necessary consequence, he conceived it badly. But this lack of success, whose cause is palpable, does not in the least prove that, with the aid of a proper co-ordination of the past, we could not indeed determine with certainty the general appearance of the society of the future.

Such an idea appears strange only because we are not yet accustomed to considering politics as a true science. For if we regarded it thus, the determination of the future by philosophical observation of the past would seem, on the contrary, a very natural idea with which all men have become familiar for other classes of phenomena.

Every science has prediction as its goal. For the general application of the laws established on the basis of observation of phenomena is to predict their sequence. In reality, all men, however backward we may think them, formulate real predictions, always founded on the same principle, knowledge of the future through that of the past. We all predict, for example, the general effects of terrestrial gravity, and a host of other phenomena, quite simple and quite frequent, so that their order of succession becomes perceptible to the least capable and the least attentive spectator. The faculty of prediction, in each individual, is proportionate to his scientific knowledge. The foresight of the astronomer who predicts, with perfect accuracy, the state of the solar system many years in advance is of absolutely the same kind as that of the savage who predicts the next sunrise. The difference is only in the extent of their knowledge.

It is therefore obviously quite in conformity with the nature of the human mind that observation of the past can unveil the future, in politics as it does in astronomy, in physics, in chemistry and in physiology.

This determination should even be regarded as the direct goal of political science, following the example of the other positive sciences. It is indeed clear that the fixing of the social system to which the course of civilization today calls the elite of the human race – a fixing which constitutes the true practical object of positive politics – is nothing other than the general determination of the imminent future of society, as it results from the past.

In short, Condorcet was the first to conceive the true nature of the general task, which is to raise politics to the rank of the sciences of observation. But he executed it in an absolutely pernicious spirit in the most essential respects. He entirely missed his goal, first in terms of theory, and consequently in terms of practice. Thus, this work must be wholly rethought from scratch, in accordance with true philosophical perspectives, considering Condorcet's attempt as marking the real goal of scientific politics.

In order to complete the summary examination of the efforts hitherto made to raise politics to the rank of the positive sciences, it remains for us to consider two other attempts which it is useful to mention even though they are not, like the two preceding ones, truly in line with the course of the progress of the human mind in politics.

The need to render social science positive is so real today, this great enterprise has so fully arrived at maturity, that several superior minds have tried to reach this goal by treating politics as an application of other sciences which are already positive, believing it possible to bring it within their domain. As these attempts were, by their nature, incapable of being accomplished, they have been much more planned than followed through. It will be sufficient therefore to consider them from the most general point of view.

The first consisted in the efforts made to apply to social science mathematical analysis in general, and especially the branch which relates to the calculus of probabilities. This way was opened by Condorcet,[g] and followed mainly by him. Other geometers have traced his footsteps and shared his hopes, without adding anything truly essential to his labours, at least from a philosophical point of view. All agreed in regarding this way of proceeding as the only one capable of stamping politics with a positive character.

The considerations set out in this chapter seem to me to establish sufficiently that such a condition is by no means necessary for politics to become a positive science. But there is more: this way of regarding social science is purely chimerical, and as a consequence, completely pernicious, as will easily be recognized.

If it were a question here of making a detailed judgement of the work of this kind accomplished hitherto, we should soon discover that it has really added no notion of much importance to the mass of accepted ideas. We should see, for example, that the efforts of the geometers to extend the calculus of probabilities beyond its natural applications have, in their most essential and most positive part, led only (as regards the theory of certainty) to presenting certain almost trivial propositions as the culmination of a long and tiresome algebraic work. Any man of common sense will perceive at a glance that these propositions are self-evidently correct. But we must restrict ourselves to examining the enterprise in itself, and in its fullest generality.

In the first place, the considerations by which several physiologists, and especially Bichat, have shown, in general, the radical impossibility of a real and significant application of mathematical analysis to the phenomena of organized bodies are directly and specially applicable to moral and political phenomena, which are only a special case of the former.

These considerations are founded on the fact that the most essential preliminary condition for phenomena to be capable of being reduced to mathematical laws is that their degrees of quantity are

---

[g] Such a project on Condorcet's part proves, in conformity with the foregoing analysis, that he was very far from having a clear conception of the fundamental importance of the history of civilization, since if he had clearly seen the philosophical observation of the past as the means to render social science positive, he would not have looked elsewhere.

fixed. And in all physiological phenomena, each effect, partial or total, is subject to immense variations of quantity, which succeed each other with the greatest speed, and in a totally irregular manner, under the influence of a mass of different causes which are not capable of being accurately estimated. This extreme variability is one of the great characteristics of the distinctive phenomena of organized bodies; it constitutes one of their clearest differences from those of inorganic bodies. It obviously excludes any hope of ever subjecting them to true calculations, such as, for example, those of astronomical phenomena, which are the ones most suited to serve as a type in comparisons of this kind.

That stated, it can easily be grasped that this constant variability of effects, due to the excessive complexity of the causes which come together to produce them, must be at its greatest in the case of the moral and political phenomena of the human race, which form the most complicated class of physiological phenomena. Of all phenomena, they are in fact the ones whose degrees of quantity present the widest, the most numerous and the most irregular variations.

If we weigh these considerations properly, I think we shall not hesitate to affirm – without fear of underestimating the capacity of the human mind – that not only in the present state of our knowledge, but even when it has progressed to the limits of its capacity, any large-scale application of calculus to social science is and will necessarily remain impossible.

In the second place, even if we were to suppose that such a hope could ever be realized, it would remain incontestable that to get there political science must first be studied directly, that is by concerning ourselves solely with co-ordinating the series of political phenomena.

In fact, however important mathematical analysis may be, when considered in its true applications, we must not lose sight of the fact that it is only a purely instrumental science, a science of method. By itself it teaches nothing real; it becomes a fruitful source of positive discoveries only when it is applied to observed phenomena.

In the sphere of phenomena which entail this application, it could never take place immediately. It always supposes in the corresponding science a preliminary degree of cultivation and advancement, whose natural end is the knowledge of the precise laws revealed by observation relative to the quantity of phenomena. As soon as these laws are discovered, however imperfect they may be, mathematical analysis becomes applicable. From that point, by the powerful means of deduction it provides, it allows us to reduce these laws to a very small number, often to a single one, and to bring within their scope, in the most exact manner, a mass of phenomena which it at first did not seem to encompass. In short, it establishes in the science in question a perfect co-ordination which could not have been achieved to the same extent by any other means. But it is obvious that any application of mathematical analysis attempted before this preliminary condition of the discovery of certain calculable laws has been fulfilled would be totally illusory. Far from making any branch of our knowledge positive, it would only have the effect of plunging the study of nature back into the domain of metaphysics, by transferring to abstractions the role that belongs exclusively to observations.

Thus, for example, we can see that mathematical analysis has been applied very successfully to astronomy (whether geometrical or mechanical), to optics, to acoustics, and most recently to the theory of heat, once the progress of observation led the different parts of physics to establish some precise quantitative laws of the relation between phenomena; whereas, prior to these discoveries, such an application would have had no real basis, no positive point of departure. In the same way again, chemists who today believe most strongly in the possibility of one day applying mathematical analysis to chemical phenomena, in a way that is both wide-ranging and positive, nevertheless do not cease to study them directly; for they are thoroughly convinced that only a long series of investigations, observations and experiments can reveal the numerical laws on which this application must be founded if it is to have any reality.

The essential condition just indicated is all the more difficult to fulfil because the more complicated the phenomena concerned, the greater the prior degree of cultivation and improvement it demands in the corresponding science. Thus astronomy became, at least in its geometrical part, a branch of applied mathematics before optics did, optics before acoustics, and the theory of heat last of all. Thus chemistry is today very far from this state, if it is ever to reach it.

In considering, in accordance with these incontestable principles, the application of calculus to physiological phenomena in general and in particular to the social phenomena of the human race, we can see first that even if we admit the possibility of this application, it would not in the least exempt us from the direct study of phenomena, which, on the contrary, it prescribes as a prior condition. Furthermore, if we were to consider carefully the nature of this condition, we should feel that it requires, in the physics of organized bodies in general and in social physics in particular, a degree of improvement which, even if it were not chimerical, could obviously not be attained without centuries of cultivation. The discovery of exact and calculable laws in physiology would represent a degree of progress far superior to that imagined even by those physiologists who conceive the most extensive hopes for the future destinies of that science. In reality, in accordance with the reasons indicated above, such a state of perfection must be regarded as absolutely chimerical, incompatible with the nature of phenomena, and completely disproportionate to the true scope of the human mind.

The same reasons obviously apply, and with still more force, to political science, given the greater degree of complexity of its phenomena. To imagine that it could one day be possible to discover some quantifiable relations between the phenomena of this science is to suppose that it could attain such a degree of perfection that, before it has even arrived at that point, everything really interesting that it has to find would be discovered, to a degree which would far surpass all the desires one might reasonably form. Thus mathematical analysis would only become applicable in an era where its application could no longer have any real importance.

It follows from the foregoing points that, on the one hand, the nature of political phenomena totally excludes any hope of ever applying mathematical analysis to them; and on the other hand that this application, supposing it to be possible, could not possibly serve to raise politics to the rank of the positive sciences, since it would not be practicable until the science was already formed.

Up to the present geometers have not paid enough attention to the great and fundamental division in our positive knowledge between the study of inorganic bodies and the study of organized bodies. This division, which the human mind owes to the physiologists, is today established on unshakeable foundations, and is confirmed more and more as people reflect upon it further. It imposes precise and irrevocable limits on the true application of mathematics in its furthest possible extension. We can establish in principle that mathematical analysis could never extend its domain beyond the physics of inorganic bodies, whose phenomena are the only ones to offer the degree of simplicity and hence of stability necessary if they are to be capable of being reduced to numerical laws.

If we consider how much, even in the simplest applications of mathematical analysis, its course becomes obstructed when it brings the abstract state and the concrete state close enough together, and how this obstruction increases as phenomena become more complicated, we shall see that the foregoing principle tends rather to exaggerate than to understate the scope of its real competence.

The project of treating social science as an application of mathematics, in order to make it positive, has its source in the metaphysical prejudice that no true certainty can exist outside mathematics. This prejudice was natural at a time when the only positive knowledge was to be found in the domain of applied mathematics and when, as a consequence, everything it did not embrace was vague and conjectural. But since the formation of two great positive sciences, chemistry and above all physiology, in which mathematical analysis plays no role, and which are nonetheless recognized to be as certain as the others, such a prejudice is absolutely inexcusable.

It is not as applications of mathematical analysis that astronomy, optics, etc., are positive and certain sciences. This character comes from themselves, it results from their being founded on observed facts, and it could only result from that, for mathematical analysis, when isolated from the observation of nature, has only a metaphysical character. But it is certain that in the sciences to which mathematics is not applicable it is still more important for us not to lose sight of strict direct observation; deductions cannot be extended as far with certainty, because the means of reasoning are less perfect. Apart from that, certainty is just as complete, if we confine ourselves within the proper limits. No doubt the co-ordination we obtain is not as good, but it is sufficient for the real needs of the applications of the science.

The chimerical search for an unattainable perfection could only end up necessarily retarding the progress of the human mind, by wastefully eating up the great intellectual forces, and diverting the efforts of scientists from their true direction of positive efficacy. This is the definitive judgement which I think I can make on the attempts made – or being made – to apply mathematical analysis to social physics.

A second attempt, much less pernicious in nature than the preceding one, but equally incapable of being realized, is the one whose object is to make social science positive by reducing it essentially to a simple logical inference from physiology. Cabanis is the author of this conception and it is above all by him that it was pursued. It constitutes the real philosophical goal of his famous work on the *Rapports du physique et du moral de l'homme*, as is clear to anyone who has considered the general doctrine expounded in that work as organic and not as purely critical.

The points put forward in this chapter about the spirit of positive politics prove that this attempt, like the previous one, was necessarily ill-conceived. But it is now time to indicate the vice precisely.

It consists in the fact that this way of proceeding cancels the direct observation of the social past, which must serve as the fundamental basis of positive politics.

The superiority of man over other animals cannot and indeed does not have any other cause than the relative perfection of his organization. Everything the human race has done and everything it can do must therefore obviously be regarded in the last analysis as a necessary consequence of its organization, modified in its effects by the state of its environment. In this sense social physics – that is, the study of the collective development of the human race – is really a branch of physiology, that is to say of the study of man conceived as a whole. In other words, the history of civilization is nothing other than the consequence and essential complement of the natural history of man.

But just as it is important to grasp this incontestable connection properly and never to lose sight of it, so it would be a misunderstanding to conclude from it that we should not establish a clear division between social physics and physiology properly so called.

When physiologists study the natural history of an animal species endowed with sociability – of beavers, for example – they rightly conceive it as the history of collective action exercised by the community. They do not judge it necessary to establish a line of demarcation between the study of the social phenomena of the race and that of phenomena relative to the isolated individual. This lack of precision has no real disadvantage in this case, although the two orders of phenomena are distinct. For the civilization of the most intelligent social species having been halted almost at its origin, chiefly by the imperfection of their organization and secondly by the preponderance of the human race, the mind experiences no difficulty, in such a restricted causal chain, in directly connecting all collective phenomena with individual phenomena. Thus the general reason which leads us to establish distinctions in order to facilitate study – namely the inability of the human intelligence to pursue too extended a chain of deductions – does not exist here.

If we imagine, by contrast, that the species of beavers had become more intelligent so that its civilization could develop freely with a continuous chain of progress from one generation to another, we shall soon sense the necessity of treating separately the history of the social phenomena of the species. We could still, for the first generations, connect this study with that of the phenomena of the individual; but as we move away from the origins, this deduction will become more difficult to accomplish, and in the end it will be totally impossible to pursue it. This is precisely the case, in the highest degree, as regards man.

No doubt the collective phenomena of the human race, like its individual phenomena, recognize as their final cause the special nature of its organization. But the state of human civilization in each generation directly depends only on that of the preceding generation, and directly produces only that of the following. It is possible to follow, with all the necessary precision, this causal chain from its origin, establishing a direct link only between each term and the preceding and the following terms. By contrast it would be quite beyond the powers of the mind to connect any term in the series to the primitive point of departure, if we suppressed all the intermediate links.

The temerity of such an enterprise in the study of the species could be compared, in the study of the individual, to that of a physiologist who, considering that the various phenomena of the successive ages are solely the consequence and necessary development of the primitive organization, strove to deduce the history of a particular era of life from the state of the individual at his birth, determined with great precision, and thought himself thus dispensed from directly examining the different ages to understand the overall development accurately. The error is much greater still with regard to the species than with regard to the individual, given that in the first case the successive terms to be co-ordinated are both much more complicated and much more numerous than in the second.

By insisting on following this impracticable course, we should not only make ourselves incapable of satisfactorily studying the history of civilization, but we should inevitably be led into some fundamental errors. For, given the absolute impossibility of directly connecting the various states of civilization with the primitive and general point of departure established by the special nature of man, we should soon be led into directly attributing to secondary organic circumstances what is a distant consequence of the fundamental laws of organization.

It is thus, for example, that several estimable physiologists have been led to suppose that national characters have an importance which is obviously exaggerated in the explanation of political phenomena. They have attributed to them differences between people and people which in almost all cases stem only from unequal stages of civilization. This has had the deplorable effect of leading us to regard as invariable what is certainly only transitory. Such deviations, examples of which could easily be multiplied, and which are all derived from the same original error in the way of proceeding, clearly confirm the need to separate the study of social phenomena from that of ordinary physiological phenomena.

Geometers who have risen to the height of philosophical ideas as a general rule conceive all the phenomena of the universe – those of organized bodies as well as those of inorganic bodies – as stemming from a small number of common and unchanging laws. Physiologists rightly observe in this regard that, even if all these laws were one day to be perfectly known, the impossibility of making a continuous series of deductions would force us to retain the same distinction between the study of living bodies and that of inert bodies which is today founded on the diversity of laws. A precisely analogous reason applies directly to the distinction between social physics and physiology properly so called, that is between the physiology of the species and that of the individual. The distance is no doubt much less great, since it is only a matter of a secondary distinction, whereas the other is of first order. But there is a similar impossibility of making deductions, even though not to the same degree.

The total inadequacy of this way of proceeding can easily be verified if, instead of considering it only in relation to the theory of positive politics, we were to think of it in relation to the current practical goal of this science, that is, the determination of the system according to which society is today to be reorganized.

One can no doubt establish, on the basis of physiological laws, what is in general the state of civilization that is truest to the nature of the human race. But in the light of the foregoing it is clear that we could not go any further by this means. And such a notion, in isolation, is purely speculative, and can lead to no real and positive result in practice. For it does not in the least put us in a position to know positively at how great a distance the human race currently stands from that state, nor the course it must follow to reach it, nor, finally, the general plan of the corresponding social organization. These essential items of knowledge can obviously result only from the direct study of the history of civilization.

If, even so, we wished to strive to give some practical existence to this speculative and necessarily incomplete insight, we could not avoid falling immediately into the realm of the absolute; for then we should be reducing the whole real application of science to the formation of an unchanging type of vague perfection, without any distinction between eras, after the manner of conjectural politics. The excellence of this type is certainly established by criteria that are much more positive than those which serve as guides for theological and metaphysical politics. But this modification does not alter the absolute character which is inherent in such a question, in whatever manner we might imagine it addressed. Politics could therefore never become truly positive by this way of proceeding.

Thus, whether from the theoretical point of view or from the practical point of view, it is equally pernicious to conceive of social science as a simple consequence of physiology.

The true direct relation between knowledge of human organization and political science, as this chapter has characterized it, consists in the former providing the latter with its point of departure.

It is exclusively to physiology that the task belongs of establishing in a positive manner the causes that make the human race capable of a constantly progressive civilization, as long as the state of the planet it inhabits presents no insurmountable obstacle. It alone can trace the true character and the necessary general course of this civilization. It alone, finally, allows us to illuminate the formation of the first aggregations of men, and to lead history from the infancy of our species up to the era when it allowed its civilization to flourish by the creation of language.

This is the natural terminus for the role of direct physiological considerations in social physics, which must then be founded solely on the immediate observation of the progress of the human race. Beyond this point, the difficulty of deduction would immediately become very great, because from this era the course of civilization suddenly becomes much more rapid, in such a way that the terms to be co-ordinated suddenly multiply. On the other hand, the functions which physiology has to fill in the study of the social past would then no longer be necessary; it would no longer have as its point to make up for the lack of direct observations. For, from the point at which a language is established, there exist immediate data on the development of civilization, so that there is no lacuna in the aggregate of positive considerations.

There is something we must add to the foregoing if we are to have a complete survey of the true role of physiology in social physics. As Condorcet saw clearly, because the development of the species is only the result of individual developments, which are linked in a chain from one generation to the next, it must necessarily display characteristics in general conformity with the natural history of the individual. By this analogy, the study of man in isolation still provides certain means of verification and of reasoning for the study of the species, means which are distinct from those just indicated and which, though less important, have the advantage of extending to all eras.

In short, although the physiology of the species and that of the individual are two sciences of exactly the same order, or rather two distinct portions of a single science, it is nonetheless essential to conceive them and to treat them separately. The first must take its basis and its point of departure from the second if it is to be truly positive. But thereafter it must be studied in isolation, resting on the direct observation of social phenomena.

It was natural for us to seek to bring social physics wholly within the domain of physiology, when we could see no other way of stamping it with a positive character. But this error could no longer have any excuse today, now that it is easy to persuade oneself of the possibility of making political science positive by building it on the immediate observation of the social past.

In the second place, at the moment when the study of intellectual and affective functions left the domain of metaphysics to enter that of physiology, it was very difficult to avoid all exaggeration in determining the true scope of physiology, and not to include in it also the examination of social phenomena. The era of conquests is not a time for prescribing exact limits. Thus Cabanis, who was one of the principal collaborators in this great revolution, is particularly to be pardoned for his illusions in this regard. But today, when a strict analysis can and must replace the heady enthusiasm of the first wave, no cause can any longer stop us recognizing the necessity of a division which is unavoidably required by the weakness of the human mind.

No real reason can any longer lead us to isolate phenomena specially labelled moral from other phenomena in the study of the individual. The revolution which bound them all together must be regarded as the most essential move hitherto made by physiology from a philosophical point of view.

By contrast, considerations of the first importance demonstrate the absolute necessity of separating the study of the collective phenomena of the human race from that of the individual phenomena, establishing, furthermore, the natural relationship between these two great sections of physiology as a whole. To strive to eradicate this indispensable division would be to fall into an error analogous to, though less important than, that so rightly combated by true physiologists, which presents the study of living bodies as a consequence of and appendix to that of inert bodies.

These are the four principal attempts made hitherto with the goal of raising politics to the rank of the sciences of observation. Taken together they decisively certify the necessity and maturity of this great enterprise. The special examination of each of them confirms, each from a different point of view, the principles previously expounded in this chapter of the true means to give politics a positive character, and hence to settle with certainty the general conception of the new social system, which alone can terminate the current crisis of civilized Europe.

We can therefore regard it as established, on the basis of *a priori* and *a posteriori* proofs, that to attain this fundamental goal we must regard political science as a particular branch of physics, founded on the direct observation of phenomena relative to the collective development of the human race. Its object is the co-ordination of the social past, and its result is the determination of the system which the course of civilization is tending to produce today.

This social physics is obviously as positive as any other science of observation. Its intrinsic certainty is just as real.[h] As the laws it discovers satisfy the totality of phenomena observed, their application deserves our entire confidence.

This science, like all others, also possesses general means of verification, even independently of its necessary relation with physiology. These means are founded on the fact that in the present state of the human race, considered as a whole, all the degrees of civilization coexist on the different points of the globe, from that of the savages of New Zealand to that of the French and the English. Thus, the causal chain established on the basis of the succession in time can be verified by comparison of places.

At first sight, this new science would seem to be confined to observation alone, and totally deprived of the aid of experiments, which would not prevent it from being positive, witness the case of astronomy. But in physiology, independently of experiments on animals, pathological cases are in reality an equivalent of direct experiments on man, because they alter the usual order of phenomena. In the same way, and for a similar reason, the numerous eras when political combinations have tended – to a greater or lesser extent – to halt the development of civilization, must be considered as providing social physics with true experiments, still better able than pure observation to reveal or confirm the natural laws which govern the collective course of the human race.

If, as we dare to hope, the considerations presented in this chapter make scientists sense the importance and the possibility of estab-

---

[h] It is, no doubt, superfluous to stop to refute the extremely exaggerated objections presented by several authors, and above all by Volney, against the certainty of historical facts. Even if we were to accord to these objections all the latitude which these writers have given them, they would in no way apply to facts of a certain degree of importance and generality, which are the only ones to be considered in the study of civilization. [The reference is to C.-F. Volney, *Leçons d'histoire* (1795), *passim*.]

lishing a positive politics in the spirit indicated above, I shall then present in more detail my view of the means to execute this first series of works. But I think it useful to conclude by recalling the necessity of dividing it, first of all, into two orders: the first consisting of general works, the second of particular works.

The first order must have as their object to establish the general course of the human race, in abstraction from all the various causes which can modify the rate at which civilization develops, and hence from all the differences observed between peoples, however great they may be. In the second order, the aim will be to assess the influence of these modifying causes, and hence to form a definitive chart in which each people will occupy a special place corresponding to its own development.

Besides, in their execution both classes of works, and especially the latter, are susceptible of several degrees of generality, whose necessity will probably make itself felt by scientists.

The obligation to treat the first order of works before the second is based on this obvious principle, applicable to the physiology of the species as to that of the individual, that idiosyncrasies should only be studied after the establishment of general laws. We should have to abandon totally any idea of obtaining any clear notion if this rule were to be violated.

As for the possibility of proceeding thus, it results from the fact that there are today a sufficiently large number of particular points which are well clarified for us to concern ourselves immediately with general co-ordination. Physiologists did not wait until all special functions were understood before they formed an idea of the overall shape of the organization. It must be the same in social physics.[36]

Further clarifying the foregoing considerations, we can see that they tend to establish that, in the formation of political science, we must proceed from the general to the particular. And if we examine this precept directly, we can easily recognize its correctness.

The course which the human mind follows in the investigation of the laws which govern natural phenomena presents an important difference – from the point of view which concerns us – according

[36] The 1822 text finishes here. The following was added in 1824.

to whether it studies the physics of inorganic bodies or that of organized bodies.

In the first, because man forms an imperceptible part of an immense succession of phenomena, whose overall shape he can never hope to glimpse unless he is insanely presumptuous, he is forced, as soon as he begins to study them in a positive spirit, first to consider the most particular facts, and then to rise gradually to the discovery of some general laws, which later become the point of departure for his investigations. By contrast, in the physics of organized bodies, because man is himself the most complete type of the overall shape of phenomena, his positive discoveries necessarily begin with the most general facts, which then shed essential light which illuminates the study of the kind of details of which, by their nature, precise knowledge is forever denied him. In short, in the two cases the human mind proceeds from the known to the unknown; but in the first it initially rises from the particular to the general, because knowledge of the details is more immediate for it than that of totalities; whereas in the second it begins by descending from the general to the particular, because it knows the whole more directly than the parts. From a philosophical point of view the progress of each of the two sciences consists essentially in allowing it to adopt the method of the other, provided that the latter never becomes as characteristic as its original method.

Having considered this law from the highest perspective of positive philosophy, we can easily verify it by observing the course which the development of the natural sciences has hitherto followed, from the moment when each definitively ceased to have a theological or metaphysical character.[i]

Indeed, in the study of inorganic bodies, if we examine it first of all in its principal divisions, we can see astronomy, physics and chemistry beginning by being wholly isolated from each other, and then converging from increasingly numerous points of view, so that at last today we can detect in them a manifest tendency to form one single body of doctrine. In the same way, if we consider each of them separately, we see each emerging in the study of facts that are at first incoherent, and arriving by degrees at the generalities we

---

[i] It is essential to draw attention to this qualification; for we do not believe that this law is exactly applicable to the theological or metaphysical era which is destined to bring about the positive era for each science. [1824 footnote, omitted in 1854.]

now know. It is only in astronomy, and in some sections of terrestrial physics, that the human mind has hitherto been able to follow the opposite course in fundamental respects. We can even say that in astronomy as far as the totality of phenomena were concerned the law of universal gravitation changed the original course only in a secondary aspect, though it was of prime importance to us. For the applications of this law do not yet embrace, and probably even will never embrace the most general astronomical facts, which consist of the relations of the different solar systems, of which we as yet have no knowledge. This comment, bearing on the most perfect branch of inorganic physics, offers a striking verification of the principle we are considering.

If we now examine the part of this principle which relates to the study of living bodies, confirmation is just as palpable. In the first place, the general system of functions of which an organization consists is certainly better known today than the partial action of each organ; and in the same way, from a more extended perspective, the study of the general relations which exist between the various organizations, animal or plant, is no doubt more advanced than that of each particular organization. In the second place, the main branches of which organic physics is today composed were at first confused, and it is only by virtue of the progress of positive physiology that we have arrived at a precise analysis of the different general points of view from which a living body can be considered, in such a way as to build on these distinctions a rational division of the science. This is indeed so certain that, in view of the short length of time since the physics of organized bodies became truly positive, the distribution of its main parts has not yet been clearly settled. This fact is still more tangible if we pass from the science to the scientists, for they are obviously much less specialized in their order of work than scientists engaged in the study of inanimate bodies.

We can therefore regard it as established, by observation and reasoning, that the human mind proceeds chiefly from the particular to the general in inorganic physics, and, by contrast, from the general to the particular in organic physics; that, at least, it is incontestably in accordance with this course that the progress of science has long been accomplished, since the moment it assumed a positive character.

If the second part of this law has been misunderstood up to now, if people have believed that in any particular order of investigations the human mind always necessarily proceeded from the particular to the general, this error can be explained quite naturally. We need only reflect that, as the physics of inanimate bodies had to develop first, the precepts of positive philosophy initially had to be founded on the observation of its distinctive course. But the prolongation of such an error should surely cease to be pardonable now that philosophical observation can bear on the two orders of natural sciences.

If we apply to social physics, which is only a branch of physiology, the principle we have just established, it obviously demonstrates the need to begin the study of the development of the human race with the co-ordination of the most general facts, and then gradually to descend to a more and more precise causal chain. But, so as to leave no uncertainty on this essential point, it is appropriate to verify the principle directly in this particular case.

All historical works written up to now, even the most commendable, have essentially been – necessarily had to be – no more than *annals*, that is to say, descriptions and chronological arrangements of a certain sequence of particular facts, more or less important and more or less accurate, but always isolated from each other. No doubt, considerations relative to the co-ordination and connection of political phenomena have not been wholly neglected, especially in the last half-century. But it is clear that this synthesis has not yet in the least recast the character of this kind of composition, which has not shed its literary character.[j] Up to now there exists no true *history*, conceived in a scientific spirit, that is, having as its goal the investigation of the laws governing the social development of the human race, which is precisely the object of the series of work we are considering in this chapter.

The above distinction is sufficient to explain why it has hitherto been almost universally believed that in history we must proceed from the particular to the general, and why, on the contrary, we

---

[j] It is only a case here of establishing a fact, and not of judging it. We are, besides, wholly convinced of the utility and even of the absolute necessity of this class of writings as a preliminary task. We shall no doubt not be suspected of thinking that there could be a history without annals. But it is equally certain that annals are no more history than collections of meteorological observations are physics.

must today proceed from the general to the particular. Otherwise nothing will be achieved.

For when it is only a matter of accurately constructing general *annals* of the human race, we must obviously begin by forming those of the different peoples, and these can only be founded on chronicles of provinces and towns, or even on simple biographies. Similarly, from another point of view, to form complete annals of each particular fraction of the population, it is essential to gather together a collection of separate documents relative to each of the points of view from which it will be considered. It is in this way that we must necessarily proceed to succeed in composing the general facts that are the materials of political science, or rather the object with which its combinations are concerned. But a quite opposite course becomes essential, once we reach the direct formation of the science, that is the study of the causal relations of phenomena.

In fact, by their very nature, all classes of social phenomena develop simultaneously, and under each other's influence, in such a way that it is quite impossible to explain the course followed by any one of them, without first achieving a general grasp of the progression of the whole.

For example, everyone today recognizes that the reciprocal influence of the different European states is too important for their histories to be capable of being truly separated. But the same is true, just as palpably, of the different orders of political facts to be observed in a single society. Is not the progress of a science or an art obviously connected with that of the other sciences or the other arts? Do not the progress of the study of nature and that of our ability to act on nature depend upon one another? Are not both closely linked to the state of social organization, and vice versa? Thus, to understand accurately the real laws of the special development of the simplest branch of the social body, we must necessarily obtain at the same time the same degree of accuracy for all the others, which is a manifest absurdity.

On the contrary, we must first of all set ourselves the task of grasping in its largest generality the phenomenon of the development of the human race, that is, to observe and to connect with each other the most important progressive achievements successively made in the different principal directions. We shall then tend step by step to give this table a greater and greater degree of precision, by always further subdividing the intervals between observations and the classes of phenomena to be observed. In the same way, from a practical point of view, the appearance of the future of society, first determined in a general way as the result of an initial study of the past, will become more and more detailed as our knowledge of the prior course of the human race develops further. The final perfection of the science, which will probably never be completely achieved, would consist, from a theoretical angle, in precisely conceiving, from its origin, the connected sequence of progress from one generation to the next – whether for the totality of the social body, or for each science, each art and each part of the political organization. And from a practical angle it will consist in the rigorous determination, in all its essential details, of the system which the natural course of civilization will make prevail.

This is the method strictly dictated by the nature of social physics.

Essay 4
Philosophical Considerations on the Sciences and Scientists[1]

If we study as a whole the phenomenon of the development of the human mind, whether by the rational method or by the empirical method, we discover beneath all the apparent irregularities a fundamental law to which its course is necessarily and invariably subject. This law consists in the proposition that man's intellectual system, considered in all its parts, has necessarily assumed in turn three distinct characters: a theological character, a metaphysical character, and lastly a positive or physical character. Thus man began by conceiving phenomena of all kinds as due to the direct and continuous influence of supernatural agents; he next considered them as produced by different abstract forces residing in matter, but distinct and heterogeneous; finally, he limited himself to considering them as subject to a certain number of invariable natural laws, which are nothing other than the general expression of relations observed in their development.

All those who have sufficient understanding of the state of the human mind in the different ages of civilization can easily verify the truth of this general fact. One very simple observation can guide us towards this confirmation, now that this revolution has been carried out for the major part of our ideas. The education of the

---

[1] This essay was first published as a series of three articles in *Le Producteur* on 12 and 19 November and 3 December 1825.

individual, insofar as it is spontaneous, necessarily displays the same principal phases as does that of the species, and vice versa. And today any man in tune with his times will readily certify of himself that he has been by nature a theologian in his childhood, a metaphysician in his youth, and a physicist in his manhood. The history of the sciences proves directly that the same has been true of the human race as a whole. But it is, moreover, possible to explain why the formation of human ideas necessarily had to follow such a course.

To understand it clearly and fully, we must consider this law, like all other social facts, from a dual perspective: from the physical point of view of its necessity, that is as deriving from the natural laws of human organization; and from the moral point of view of its indispensability, that is as the only way suited to the development of the human mind.

In the first aspect, the law is easy to conceive.

A natural and irresistible tendency leads the human race to be a theologian before becoming a physicist. The personal action of man upon other beings is the only kind whose operation he understands, because of the feeling he has for it. He is therefore led to imagine analogously the reaction which external objects exercise upon him, as well as the action they exercise upon each other, only the results of which he can see directly. At least this is how he must conceive them as long as the progress of observation has not yet led him to recognize the very striking differences between the course of these phenomena and that of his own. If he later changes his ideas on this subject, it is solely because, as experience and reflection have disabused him of his primitive illusions, he absolutely renounces his attempt to penetrate the mystery of the mode of production of phenomena – for his nature prevents him having any knowledge of that – in order to confine himself to observing their real laws. For if, even today with all the positive notions that we have acquired, we wished to try to conceive, for the simplest phenomenon, by what power the fact that we call the *cause* engenders that which we call the *effect*, we should inevitably be induced to create images similar to those which served as the basis for the first human theories, as Barthez has very properly remarked, extending an idea of Hume's.[2]

[2] P.-J. Barthez, *Nouveaux éléments de la science de l'homme* (1858 edn) I 'Notes', 11–13.

Man therefore necessarily begins by seeing all the objects that attract his attention as if they were living beings, with a life analogous to his own, but in general superior because most of them exert more power. Next, the development of his observations makes him convert this first hypothesis into the much less durable one of an inert nature directed by a greater or smaller number of invisible superhuman agents, distinct and independent of each other, whose character and authority correspond to the nature and extent of the phenomena attributed to their influence. This theory, which at first was applied only to the phenomena of external objects, later extends even to those of man and society, when human contemplation turns its attention to them. It is then that theological philosophy begins to acquire a real consistency, and to exercise a powerful influence on the progress of the human mind.

But the inevitable and continuous progress of our knowledge of nature is not slow to modify this system, and in the end destroys it.

Properly speaking, man was never completely a theologian. There were always some phenomena simple enough and regular enough for him to regard them, even at the outset, as subject to natural laws, as Adam Smith explained very well.[a] But at first these were neither the most numerous nor the most important phenomena; far from it. As for the others, we could say that man had recourse to theological explanations only as long as physical conceptions were not possible; for when they became possible, he became exclusively attached to them.

The first effect of the progress of observation was to lead the human mind continually to reduce the number of supernatural agents, attributing to just one the functions which originally required several, as the relations of phenomena acquired more generality. This effect, pushed to its limits, in the end simplified the theological system to the point of reducing it to unity.

From that time, the continuous influence of the same principle which had first led the human mind from fetishism to polytheism,

[a] See, in his *Posthumous Works*, the *Philosophical Essay on the History of Astronomy*. This work, too little known on the continent, and generally undervalued, has a more positive character than the other productions of Scottish philosophy, if we except those of Hume. Very remarkable for its time, it could be reflected upon very fruitfully, even today. [*The History of Astronomy* III.3, in Adam Smith, *Essays on Philosophical Subjects*, ed. W. P. D. Wightman, J. C. Bryce and I. S. Ross (1980), pp. 50–1.]

and then from polytheism to theism, led it to confine the direct intervention of the great supernatural cause within narrower and narrower limits, while still reserving for it the direction of the phenomena whose positive laws were unknown. For the others, as the discovery of their laws allowed man to predict them with greater accuracy, and consequently to act upon them more effectively than special theological theories did, man increasingly ceased to employ the latter in his normal speculations, and made ever increasing use of those which best satisfied his two great needs of foresight and action. Finally, when natural conceptions acquired a sufficient extent and generality (that is, nowadays), when they embraced at a number of major points all orders of investigation really accessible to our powers, the human mind, extending by analogy to all phenomena, even unknown ones, what had been verified only for a certain number, considered them all as subject to invariable physical laws, whose discovery – more and more accurate – is henceforth the sole reasonable goal of our speculative work. Then the theological method, which up to then had not entirely fallen into disuse, was regarded as no longer able to be employed in our investigations, and the positive method began completely and exclusively to direct the activity of our intellect.

Having conceived this great revolution as an inevitable fact, we must explain why such a course has been indispensable to the development of human reason. Positive philosophy has today obtained such an ascendancy over the mind that it is difficult to conceive how, in any era, theological philosophy and metaphysical philosophy could have been useful – still less necessary – as means of investigation. They are almost universally regarded – especially the first – as aberrations of the human mind, even by the small number of people who conceive of these aberrations as having been inevitable. It is therefore necessary to rectify people's ideas on this essential point, since without this clarification it would be possible to understand the law of the succession of the three philosophies only very imperfectly, and that would singularly limit the extent and value of its applications. It is no doubt important to establish that the human mind has not up to our day been in a state of insanity, and that it has constantly employed in each era the method best able to favour its progress, at least if we take in its overall course.

It is certainly incontestable today that observation of the facts is the only solid basis for human knowledge. We can even say strictly, taking this principle in its greatest rigour, that no proposition which is not reducible to the simple enunciation of a fact, whether particular or general, can have any real and intelligible sense. But it is not less certain that the development of the capacity of imagination must precede that of the capacity of observation. The same causes that determine this order in the education of the individual make it still more essential in that of the species.

The positive method is the one that is surest in its course; perhaps even the only one that is sure. But at the same time it is the slowest, and for this reason not at all suited to the infancy of the human mind. If this disadvantage is apparent even when our intellect has been in full swing for a long time, just think what it must have been in the age of our first efforts. Even the possibility of such a method presupposes a prior series of observations, all the longer because the first natural laws are always those whose discovery demands most time. And on the other hand absolute empiricism is impossible, whatever people may say. Man is by his nature incapable not only of comparing facts and deducing some consequences from them, but even simply of observing them carefully, and remembering them reliably, if he does not immediately connect them with some explanation. In short, there can no more be sustained observations without a theory of some kind than a positive theory without sustained observations. It is therefore obvious that human faculties would necessarily have remained in an indefinite state of torpidity if in order to reason about phenomena we had to wait until their relationship and their mode of exploration emerged from their observation itself. Thus the earliest progress of the human mind could only have been produced by the theological method, the only method which can develop spontaneously. It alone had the important property of offering us, from the outset, a provisional theory, vague and arbitrary it is true, but direct and easy to understand, which immediately grouped the first facts; with its help, by cultivating our capacity for observation, we were able to prepare the age of a wholly positive philosophy.

If it were possible here to go into a few details on this great subject we should see clearly not only that theological philosophy –

taken as a whole – was indispensable in facilitating the development of the positive method, but also that the different improvements which it experienced, and which were moreover produced by the progress of observation, by a necessary reaction made a powerful contribution to accelerating that progress. To cite only the most remarkable fact of this kind, it is obvious that, without the passage from polytheism to theism, theories of nature would never have been able really to expand. This admirable simplification of theological philosophy reduced the influence of the great supernatural power, in each particular case, to a certain general direction, whose character was necessarily vague. By this means, the human mind was fully authorized and even strongly encouraged to study the physical laws of each phenomenon as the mode of action of this supernatural power. Before this time, by contrast, the intellect which inclined towards positive investigations came across so many special and very detailed theological explanations for all phenomena, even the simplest, that each physicist was necessarily ungodly.

The necessity of the course we are examining becomes even more apparent when we consider that at the same time as theological philosophy was the only one possible at the outset, it was also the only one appropriate to the nature of the investigations which had first to occupy the human mind.

It was only by experience founded on the actual exercise of his faculties that man could have come to know their true range. At the outset, we find him constantly inclined to exaggerate it. This tendency was at that time peculiarly strengthened by ignorance of the natural laws, which bound him to the hope of exercising over the external world a power which was, so to speak, arbitrary. In this state of the intellect, investigations about the secret nature of beings, about the origin and the end of the universe and of all phenomena, alone appear worthy of occupying the human mind to any great extent. Indeed, they alone were capable of doing so. At first we are astonished to find such temerity combined with such deep ignorance. But when we think about it, we recognize that it is impossible to conceive of any motive powerful enough to draw the human intellect in its first age into purely theoretical investigations, and to sustain it, without the potent attraction which was inspired in it, especially at that time, by these immense questions which embraced all others, even without the chimerical hopes of limitless power which were linked to them. Kepler vividly saw this necessity for astrology relative to astronomy; and Berthollet made the same observation for alchemy relative to chemistry. But whatever one may think of this explanation, the fact itself, which is incontestable, is enough to show clearly to what extent theological philosophy is alone adapted to the primitive state of the human mind. For the first character of positive philosophy is, precisely, to regard all these big questions as necessarily insoluble for man. By forbidding our intellect to undertake any investigation into the first and final causes of phenomena, it limits the field of its operations to the discovery of their present relations. It is therefore apparent that, even if at the outset it had been possible to choose between these two methods, the human mind would not have hesitated to reject with disdain that which, in the humility of its promises as in the slowness of its procedures, is so ill-matched with the extent and vivacity of our primitive intellectual needs.

The foregoing reflections therefore prove that, considering only the philosophical conditions for the development of the human mind, it necessarily had to employ the theological method for a long time, before taking the positive method as its guide. But this necessity becomes still more striking if we take account of the political conditions, which, no less than the philosophical, are essential to the intellectual education of the human race.

It is only by an abstraction, and a necessary one, that we can study the spiritual development of man separately from his temporal development, or that of the human mind without that of society; for these two developments, although distinct from one another, are not independent. On the contrary, they exert on one another an influence that is continuous and indispensable to both.

It is not enough to sense in a general way that the cultivation of our intellect is possible only in society and through society; we must in addition recognize that the nature and extent of social relations determine in every age the character and the pace of our spiritual progress, and vice versa. We all know today, for example, that it is impossible to conceive of any real and durable progress in the human mind in that state of society where each individual is constantly obliged to provide for his subsistence by himself. For the division between theory and practice, the general cause of our progress, could not then exist to any degree. But among pastoral peoples, and even among agricultural peoples, though their mode of existence has eliminated this firm obstacle, this fundamental condition is often very far from being fulfilled. It is necessary, besides, that the social organization should be sufficiently advanced to permit the regular establishment of a class of men who, dispensed from the cares of material production and those of war, can devote themselves consistently to the contemplation of nature. In a word, in this respect as in many other no less important ones, the formation of human knowledge presupposes an already very complicated state of society. And on the other hand no real and compact society could be formed and maintained without the influence of some kind of system of ideas capable of overcoming the opposition between individual propensities, which are so pronounced at the outset, and making them co-operate in a stable order. This essential function could only be performed by a philosophical theory which was dispensed by its nature from that slow preliminary elaboration that is necessary to the development of real knowledge, and which requires the prolonged existence of a regular and complete political order. This is the admirable character of theological philosophy, and is exclusive to it. It is to theological philosophy that, by the nature of things, the original establishment of any social organization is due. Without the powerful and happy influence that it alone can exert on the mind in the infancy of peoples, we could conceive of no permanent classification capable of entailing and assisting, up to a certain point, the blossoming of human faculties. From the point of view that concerns us here, what other ascendancy than that of theological doctrines could have permitted and maintained, in the midst of a population of warriors and slaves, the existence of a corporation solely occupied in intellectual work; still less ensured its predominance, which is indispensable to its earliest operations as to the stability of society?

Thus, having regard to the conditions, moral or political, for the development of the human mind, we find that it necessarily had to begin with theological philosophy, before attaining positive philosophy. It is easy to establish, with the same certainty, that it could only pass from the one to the other by employing metaphysical philosophy.

Theological conceptions and positive conceptions are too different in character, even too opposed, for our minds, which proceed only by almost imperceptible degrees, to be able to pass from the former to the latter without any intermediaries. These indispensable intermediaries were and had to be metaphysical conceptions, which – deriving both from theology and from physics, or rather being only the first modified by the second – are by their nature splendidly suited to this operation, which comprises the whole of their utility.

Theological philosophy, placing itself directly at the primary source of all phenomena, concerns itself essentially with revealing their generating causes, whereas positive philosophy, setting aside any investigation into *cause*, which it proclaims to be inaccessible to the human mind, is simply attached to the discovery of *law*, that is, the constant relations of similarity and succession which the facts have with each other. Between these two points of view the metaphysical point of view is naturally interposed; it considers each phenomenon as produced by an abstract force which is unique to it. This method is invaluable in the facility with which it enables us to reason about phenomena without directly considering the supernatural causes which the human mind has thus been able gradually to eliminate from its operations.

It is in fact by such a process that this change has occurred in all intellectual areas. When the progress of observation led man to generalize and to simplify his theological conceptions, for each particular phenomenon he replaced the primitive supernatural agent with a corresponding entity, and that was from then on the exclusive focus of his consideration. These entities were at first kinds of emanations from the supreme power; but thanks to the indeterminacy of their character, they ended by being spiritualized to the point of no longer being regarded as anything other than the abstract names of phenomena, as the increase in natural knowledge made us feel the emptiness of this kind of explanation, and allowed us at the same time to substitute another kind for it. It was thus that metaphysics was a means of transition, both natural and indispensable, from theology to physics. Its triumph is, on the one hand, the infallible sign, and on the other hand the direct cause, of the decadence of the former and the elevation of the latter.

If the various foregoing considerations clearly prove that theological and metaphysical theories were an indispensable preliminary for the human mind, they show just as clearly that these doctrines could not have had any other natural destination, since their development was never other than a continuous and progressive tendency towards positive theories. For the very reason that they were fitted to direct the infancy of human reason, they are necessarily impotent to serve as its guides once it has reached its maturity. Once the human mind has really abandoned a theory, it never returns to it. The vigour and influence of a method can be measured by the number and importance of its applications: those which no longer produce anything soon completely cease to be employed. And as for two centuries at least theological and metaphysical methods, which had governed our intellect's earliest efforts, have become wholly sterile; as the most extensive and the most important discoveries, those which do most honour to the human mind, have since that time been solely due to the employment of the positive method, it is obvious, by this fact alone, that it is to it that will henceforth belong the exclusive direction of human thought.[b]

Without underestimating the important and innumerable services of all kinds previously performed by theology and metaphysics, we cannot hide the fact that our mind is not intended indefinitely to compose theogonies, nor to be forever content with logomachies. The most exact and the most complete possible knowledge of the laws of nature, and consequently investigation of the action which the human race is called to exert upon the external world, these are the true and constant objects of the efforts of human genius, when its preliminary education is over. Positive philosophy is therefore the definitive state of man, and must cease only with the activity of our intellect. The appeal it has for us, its perfect suitability for the nature of our spiritual needs, are such that as soon as it begins to form through the discovery of some great laws, the most distinguished minds renounce with singular facility, at corresponding points, the seductive hopes of sublime and absolute knowledge which theology and metaphysics gave them, to seek with enthusiasm the pure intellectual satisfaction associated with real and precise knowledge. No doubt today it is not necessary to dwell much on demonstrating a tendency which is manifest at every moment and

[b] At the end of the sixteenth century, Bacon was already comparing theological ideas to virgins consecrated to the Lord, who became sterile. Nowadays he would certainly have extended his comparison to metaphysical ideas, whose sterility is not less manifest.

in a thousand ways, even in the least advanced intellects. Wherever positive conceptions could be brought into competition with mystical and vague conceptions, distaste for the latter has not been slow to make itself felt.*

From all the considerations set out above there results the demonstration, both theoretical and experimental, of the general fact enunciated at the start: in all the fields in which it is exercised, the human mind, by its nature, passes in turn through three different theoretical states: the theological state, the metaphysical state, and the positive state. The first is provisional, the second transitory, and the third definitive.

This fundamental law must today be, in my eyes, the starting-point for all philosophical investigation of man and society.

Since theological and metaphysical doctrines still retain some activity, or at least quite a large influence, it is obvious that this important revolution is not complete. At what point is it? What remains to be done to accomplish it? This is what must be examined.

This is not the place to explain by what sequence of work this great change was produced. It is enough to note in fact, to settle our ideas, that it is to the movement brought about in the human mind by Bacon's precepts, by Descartes's conceptions, by Galileo's discoveries (a movement which was itself only the final and inevitable result of all previous work) that we must trace the direct origin of a truly positive philosophy, that is a philosophy wholly freed from the theological and metaphysical hotchpotch which had up to then distorted the character of theories of nature.

It is during the two centuries that have passed since that memorable era that the different branches of our knowledge have finally reached the positive state. But if it is of little importance, for our present purpose, to examine by what means this passage has

---

* Language, which when examined historically presents a faithful picture of the revolutions of the human mind, offers us a very tangible piece of evidence of this. The word *sciences*, which at first had been applied only to theological and metaphysical speculations, and later to the purely learned investigations they engendered, today no longer indicates, when unqualified, anything other than positive knowledge, even in popular usage. When people want to give it some other meaning they are obliged, in order to make themselves understood, to have recourse to circumlocutions whose use shows well that, in the eyes of the public of today, it is only in this that true knowledge consists.

occurred, it is by contrast essential to observe attentively in what order our different classes of ideas have undergone this transformation; for this notion is indispensable to complete our knowledge of the law previously expounded.

A very simple and very natural course of development manifests itself in this respect.

Our different conceptions have become positive in turn, in the same order which they followed in becoming first theological and later metaphysical. This order is that of the degree of ease presented by the study of the corresponding phenomena. It is determined by whether they are more or less complex, more or less independent, more or less special, and by whether their relation with man is more or less direct: four causes which, though each has a distinct influence, are basically inseparable. And this is, in this respect, the classification dictated by the nature of phenomena as we know it today.

Astronomical phenomena are at once the simplest, the most general and the most remote from man; they influence all the others without being influenced by them, at least to a degree apparent to us; they obey only one single law, the most universal in nature, that of gravitation. After them come the phenomena of terrestrial physics properly so called, which are dependent upon the previous ones and which, besides, follow special laws more limited in their results. Next, chemical phenomena, which depend upon the two preceding classes, and in which we can see in addition a new series of laws, that of affinities, whose effects are less extensive. Finally, physiological phenomena, in which we can observe all the laws of physics, whether celestial or terrestrial, and of chemistry, but modified by other laws which are proper to them, and whose influence is still more limited.

It results from this simple exposition that human conceptions, in any of the three general forms previously assigned, could develop quite extensively in relation to phenomena that are early in this encyclopaedic scale, without yet being developed in relation to the later ones, since the first are independent of the second; whereas, by contrast, they could not begin to form in relation to the latter without having already acquired a certain consistency in relation to the others whose influence must inevitably be taken into consideration in any theory. This classification therefore irresistibly settles the order of development of each of the three philosophies. The facts are consistent with this principle, as can easily be verified: that is especially easy for positive philosophy, whose formation, which was in any case very recent, was naturally slower and therefore presents more distinct intervals.

If we observe from this perspective the course of the human mind over two centuries, we find that astronomy was indeed the first to become a positive science; after it, physics, then chemistry, and finally today physiology. This is the present state of our intellectual development.

In order to understand with all the necessary precision the true stage which this great revolution has now reached, we must distinguish in the last science (physiology) the section that relates to the intellectual and affective functions from that which takes in the other organic functions.

Moral phenomena have been the last of all to leave the domain of theology and metaphysics to enter that of physics. No doubt nothing was more natural according to the encyclopaedic scale established above. But if this inevitable circumstance makes the transformation less apparent in relation to them, it is no less real, although still unnoticed by the greater number of minds. All those who are truly in tune with their age know as a matter of fact that physiologists today consider moral phenomena in absolutely the same spirit as all other animal phenomena. Very extensive work has been undertaken in this area, and has been enthusiastically pursued for more than twenty years; positive conceptions, more or less fruitful, have come into being; schools have formed spontaneously to develop them and propagate them; in short, all the signs of human activity have been displayed unequivocally with regard to moral physiology. It is useless here to take sides for or against any of the different opinions which today fight for dominance, about the kind, the number, the extent, and the mutual influence of the organs assignable to the different functions, whether intellectual or affective. No doubt science has not yet found its definitive foundations in this regard; and the only things solidly established here are a few generalities that are insufficient, though very valuable. But the very fact of this diversity of theories, which indicates an inevitable uncertainty in any emerging science, clearly establishes that the great philosophical revolution has taken place in this branch of our knowledge, as in all the others, at least in the minds which in this respect form the avant-garde of the human race, and which sooner or later are followed by the mass. For in the disagreements that are taking place, the positive method is recognized on both sides as the only admissible instrument; the formation of a physical theory, which here consists in the combination of the anatomical point of view with the physiological point of view, is regarded in the opinion of all as the only reasonable goal; theology and metaphysics are, by common accord, eliminated from the question, or at least they have no important role to play there; and whatever must be the final result of the debate, it can only still further diminish their activity. In short, the debates are henceforth confined within the field of science, and philosophy is no longer at issue.

I have particularly insisted upon this last philosophical fact, first because it is still barely noticed and often even disputed, and above all because, for anyone who has properly understood my classification of the sciences, this last observation presents both a new incontestable proof – though an indirect one – and an exact résumé of the totality of the great intellectual change.

Having thus established, as a matter of fact, the point now reached in the formation of positive philosophy, we must examine what remains to be done to complete it.

The natural series of phenomena provides, as it were of itself, the reply to this question.

The four large classes of observations already established do not include, at least explicitly, all the points of view from which living beings can be considered. Obviously the social point of view is missing for beings who are capable of it, and especially for man; but we can see just as clearly that this gap is the only one. Thus we now possess a celestial physics, a terrestrial physics whether mechanical or chemical, a vegetal physics and an animal physics: we still need one final one, social physics, in order that the system of our natural knowledge may be complete. Once this condition is fulfilled, we shall at last be able, by a general summary of all our different notions, to build a true positive philosophy, capable of satisfying all the real needs of our intellect. From this moment, human thought will no longer be forced at any point to have recourse to the theological method or the metaphysical method; and these, having lost the remains of their utility, will no longer have anything but a historical existence. In short, the human race will have entirely completed its intellectual education, and will henceforth be able to pursue its final destination directly.

These are the important considerations which I must now develop.

The present framework does not allow me to characterize sufficiently closely the particular spirit and the special method of this last branch of natural philosophy. Here I shall limit myself to saying, to avoid any confusion, that I understand by *social physics* the science whose distinctive object is the study of social phenomena,[d] considered in the same spirit as astronomical, physical, chemical and physiological phenomena, that is as subject to invariable natural laws whose discovery is the special goal of its investigations. Thus it sets out directly to *explain*, with as much accuracy as possible, the great phenomenon of the development of the human race, considered in all its essential parts: that is to discover by what necessary chain of successive transformation mankind, starting from a state which was barely superior to that of societies of apes, was gradually led to the point it is today at in civilized Europe. The spirit of this science consists above all in seeing in the detailed study of the past the true explanation of the present and the general manifestation of the future. Always considering social facts, not as objects to be admired or criticized, but as objects to be observed, it is solely concerned with establishing their mutual relations and grasping the influence exercised by each of them on the overall pattern of human development. In its relations with practice it removes any absolute idea of good or evil from the different institutions and regards them consistently as relative to the particular state of society, and variable according to it. At the same time it conceives them as always able to establish themselves spontaneously by the sole force of antecedents, independently of any direct political intervention. Its applied investigations can therefore be reduced to bringing to the fore the various tendencies peculiar to each age, according to the natural laws of civilization combined with immediate observation. These

[d] Social phenomena, as human phenomena, are no doubt included among physiological phenomena. But although for this reason social physics must necessarily take its point of departure in individual physiology, and remain in continuous relations with it, it must nevertheless be conceived and cultivated as a wholly distinct science, because of the progressive influence of human generations on one another. This influence, which is the prime consideration in social physics, cannot be properly studied from a purely physiological point of view.

general results in turn become the positive point of departure for the work of the statesman, which thus no longer has any other real object than to discover and institute the practical forms corresponding to these fundamental data, in order to avoid or at least to soften as much as possible the crises – more or less serious – which spontaneous development brings about when it has not been foreseen. In short, in this order of phenomena as in any other, science leads to foresight, and foresight allows us to regulate action.

To this necessarily very imperfect description of the character of social physics, we must add – in order that this survey might have some utility – a brief indication of the fundamental principle that distinguishes the positive method particular to this science. It consists in the fact that, in the investigation of social laws, the mind must necessarily proceed from the general to the particular, that is, it must begin by conceiving as a whole the total development of the human race, at first distinguishing in it just a very small number of successive states, and then gradually descend, by multiplying the intermediate points, to an ever-growing precision whose natural limit would consist in supposing an interval of only a single generation in the co-ordination of the terms of this large series. This course is essentially common to all parts of the physics of organized bodies, but it is particularly necessary in social physics.*

This is therefore as much as I can here present of the nature of the new physical science that is destined to complete the system of our positive knowledge.

Having given this definition, which seemed to me indispensable in settling our ideas, we can easily explain why this last branch of natural philosophy could not be formed before now, and why it must inevitably begin today.

Social theories, even if considered only from a purely philosophical point of view, necessarily retained their theological character and their metaphysical character longer than all the others, in accordance with the law of formation established above. For their phenom-

---

* Besides, it would be easy to see very clearly, as a matter of fact, what social physics consists in, if the fundamental law expounded above were regarded as irrevocably established. For on this assumption the science would really have begun. The discovery of this law, if its accuracy were accepted, would be a first direct step in social physics, since it sets out the first natural causal chain of social phenomena, and the most general possible.

ena obviously occupy the last rung in our encyclopaedic scale, being
at once the most complicated, the most particular, the most directly
related to man, and the ones that depend upon all the others. It
would no doubt be impossible to conceive that the human mind
could rise to positive ideas about social phenomena without having
first acquired quite an extended knowledge of the fundamental laws
of human organization. And this knowledge for its part presupposes
the preliminary discovery of the principal laws of the inorganic
world. And these, besides, also have a direct influence upon the
character and conditions of existence of human societies.

Readers who are used to considering natural laws will easily see
the full force and extent of this universal and profound relation. To
indicate here only the most decisive case, that where the relationship
is least apparent, it is easy to persuade oneself that astronomical
phenomena, through their extreme generality, exercise a dominant
influence over social phenomena. Their laws could not experience
the least change without it bringing about a profound alteration in
the mode of existence and development of human societies. Who
cannot see, for example, that the fact that the earth moves – at first
ignored, and then discovered – must have had the highest degree
of influence over our whole intellectual system? We can even say
that the simplest circumstances of form or position, insignificant in
the astronomical order, have a supreme importance in the political
order. Thus, imagine a variation of a few degrees in the obliquity
of the ecliptic, which established a new distribution of climates; a
slight increase or diminution in the distance of the earth from the
sun, which changed the length of the year and the temperature of
the globe, and in consequence probably the length of human life,
or a host of other analogous modifications whose astronomical
importance would be almost non-existent. We can see, by contrast,
that human development could no longer be conceived in anything
like the form that has taken place. Such hypotheses, which are capable of bringing out the actual relations of different orders of
phenomena, can easily be multiplied to infinity in their different
kinds. They make us see that the conditions of existence of human
societies are in a necessary and continuous relationship not only
with the laws of our organization – which is obvious – but also with
all the physical and chemical laws of our planet and those of the
solar system of which it forms a part. This relation is so close that

if any change of note came to be introduced into just one of these innumerable influences of all kinds under whose absolute rule our societies exist, the course of mankind would be profoundly altered, even supposing only variations that do not compromise its existence.

It is therefore apparent that social phenomena could not by their nature be reduced to positive theories before a similar revolution had been effected for astronomical, physical, chemical and physiological phenomena. As, in relation to these last, the transformation has taken place only in our age, and is still barely to be felt for moral phenomena, the theory of which is the most directly indispensable to social physics, we can easily imagine why this science has not been possible up to the present.

This explanation acquires a new degree of clarity if we consider another circumstance which is wholly peculiar to social phenomena. In fact their positive study, if it is to become possible, would obviously require that the course of the human race should be sufficiently advanced to be able of itself to display to observers some natural laws of succession. In trying to assess the scope of this condition, it seems to me that the experimental base of social physics would not have had sufficient breadth if it had not been able to embrace the totality of the development which has taken place hitherto in the human race. This conjecture will be logically demonstrated for all those who accept the law set out above; for this law could only be revealed once the human race in the greater part of our ideas had completely undergone the revolution to which the law relates. This brings us precisely to the era which we have just assigned for other reasons.

The same considerations which explain what has hitherto prevented the positive method from being extended to social theories prove no less strongly that this last part of the great intellectual renovation must necessarily occur today.

The human mind constantly tends to unity of method and doctrine; that is its regular and permanent state: any other can only be transitory. It is inconceivable that we should habitually employ a certain method in most of our operations, and should not in the end either renounce it altogether or extend it to all the others; and the latter outcome alone is conceivable for methods whose superiority has been established by experience. It would therefore be contradictory to imagine that the human mind, now raised to reason in a positive manner about all astronomical, physical, chemical and physiological phenomena, should have to continue for ever to reason theologically and metaphysically when social phenomena are in question. Anyone who has studied the intellectual character of man will see that it cannot be so. What must inevitably happen, therefore, is either that astronomy, physics, chemistry and physiology will again become metaphysical and even theological – which it would be absurd to imagine – or that politics will become positive, which is consequently certain.

A philosopher of the nineteenth century who has gone deeper than anyone into the nature of the former state of the human race, M. de Maistre, has very convincingly seen the necessity of this choice. He has seen very clearly that the development of the natural sciences tended radically to destroy the rule of theology and metaphysics; he has understood that, to be truly logical in his regrets about the decadence of the old intellectual and social system, he must audaciously return to those ancient times where there was unity in the human mind, by means of a uniform subordination of all our ideas to supernatural phenomena.*f*

No doubt, since not all positive sciences have been able to form simultaneously, there must have existed periods, longer or shorter, during which the human mind employed the three methods at once, each for a certain order of ideas.*g* Since metaphysical philosophy by custom erects an essentially transitory state into an immutable principle, it has in accordance with this practice established the maxim of a fundamental and absolute separation between the theological method and the positive method, under the abstract names of faith and reason. But experience proves clearly that such a

---

f See in the *Soirées de Saint-Pétersbourg*, among other insights, a very remarkable comparison between the character of ancient science and that of modern science. [J. de Maistre, *Les Soirées de Saint-Pétersbourg*, pp. 71–6 and 245.]

g This temporary and inevitable confusion is the main difficulty which the verification of the law expounded above can experience. But if we observe that the three methods have never been employed at the same time for the same order of ideas, the difficulty will disappear when we have regard to the encyclopaedic order already established.

The fact of this mixed state is, moreover, the only serious objection that has hitherto been made, to my knowledge, against this fundamental law. And this objection is only put forward by minds that are by their education unfortunately alien to the positive sciences, although they are in themselves very distinguished.

doctrine has never served to do anything but to extend the domain of reason at the expense of the domain of faith, which was besides the natural destination of this principle of transition, which was for a long time useful. In spite of this eternal truce between theology and physics, the latter always tended more and more to invade the entire system of our ideas, and ability to do that increased in proportion to the conquests already effected. As it only remains for it today to take hold of social ideas, it is therefore obvious that it must end up embracing them too within its domain, and even very imminently, if we appreciate the immense power given to it by its exclusive domination of all our other classes of ideas.

The conclusion drawn from this consideration of unity becomes still more apparent when we examine the formation of theological or metaphysical theory in relation to social phenomena.

The superficial philosophy of the eighteenth century generally represented theological social doctrine as the work of non-believing legislators who saw in it only an instrument of domination. Without dwelling here on the shocking absurdity of such an assumption, which we no longer need to refute today, experience shows us, in conformity with the general order of formation established at the beginning of this article, that theological philosophy was extended to social phenomena, and was able in consequence to become a means of organization, solely by virtue of the ascendancy it had first acquired in explaining all the phenomena of external bodies and of man himself. This explanation is the first origin and the fundamental condition of the general ascendancy attained by the theological system. The same relation can always be observed in the different forms that it successively takes. Is it not evident, for example, that as soon as the human mind could rise to the idea of a single great supernatural cause producing all the phenomena of the external world and the individual phenomena of man, it could not but apply the same doctrine to the direction of societies? It was the same again when human conceptions became metaphysical. When this transformation occurred for astronomical, physical, chemical and physiological ideas, it would have been possible to foresee that it would not be slow in extending itself to political ideas. There is a deep though indirect connection between Aristotle's ideas on celestial and terrestrial physics, the scholastic doctrines of the Middle

Ages, and Rousseau's *Social Contract*: it is the same spirit embracing a new order of ideas. Thus, since social theories have always been as a matter of fact in close and necessary relation with those of other phenomena, and since the transformations which have hitherto affected the former have constantly followed those experienced by the latter; the same must apply – all the more so, given the greater discordance – to the changes which have brought them to the positive state. This consequently cannot fail to manifest itself also in doctrine relating to political phenomena.

All the symptoms, general or particular, which could indicate such a revolution have in fact already made their mark with an energy that is easily sufficient to leave no doubt about its imminent accomplishment.

The total primacy gained in the last century by metaphysics in relation to social ideas is an indisputable sign of the complete decadence of theology. On the other hand the deep distaste for metaphysical politics which has generally arisen since the experience of the French Revolution, and which however has not brought minds back to theological doctrines, is no less certain an indication of the imminent formation of positive politics, which alone is capable of eliciting universal assent on the part of minds that have become as resistant to the power of abstractions as to the authority of oracles, and that no longer wish to yield to anything but the force of facts.

We might even say that the most distinguished thinkers have already made direct attempts, more or less complete, to satisfy this new need of the human mind. This is essentially the character of the great Montesquieu's works. First, in his work on the Romans, and especially thereafter in *L'Esprit des lois*, he strove to connect political phenomena with one another, and to grasp the laws of their causal relations. This attempt was no doubt too premature to be able to succeed; but the fact itself clearly testifies to the tendency of the human mind. Later, Condorcet ascended in the same direction to the direct and definitive conception by setting out to study the successive development of the human race; and, although the execution of this project was a complete failure, it nevertheless shows how much the need was felt. We should consider in the same light the efforts made in England in the last century to perfect the nature of history by giving it an explanatory or scientific character, instead of the descriptive or literary character it had had up to then. In Germany the works of Kant[h] and Herder on the philosophy of history, and subsequently the formation among jurists of a school which conceives legislation as always necessarily determined by the state of civilization, display just as obviously the general tendency of our century towards positive doctrines in politics. An exclusive taste for books which tend to reveal this character asserts itself more every day; and it even dominates party spirit, which is a very decisive observation. The men who strive most to re-establish the old dominance of theology unknowingly yield to the spirit of the age and regard it as a matter of honour to establish their opinions above all by using the authority of positive considerations.[i]

The time has therefore at last come when, as the final result of all previous work, the human mind can complete the general system of natural philosophy by reducing social phenomena, following all the others, to positive theories. The different preliminary attempts that we have just briefly indicated are sufficient to indicate this operation and to make it immediately practicable, but they leave it wholly to be effected. This is the great philosophical task reserved for the nineteenth century by the natural course of our intellectual development.

When this work has been completed, or rather when it is sufficiently advanced for the human mind to be henceforth regarded as irrevocably set in this new direction, we can and even must at last proceed to the construction of a general system of human knowledge, all the elements being by then developed.

Before and after the eighteenth-century *Encyclopaedia*, a host of attempts were made at this goal, but none succeeded. Every day we

[h] Kant, in a little work written in 1784 under a very remarkable title (*Introduction to a General History of the Human Race*), formally established that social phenomena must be considered just as reducible to natural laws as are all other phenomena in the universe. [The text to which Comte is referring here is Kant's *Idee zu einer allgemeinen Geschichte in weltbürgerlicher Absicht*, or *Idea for a Universal History with a Cosmopolitan Purpose*, which was first published in the *Berlinische Monatsschrift* in November 1784. Comte read this in a translation prepared at his instigation by Gustave d'Eichthal, and sent to Comte in November 1824. See Pickering, *Auguste Comte*, p. 290.]

[i] If, for example, the book *Du pape* has great philosophical value, as cannot be doubted, it owes it essentially to the fact that, by a fundamental consideration, the author sought as much as he could to employ only the positive method in his reasonings, and made only a secondary use of considerations drawn from theological or metaphysical philosophy. [Joseph de Maistre, *Du pape*, 1819, 2 vols.]

see new ones arising which have no more success, and which serve only to witness to the need which our intellect feels deeply to bring order and unity to its acquisitions. The nullity of all these efforts stems from the fact that, since the different branches of human knowledge have not hitherto all had the same character, it has necessarily been impossible to combine them in a single system. At other times it was possible to construct a theological or metaphysical encyclopaedia, and indeed, for example, all the systems of the Greek philosophers were for their time so many encyclopaedias. Later it will be possible to construct a positive encyclopaedia, when social physics has assumed some consistency. But to seek, as people have hitherto always presumed, to form an encyclopaedia that is at once theological, metaphysical and positive is to seek to compose a whole of elements that are mutually exclusive. It is not surprising that such ill-conceived enterprises have ended up discrediting this project among the best minds. But it cannot be the same once social science has become positive, theology and metaphysics have been chased from their last refuge, and hence the system of our ideas comes to consist solely of homogeneous elements. Then it will be enough to sum up the state of knowledge in relation to the different orders of phenomena in order to discover immediately their natural causal relations and thus to form a true positive philosophy, much more complete and much more coherent than metaphysical philosophy and even theological philosophy were ever able to be; for they were by nature provisional, and hence were at no time strictly universal.

This vast enterprise, which the present century will no doubt see accomplished, should be regarded as the last act and the final goal of the great revolution begun by Bacon, by Descartes, and by Galileo. It is indispensable as the only possible spiritual basis for the new social state towards which the human race is today moving so forcefully; for it is only by its strength as a whole that any doctrine can succeed in directing society. As long as positive conceptions remain isolated from one another, as long as they do not appear to the mind as different parts of a single and complete system, they can remain very important in particular cases, they can even fight to great advantage against the political authority of theology and metaphysics, but they cannot replace them in the supreme direction of the social order. The progress of our knowledge no doubt essentially demands that a permanent division of labour be established at the heart of science, and even that the specialization of research be pushed to its limits. But it is just as incontestable that the mass of society, which continually needs all these various results at once, and which cannot and must not concern itself with this internal mechanism, needs to see scientific doctrines as only the different branches of one and the same trunk if it is to adopt them exclusively as its habitual guides. This condition is no less essential for the unity and homogeneity of the political action of the body of scientists, which will always be very weak when it is not concentrated. Thus, as long as this state of things continues, theology and metaphysics, in spite of their obvious decrepitude, will still retain legitimate pretensions to moral sovereignty by virtue of their generality alone.

This final consideration brings me back by another route to the necessity of social physics. In the reasons I previously used to demonstrate it, I deliberately set aside the point of view of social organization in order to focus all our attention on the philosophical movement which should bring about this change on its own. But the conclusion deduced from this unique class of considerations is singularly strengthened if, as we should, we have regard to the great political needs of present-day society. I shall restrict myself here to a simple sketch of this important part of the question, which I shall later treat in detail.

Today society is from a moral point of view obviously in a state of true and profound anarchy which is recognized by all observers, whatever their speculative opinions. In the last analysis this anarchy stems from the absence of any preponderant system which is capable of uniting all minds in a single communion of ideas. Positive conceptions have become sufficiently widespread to cancel *de facto* the political influence of theology and even of metaphysics, without having yet become sufficiently general to replace them in the spiritual direction of society. It follows from this fundamental and continuous opposition that, because minds no longer have any real bond between them, they diverge on all essential points with that licence that is inevitably produced by unrestrained individuality. Hence the complete absence of public morality; consequently, the universal excesses of egoism and the preponderance of purely material considerations; and as the last necessary consequence, corruption erected into a system of government, being the sole means of order applicable to a population which has become deaf to any appeal made in the name of a general idea and which is sensitive only to the voice of private interest. If this disorder were to be prolonged, there could be no other result than the complete dissolution of social relations. The only way to bring a complete end to it is to destroy it in its principle by bringing the intellectual system to unity by some process or other. And that can be done only in two ways: either by restoring to theological philosophy all the influence it has lost (it is useless to speak here of metaphysics, which could never be anything more than a transition); or by completing positive philosophy in such a way as to make it capable of definitively replacing theology. It is to these simple terms that the great social question can now be reduced. If therefore we regard it as demonstrated that it is impossible to re-establish theology in all the breadth of its former empire (and certainly no one any longer doubts it), then there is no other acceptable solution than the definitive formation of positive philosophy. It is not a matter of examining whether that is advantageous or deplorable, whether such an operation is difficult or easy, whether it will require a lot of time or little. All these idle questions are set aside by this fatal decision made by observation: there is no other way out for society, and we must therefore immediately set to work. And furthermore, the other considerations set out here show that this final revolution, which must at last re-establish stable order in society, is not as far beyond the present state of the human mind as is believed; rather, it is so completely prepared by its antecedents that it has become inevitable.

Thus the formation of social physics, which from a purely intellectual point of view has already been demonstrated to be essential if we are to arrive at a complete philosophical system, is no less necessary, from the political point of view, to produce an entirely homogeneous social education capable of serving as the basis for a fixed and regular hierarchy. These two great conditions are obviously the consequences of one another, for education and philosophy are in a close and necessary relationship, given the impossibility of raising a society other than under the influence of the preponderant system of ideas. Social education was at first theological, and later metaphysical, because philosophy was in turn one and then the other. It is today at once theological, metaphysical and positive, because philosophy simultaneously displays these three characteristics relative to the different classes of ideas; or, rather, there is today neither real education nor real philosophy, for this very reason that there are three of each and they are mutually exclusive. Finally, in the new social era that the human race is close to entering, philosophy and consequently general education must become entirely positive. These two great operations, of which the first must serve as the basis for the second, correspond to the same fundamental need of present-day civilization, considered in two different aspects, the need for doctrine and direction.

For me, the work is already under way, for I regard social physics as having even today the beginnings of an existence, and this point of view will always hold sway in my philosophical considerations. But I do not ask our readers immediately to share my conviction in this regard. I only wish to direct their attention upon this natural and continuous course of the human mind, which is always committing it further in the direction of positive philosophy; I hope to make them see that the time has arrived when this revolution must inevitably be extended to social theories; and finally to prove to them that its accomplishment is the only real means of re-establishing moral order in society, without presuming to embark upon any idle discussion about precisely how opportune this change is, or in exactly what way it will be brought about.

The considerations set out here lead us naturally to consider the sciences from a new point of view.

They are not only, in my eyes, the rational basis for the action of man upon nature. Their importance in this respect, though certainly very great, is only indirect and secondary. It does not adequately explain the profound interest which the human mind, by an admirable instinct, has always taken in their most abstract theories, without any regard to material utility; an interest which remains today in all its strength, in spite of the pernicious preponderance accorded for three centuries to the purely practical point of view.

I look upon the sciences above all, even in their present state, as having as their direct and principal destination to satisfy this fundamental need which our intellect feels for a system of positive ideas about the different classes of phenomena which can be the subject of our observations.

Considered in the past, the sciences have freed the human mind from the tutelage which was exercised over it by theology and by metaphysics and which, indispensable at its infancy, then tended to prolong it indefinitely. Considered in the present, they are to serve, whether by their methods or by their general results, to effect the reorganization of social theories. Considered in the future, once they are systematized they will be the permanent spiritual basis of the social order, as long as our species remains active in the world.

This general summary presents the social existence of scientists from a point of view which is far removed from ordinary ideas. It therefore remains for me to develop it to form the first complete sketch of the great moral revolution which is today being accomplished in mankind.

The political history of scientists, considered collectively, reveals three great epochs which correspond precisely to the state – first theological, then metaphysical, and finally positive – of human philosophy, which is the subject of our first article. I must restrict myself here to a summary of this new series of general facts.

The first social system in which the human mind was able to begin to make real and lasting progress had as its fundamental character the confusion of the temporal power with the spiritual power, or more exactly the complete subordination of one to the other. In more precise terms, it consisted essentially in the general and absolute preponderance of a learned caste, organized under the influence of theological philosophy.

Every primitive society, insofar as its development is indigenous and spontaneous, reveals a natural tendency towards such an organization. But this regime was able to establish itself completely and acquire a good deal of consistency only in countries where, through a favourable combination of circumstances of climate and location (which this is not the place to explain), theological philosophy was able to expand to the full at an early stage, and consequently obtain an irresistible ascendancy over the other parts of the social system. These conditions were fulfilled in Egypt, in Chaldea, in Hindustan, in Tibet, in China, and in Japan, to which we can add Peru and probably also Mexico, some generations after the discovery of America.

If we consider this state of society only from an abstract point of view, we are struck above all by this profound character of unity and coherence which then so completely holds sway in the intellectual system. Never since that era has the generalizing spirit appeared to the same degree, and it can only be found again in the future by the direct construction of positive philosophy.

The homogeneity of human ideas, then uniformly theological, is no doubt the primary cause of this absolute systematization. But this cause, which was universal, did not everywhere produce this effect, at least to such an eminent degree. The organization of the scientific corporation particular to this social state was also necessary.

By the sole fact of the existence of a learned caste, we can say that from that time there was established a regular and permanent division between theory and practice; but, in the first place, this division was incomplete in a very important dimension, since it did not extend to social combinations. In the second place, there existed no determinate distribution of work in the domain of theory. This is the special nature of this first scientific organization.

Universality of knowledge, which is today so rightly regarded as an ambitious chimera, was then, on the contrary, the dominant characteristic of the members of the spiritual corporation. In the upper ranks of the hierarchy, each minister of religion was at once an astronomer (or rather astrologer), a physicist, a doctor, even an engineer, and also a legislator and a statesman. In short, the titles of priest, philosopher and scientist, which later assumed very different meanings, were then strictly synonymous; the combination of these three characteristics is marked in the person of Moses, whom we can regard as the best-known type of this first state of the human mind.

It is easy to understand this state of universality, for it depends directly upon the same causes that brought about the preponderance of the learned caste, and it is at least as inevitable. If some kind of combination of physical circumstances allowed human ideas in certain countries to develop rapidly enough for them to be able to systematize themselves in the theological form at a very early stage, it obviously had to follow from this very rapidity that, at the time of the co-ordination, the different branches of knowledge were not yet sufficiently extensive to require or allow for a real and stable division.

But this universality of operations does not only coincide, by a necessary relationship, with the social supremacy of the learned caste; it is also its firmest support. The credit obtained by priests as astronomers, doctors and engineers is the basis of their political authority; and conversely the power they enjoy is an indispensable condition for the development of their scientific speculations.

It is in the nature of this spiritual organization that we must seek the true primary explanation of the admirable vigour and coherence which have always so strongly characterized this primitive social system, by comparison with all those which have existed since. In an order in which everything hangs together so closely that, to attack any one part, it would immediately be necessary to unhinge the whole, can we be surprised at this energy of resistance which has hitherto always overcome the action of all known forces? Thus this state of society must be regarded as the true age of the triumph of the theological system. However real the power displayed by this system since, we can say without exaggeration that since this period it has been in continuous decay. This is the point to which the human race would have to return if it were able to go into reverse.

While recognizing that the theocratic regime was at once the necessary consequence and the indispensable condition of the earliest progress of the human mind, we cannot close our eyes to the fact that by nature it tended to become a permanent and almost invincible obstacle to more extended progress. Whether there is a necessary incompatibility between the extreme solidity of the social system and its perfectibility, or whether instead the combination of these two great properties was just beyond the powers that man has hitherto had at his disposal, it is certain that the most powerfully organized peoples have ended up being almost stationary. This is what happened in all countries where theocracy was able to establish itself completely. The explanation is easy.

Progress is not possible for the human mind except through the separation of works. The theocratic system itself had value, from the intellectual point of view, only as the sole means of organizing on regular and stable foundations the beginnings of a division between theory and practice. But this primary division which, once settled, was by the character of the system irrevocable, needed to be pushed much further to permit the indefinite development of human faculties. This was the radical vice of this primitive regime.

The different classes of our knowledge cannot by their nature develop at the same speed. I have established above the necessary order of succession which is constantly displayed in their formation. We can thus see that this scientific organization, by virtue of which all the different theories are cultivated at once by the same minds, must before long become a powerful obstacle to the progress of our knowledge, since it entails only such progress as can be simultaneous for all the parts of the intellectual system.

This conclusion is singularly strengthened if we combine the purely philosophical point of view with the political point of view of the fusion of the temporal power into the spiritual power, which characterizes this first social epoch. For, through this cause alone, any great progress in human theories becomes impossible since it tends to the total and immediate overturning of the political order. What important progress could we hope for, under a regime by virtue of which every essential discovery must necessarily be considered not only as an act of impiety but also as a direct act of sedition? In these earliest times, theological philosophy was alone capable of directing society; indeed, perhaps it always has been up to now. Thus, as long as the temporal power was only a derivation of the spiritual power, and even as long as physical theories and social doctrines have not been totally separated, the former could not escape from the theological state without destroying the foundations of society.

If therefore the progress of the human mind was originally possible only by means of the initial degree of division of labour regularized by the theocratic regime, it is obvious that subsequent progress no less indispensably required a much more detailed division, which could be established only under a very different regime. Above all, it was necessary for the cultivation of the human mind to become independent of the immediate direction of society, so that the division and improvement of our knowledge could take place without compromising the existence of the political order.

In the end, no doubt, the natural development of the different theories would have spontaneously effected this separation, even in theocracies, although in them for the above reasons such a change would have been considerably delayed. In fact it seems impossible that after a given period of time, however slow we imagine progress to be, the ever-growing difficulty of continually embracing the universal system of human ideas in all its extent should not lead to an ever greater specialization. Some beginnings of an improved division can even be observed in the learned castes of the different theocracies. But the course of events did not allow any known theocracy a sufficiently prolonged existence for it to be possible to observe there the development of such a revolution. Fortunately for human civilization, the new scientific organization has been established by a much quicker route.

It was in Greece that this change was accomplished which was so indispensable for the future destinies of the human mind. By the way in which knowledge was introduced into that country from Egypt and from the Orient, it was from the beginning wholly external to the social order. Military activity, towards which Greek societies necessarily tended, made the lasting establishment of pure theocracy impossible there. At the same time, other causes placed obstacles in the way of the full and free development of this activity that were too powerful for it to be able exclusively to absorb, as in Rome, all the great intellectual powers. Through this happy combination of conditions, the division between theory and practice was immediately much more complete than it was in theocracies, and theory itself could subdivide freely. There formed a class of men, as pure of political ambition as they were free of any material occupation, who were devoted to a wholly philosophical existence. Setting out from the earliest knowledge of all kinds amassed by sacerdotal castes, their sole and constant goal was to cultivate as completely as possible the domain of the human mind. This historic revolution in the organization of the scientific corporation is summed up for the observer by the clear-cut distinction which was established, from that moment, between the title of philosopher and that of priest. To this new state corresponds in the abstract the metaphysical character which then begins to appear clearly in the intellectual system.

At the origin of this second organization, there was real progress only insofar as the existence of the spiritual corporation had become purely speculative, and completely freed from any participation in the conduct of public affairs. For the rest, the first sages of Greece introduced no more specialization into their theoretical investigations than did the sacerdotal castes, except that from the beginning they assigned a wholly separate domain to the fine arts, as they were more developed. But in spite of this confusion, which was then still inevitable, the major condition was fulfilled, and as human knowledge developed its divisions were not slow to establish themselves.

The philosophers had at first hoped to tackle simultaneously the completion of ideas about the moral side of man and about society, and the completion of theories relative to physical phenomena. The results of their work at last made apparent the necessity of a total separation between these two classes of investigations. The first attempts to develop social theories, in which we can already observe a certain vague tendency to deprive them of their theological character, made them realize that this transformation was still far beyond the powers of the human mind. The philosophical schools whose speculations had more particularly taken this direction recognized that, in this respect, and especially with regard to the needs of the social organization, it was impossible to go beyond that great generalization of theological doctrine which the superior class of the priestly hierarchies had long ago reached. From that time, knowledge relative to the external world and to the physical side of man – being capable by its nature of more rapid progress, and at the same time being bound no less directly to the political order – was entirely separated from social doctrines. The latter remained theological, whereas the former became metaphysical, and consequently came closer to the positive state.

It was thus that a spiritual organization wholly different from that of the sacerdotal castes was gradually established. The titles of scientist and philosopher, which at first, when they separated from that of priest, had remained equivalent to one another, in turn became wholly distinct from one another. The first henceforth applied only to thinkers who were engaged in the cultivation of physical knowledge and whose existence, isolated even in matters of speculation from the movement of society, was still more purely theoretical than that of the first sages of Greece.[j] The second now

---

[j] At this time we can see in Archimedes the perfect type of the scientific class properly so called. This class's activity, so purely speculative, is no doubt well characterized by the picture the historians paint of the sublime death of this great man; but it is still more profoundly characterized by the admirable naïveté with

indicated only those who were occupied exclusively with moral and social studies, and who henceforth strove to participate ever more in spiritual government. In short, from that time the distinction is essentially the same as that which still exists today. The two classes were so far separated that they were not slow to become rivals, in the later ages of Greek philosophy. It was around the time of Alexander that the division began to assert itself openly. It was profoundly characterized by two great series of works: those of Aristotle in the specially scientific direction, and those of Plato in the philosophical direction properly so called. The formation of the museum of Alexandria, so different from the older Greek schools, is incontestable testimony to this separation, and at the same time made a powerful contribution to its development.

It is by means of this division that all subsequent progress of the human mind has taken place. The sciences, completely isolated, could henceforth grow, subdivide and progress, and gradually become positive, however metaphysical they were at the origin of this period, without troubling the social economy. Philosophy, concentrating its forces on a single point, could effect in the mass of civilized nations the passage from polytheism to theism, and thus develop to its fullest potential the power of theological doctrines to civilize mankind.

This spiritual organization, born in Greece, was the first foundation of the social system established twelve centuries later which had as its essential characteristic this admirable division between the spiritual power and the temporal power, by means of which it was so superior to the theocratic system. The germ of this division no doubt existed in the purely speculative activity of philosophical sects within the Greek populations. For it to be able to develop, it was first necessary that the separation between sciences and philosophy should allow the latter to move freely towards the convergence of the different schools in a common theism. Once this goal was reached, the division required only a temporal condition to begin directly to bring about a new social organization. This condition consisted in the decadence of the system of conquest produced by the unification of the whole civilized world under a single rule

which he excused himself to posterity for having momentarily sacrificed his genius to discoveries of material utility.

which resulted from the dominance of Rome. When these two fundamental bases were in place, the course of events could accelerate or retard the development of the social system of the Middle Ages; but it necessarily had to be formed in the end.

If the earliest origin of this system must be traced back to the organization of the human mind in Greece, it is there too that we can discover the original cause of the decadence it has undergone in the last four centuries. Through the absolute separation established between sciences and philosophy, the theological system could be in contact with the special branches of knowledge only in the state they were in when this system assumed its definitive character. It was necessarily impossible for it to have anything to do with their later progress. When the special branches of knowledge began to become positive, the intellectual incompatibility between theology and physics did not take long to assume a political character, and it asserted itself more or less openly as a fundamental hostility between the spiritual power and the scientific class, which had originally formed outside the social system.[k] This is the original great schism which was later the general model of disorganization of this regime.

Plato forbade the entry into his school of all men unacquainted with geometry, which was the only science which then had a clear character. For nearly a century, his disciples had a large share in the progress of this branch of our knowledge. But soon imperious necessity fully demonstrated the impossibility of reconciling this order of investigations with the philosophical work which this sect rightly regarded as the most important they could undertake and as specially assigned to it by its original constitution. The sect gradually became forever wholly estranged from the scientific movement. Archimedes, Apollonius, Hipparchus, the three great mathematicians of antiquity, were certainly not Platonists.

For a long time, the fundamental opposition between sciences and philosophy was not profound enough for their rivalry to be able

---

[k] A number of very distinguished thinkers who can see the true cause of the decadence of the theological system would today like to restore it, to recast it with the sciences. But this is to misunderstand the fundamental observation I have just set out. Even if the radical heterogeneity of theology and physics did not make their combination absolutely impossible, to effect it we should have to be able to recommence in reverse order all the modifications that have occurred since Plato in the

to compromise the theological system. When it began to make itself felt, it was even dangerous for the sciences before being so for theology. St Augustine tried, it is true, to refute the reasonings of the astronomers of Alexandria as to the spherical shape of the earth; and such an undertaking on the part of such a great mind clearly shows just how far the isolation between philosophy and the sciences had then gone. But at the same time we can see that this discussion was for him purely philosophical, and that as a member of the spiritual power he did not at all attach to it the major importance that was later aroused by the discoveries of Copernicus and Galileo.

The reorganization of the social state under the influence of theism was too important an operation not to attract all the intellectual forces almost exclusively, and to command in addition all the attention and esteem of society. Thus, during its long life-span, the sciences were comparatively highly neglected, at least in the West.[1] Furthermore, the very slowness of their progress easily permitted the members of the spiritual power to keep up to their level, without the least alteration of the theological character.

But when the nature of the social system had been definitively developed by the work of the great pope Hildebrand and his immediate successors, the germ of dissolution which this system contained from its birth soon began to become apparent. The major forces of the human mind and public attention, gradually transferring their focus onto the sciences, effected some great and rapid progress in this direction. From this moment the spiritual power was not slow to decline, especially when the positive character of the new knowledge had begun to make itself felt.

It was in vain that the clergy at first displayed a very honourable eagerness to take hold of the new intellectual domain. Individual or even collective wills, however powerful they were, could

spiritual organization of society. No doubt present-day Europe could not again become Egyptian.
[1] We ordinarily regard this sort of neglect of the sciences as a consequence of the invasions of the barbarians; but it is obviously far older. It was evident in the first centuries of Christianity, in the state of languor into which the museum of Alexandria fell. We can even see the very palpable marks of this tendency from the moment when Platonism began to triumph over the other philosophical sects. The alienation, and even the reciprocal animosity, of the scientists and the philosophers properly so called, developed more and more from that time onwards.

not prevail against the unbending nature of things, which established an absolute incompatibility between theology and physics, nor against this character of isolation from the sciences, with which the theological philosophy of the Middle Ages had been so powerfully stamped from its origin and which had continued to develop since. We begin by sensing generally that the cultivation of positive knowledge could belong as of right only to minds which were entirely devoted to it, and did not have to uphold heterogeneous doctrines.*

The great efforts of the clergy, in the twelfth and thirteenth centuries, to take hold of the natural theories at their birth were singularly favourable to their progress, since this corporation was then the only one whose members could without obstacles devote themselves to speculative activity. But they did not change, nor could they change, the priestly character. If a number of ecclesiastics devoted themselves entirely to this new class of works, they ceased to be priests to become scientists; the natural opposition of the two intellectual systems was not in the least diminished thereby. When we think today of Albert the Great and of Roger Bacon, it is as physicists that we consider them, and not to remind ourselves that the one was an archbishop and the other a monk.

The incompatibility of natural theories with theological philosophy did not take long to make itself felt soon after these two illustrious men, by the slowness with which the clergy came to this new branch of study, and even by the kind of instinctive aversion it soon inspired in them. We can find a palpable sign of these tendencies in the obligation that kings soon found themselves under, and increasingly so, to institute a special training in the sciences, under their immediate protection and wholly independent of ecclesiastical authority. From that era date the first extension of metaphysics to moral and social ideas, and also the first direct attempts at opposition to the doctrines of the clergy. Through the influence of these various orders of facts, the separation and opposition between science and theology were

---

* Later, the new series of efforts made with such perseverance and skill by the Jesuits to take hold of the domain of the sciences, which had no more success than the previous efforts, made the radical impossibility of this enterprise still more evident.

henceforth, and before everyone's eyes, fully and irrevocably established. The still more open struggles that took place afterwards only continued to develop this antagonism.

This is not the place to enter into the details of this exposition. It is enough to have ascertained that, since the era when the theological philosophy of the Middle Ages succeeded in completely producing the corresponding social organization, its activity was essentially defensive; that a new spiritual order came into being through the development of natural theories, which from that time normally attracted the great intellectual forces; that positive knowledge penetrated general education more and more; in short, that scientists, kept outside the ranks of the spiritual power, gradually acquired all the power successively lost by the clergy.

What does it remain for them to do to constitute, in their turn, a new spiritual power, no less powerful in its way than the old one? They must complete the system of natural knowledge by forming social physics, and then proceed directly to the final construction of positive philosophy. It is thus and only thus that science, resuming a wholly general character, can come to be suited to fill the gap left by the impotence of theology in the moral government of society.

This sketch of the future of the sciences leads us to consider a third kind of organization of the scientific corporation, which corresponds to the positive state of philosophy, as the Greek organization did to its metaphysical state, and as the Egyptian or Asiatic organization did to its theological state. Scientists, having at last succeeded in constructing their own philosophy, will again be incorporated into society to be its spiritual rulers, in a mode absolutely different from the theocratic mode. It remains for me to indicate the internal work which must be effected in the scientific class for this to happen. The limits of this essay only allow me to present this important exposition very briefly. I shall return later to consider each of its essential parts in detail.

It is above all the positive intellectual system which requires and causes the division of labour. Since its origin, the study of natural theories has been constantly subdividing more and more among the different minds which are concerned with it. By the sole fact of its indefinite increase, it will necessarily continue to subdivide ever more. There can be no question, therefore, of stamping scientists with a character of generality which they still lack, by a universality of works analogous to that of the sacerdotal castes, and which would obviously be impossible, given the present extent of each order of knowledge, even if we were to suppose that such a project could be attempted. It is, on the contrary, by a fuller application of the principle of the division of labour that this indispensable progress can be achieved. It is simply a matter of attributing the study of society and philosophy, once they have become positive, to a new section of the scientific corporation. This class will be distinct from all the rest, but only to the extent that they are from one another. By the nature of its doctrines it will be continually forced to hold itself in a direct and continuous relationship with them, as they will reciprocally with it, by means of a general education which, for each class of scientists, will precede their special education.

When we observe the internal formation of the scientific corporation, we can ascertain that, from the point of view of organization, as from that of doctrines, it is only a case of bringing to its final completion a revolution which has up to now been progressing by degrees. That is easy to conceive in accordance with the encyclopaedic order established above. In fact, though all the different classes of scientists are specialized, some are more specialized than others. Geometers are naturally the most specialized, because their science does not rest on any other; being, on the contrary, the foundation of the whole of natural philosophy. When we pass to the astronomers, we already find more generality of knowledge, because in addition to the direct study of the phenomena they consider, they are necessarily liable to make continual use of the mathematical sciences. Physicists, properly so called, are still less specialized, since the nature of their studies requires permanent recourse to mathematical methods, and direct knowledge of the general laws of the system of the world. For a similar reason, chemists, who fulfil the conditions imposed by the nature of the phenomena they study, necessarily have a still greater degree of generality. Finally, physiologists, concerned with phenomena whose laws are complicated by those of all other phenomena, are naturally the least specialized of all scientists, being obliged to possess at least a general knowledge of the mathematical, astronomical, physical and chemical sciences. Scientists working on social physics will necessarily merely rise in the same direction to a degree immediately higher than that of physiologists. Studying a class of phenomena which, by their nature, depend upon the laws of all the previous ones, they will indispensably need a preliminary education which will familiarize them with knowledge of the principal methods and results of all the other positive sciences: this is the only rational basis for all their own work. Thus having constantly before their eyes the totality of physical knowledge, they will necessarily be led to the immediate construction of positive philosophy, as soon as their special science has made enough progress for it no longer to absorb exclusively all their activity."

At the same time as this new class of scientists forms, there must also occur in the scientific corporation an important subdivision that is indispensable to the precision of its philosophical character and hence to the solidity of its political action. It will consist of a new and final development of the general division between theory and practice. This division is still incomplete, in that the character of engineer has always been more or less confused with that of scientist, which even today it greatly distorts. At the origin of natural theories, this confusion was no doubt inevitable; at the same time it was indispensable in giving a sense of their importance to minds which were still too coarse to understand any theoretical utility which is not capable of being immediately realized. But today this direct and permanent relation is no longer necessary. Henceforth it is above all by their philosophical importance that the sciences must be judged. Thus the scientists, far from having to restrain their profound sense of the dignity of theory, must on the contrary stubbornly resist all attempts which might be made – given the excessively practical outlook of our century – to reduce them to the simple functions of engineers. But it is above all by means of appropriate doctrines that they can definitively extinguish pretensions which will necessarily retain a certain legitimacy as long as the relations

" Moreover, to finish with this question of universality, which has been discussed so much, it seems to me that it would be necessary to distinguish between active universality and passive universality. The former leads us to seek simultaneously to perfect all the branches of human knowledge; it is obviously absurd and chimerical. The latter consists in limiting ourselves to the specialized cultivation of a single science, but possessing enough precise ideas about all the others to be able to understand their spirit properly, and to have a profound sense of their relations with the science with which we are exclusively concerned. That is not only possible, but even indispensable in some degree or other; it exists in fact, more or less, in the different classes of scientists, in accordance with my foregoing exposition; it must develop completely among those who are called to social physics.

between theory and practice have not been regularly organized by a system of ideas that is specially adapted to this purpose. Scientists alone can construct this system, since it must derive from their positive knowledge of the relation between man and the external world. This great operation is indispensable in constituting the class of engineers, as a distinct corporation, serving as a permanent and regular intermediary between scientists and industrialists in all particular works.*

These are therefore, in brief, the different doctrines which are necessary to complete the modern organization of the scientific corporation, and which I had already represented as indispensable in completing the formation of the intellectual system proper to the new state of the human mind. No doubt this work will not be executed by present-day scientists, whose powers are irrevocably engaged in very important investigations which it would be absurd and harmful to seek to interrupt. But by their nature they could only be usefully undertaken by minds raised under the ascendancy of the different positive methods, familiarized with the main results of all the physical sciences, and subject to the direct and continuous sanction of the existing scientific corporation. It is above all the more or less prompt formation of this new class of scientists that will naturally determine the speed of this complementary work, which is destined at last to invest the positive system with the spiri-

---

* We can easily recognize in the *corps scientifique*, as it exists today, a certain number of *engineers*, as distinct from scientists properly so called. This important class has necessarily been the last to form, once theory and practice, having set out from such opposite points, have both advanced sufficiently to link hands. This is what makes its distinctive character still so ill-defined. As for its own doctrines, which must give it a clearly distinct existence, it is not easy to indicate their true nature, for up to now we have only a few rudiments. I know only the illustrious Monge's conception of descriptive geometry, which is capable of giving us a precise idea of them, being the immediate general theory of the arts of construction. The body of doctrine proper to the engineers must consist of a series of analogous conceptions relative to all the other great operations rationally analysed. Its formation naturally presupposes that the construction of positive philosophy has already progressed to a certain point, for any great application to the arts ordinarily requires the combination of bodies of knowledge that relate at once to several scientific points of view.

The establishment of the class of engineers, with their own character, is all the more important given that this class will no doubt be the direct and necessary agent of the coalition between scientists and industrialists, by which means alone the new social system can begin immediately.

tual supremacy which the invariable course of mankind assigns to it for the future.

When these different operations are sufficiently advanced to have assumed an irrevocable character, we shall see social education itself fall for ever into the hands of the scientists. Already everything is ready for this great revolution. Natural knowledge has at last become in everyone's eyes, and will increasingly become, the chief object of education. If the regular system of public education does not adequately meet this pressing need of today's minds, they seek satisfaction outside it, and they succeed in finding it. Governments, continuing to back this universal tendency, as they have since the beginning, create with this goal in mind a host of special new establishments. From the higher degrees of theoretical instruction to the simplest rudiments intended for the least cultivated intellects, they strive, with all the means they have at their disposal, to stamp minds with the positive character.*ᵖ* In short, the political measures that can truly contribute to this regeneration are already essentially developed. All that is lacking is the great philosophical condition without which all these partial efforts, however sustained they may be, could result in nothing of much importance: namely, the formation of the general positive doctrines indicated above.

ᵖ It seems to me that people have not considered from the proper point of view and with all the necessary attention the sequence of efforts made by the different European governments, particularly in the last thirty years, to diffuse scientific education throughout all classes of society, by means of special institutions independent of the regular universities. This movement was first registered by the foundation of a school (the Ecole Polytechnique) which afforded this philosophical innovation of being an establishment of theoretical instruction of a high degree of generality, whose positive character is nevertheless pure of any theological or metaphysical adulteration. This movement has since taken shape uninterruptedly and with an ever-growing intensity. At the present moment, the working class is summoned to participate immediately, by institutions of which M. Charles Dupin in France and Dr Birbeck [*sic*: Birkbeck] in England have been the most zealous promoters, and to which governments have lent powerful encouragement. Similar establishments are going to come into being even in Russia, and they exist already in Austria and in Prussia; and in a few years the whole of Europe will be covered with them. Their influence cannot fail to effect the foundation of analogous and more elevated institutes for the superior classes of industry, such as we can begin to see in England.

It is perhaps by this very direct route that social education can be entirely regenerated, when the necessary doctrines have been formed. For it would probably be too awkward to refound the universities by setting out from their present state.

The considerations presented in this article, if they are taken as a whole, can be looked upon as a first draft on the question of the spiritual power, treated only from the philosophical point of view. Having thus laid down in advance the principles of the discussion, we can now directly examine all the parts of this great question, the most fundamental that can be aired today. This will be the object of another work.

Essay 5
Considerations on the Spiritual Power[1]

All the different social systems established in antiquity had as
their common characteristic the confusion of the spiritual power
and the temporal power; whether one of these two powers was
completely subordinated to the other, or whether, as happened
more frequently, they directly rested in the same hands. From
this point of view, these systems must be distinguished into two
great classes, according to which of the two powers was dominant. Among peoples in whom, through the nature of the climate
and of the locality, theological politics was able to form rapidly,
whereas the development of military activity was restricted, as in
Egypt and in almost the whole of the Orient, the temporal power
was only a derivation and an appendix of the spiritual power,
which was the supreme and continuous regulator of the whole
social organization, even as far as the smallest details. By contrast,
in countries where, by the opposite influence of physical circumstances, human activity was at an early stage essentially turned
towards war, the temporal power was not slow in dominating
the spiritual power, and in employing it regularly as an instrument and as an auxiliary. This was, more or less equally, the
character of the social systems of Greece and Rome, in spite of
their very big differences.

---

[1] This essay was first published as a series of three articles in *Le Producteur* on 24
December 1825 and 11 and 18 February 1826.

This is not the place to explain why these two sorts of organization were necessary in the countries and the ages in which they
were established, nor how they contributed – each in its own way –
to the general progress of the human race. We mention them now
only to pinpoint the most important political difference that existed
in the whole lifetime of the theological and military system, between
the characteristics which this system had in antiquity and those it
assumed in the Middle Ages.

In the latter era, not only did the theological and military system
experience an immense improvement through the foundation of
Catholicism and feudalism; but besides, the great political fact
resulting from this formation – that is, the regular division between
the spiritual power and the temporal power – must be considered
as having brought to noble perfection the general theory of social
organization, for the whole conceivable lifetime of the human race,
under whatever regime it might ever have to exist. By this admirable division, human societies were naturally able to develop on a
larger scale, through the possibility of uniting under one and the
same government populations which were too numerous and too
varied not to require several distinct and independent temporal
governments. In short, the opposite advantages of political centralization and diffusion could thus be reconciled, to a degree which
had up to then been chimerical. It even became possible to conceive
without absurdity the union – in a distant but inevitable future –
of the entire human race, or at least of all the white race, in a single
universal community, which would have implied a contradiction as
long as the spiritual power and the temporal power were confused.
In the second place, within each particular society, the great political problem which consists in reconciling the subordination to
government which is necessary for the maintenance of all public
order with the possibility of rectifying its conduct when it becomes
pernicious was resolved – as far as it can be – by the legal separation
established between moral government and material government.
Submission could cease to be servile by taking the character of voluntary assent, and remonstrance could cease to be hostile, at least
within certain limits, by resting on a legitimately constituted moral
power. Before this era, there had been no alternative to the most
abject submission and direct revolt; and this is still the character
of societies, such as all those organized under the ascendancy of

Mohammedism, in which the two powers are legally confused at their origin.

Thus, in summary, by the fundamental division organized in the Middle Ages between the spiritual power and the temporal power, human societies could be at the same time more extended and better ordered, a combination which all the legislators and even all the philosophers of antiquity had proclaimed to be impossible.

Although the Catholic and feudal system produced, as far as was permitted by the era when it was dominant, all general advantages which I have just indicated as inherent in the division of the two powers; and although it thus contributed more powerfully than all previous systems to the progress of humanity, we must nonetheless recognize that the decay it experienced was at once absolutely inevitable and logically necessary.

I have previously demonstrated[a] that the theological philosophy and the moral power founded on it could by their nature have only a provisional sway, even in the most perfect state they were able to attain, that is Catholicism. I have established that after directing mankind in its preliminary education, they necessarily had to be replaced in its manhood by a positive philosophy and a corresponding spiritual power. It is much easier to accomplish an analogous demonstration with regard to the temporal power, which, originally founded on military superiority, must in the end be essentially attached to industrial pre-eminence, in the mode of existence towards which modern societies are increasingly tending. Thus, however eminent was the value of the Catholic and feudal system for the era of its triumph, the development of the human race, under the dual influence of science and industry, necessarily had in the end to destroy it, and all the more rapidly as that system more than any other favoured this development. I have even proved that, from the spiritual point of view, it was possible to observe in the earliest origins of that system the germ of its destruction, which developed immediately after the moment of its greatest splendour. This observation, which it is easy to extend to the temporal order (since the abolition of serfdom and the enfranchisement of the communes almost coexisted with the complete establishment of

---

[a] See the *Philosophical Considerations on the Sciences and Scientists*.

feudalism), is a salient manifestation of the provisional nature of the social system of the Middle Ages.

I am not here writing the history of the formation of that regime, nor that of its dissolution. But in order to shed as much light as possible on the moral state of present-day society, which is the proper subject of this essay, I must quickly survey the way in which the spiritual disorganization of that system occurred, and the main consequences it engendered.

The destruction of one social system, and the establishment of another, are two operations which by their nature are too complicated, and each of them demands too much time for them ever to be tackled head on. First, the institution of a new political order presupposes the prior overturning of the preceding order, whether to make reorganization possible by removing the obstacles which prevented it, or to make us properly appreciate its necessity by experiencing the disadvantages of anarchy. But we can even say, from a purely intellectual point of view, that the human mind, given the weakness of its native powers, could not rise to a clear conception of a new social system as long as the prior system has not been fully dissolved. It would be easy to verify this deplorable necessity by numerous examples.

Every time the human race is called to pass from one political regime to another, there is therefore in the nature of things an inevitable era of anarchy, at least in a moral sense, whose duration and intensity are determined by the extent and importance of the change. This anarchic character necessarily had to develop to its highest degree, therefore, in the period of disorganization of the feudal and Catholic system, since what was happening then was the greatest revolution which could ever take place in the human race, the direct transition from the theological and military state to the positive and industrial state; in comparison with this, all previous revolutions were only simple modifications. This is thus what took place in the sixteenth, seventeenth and eighteenth centuries, during which period this disorganization occurred.

In the entire course of this period, which can justly be termed revolutionary, all antisocial ideas were aroused and reduced to dogmas, to be employed continuously in the demolition of the Catholic and feudal system, and to rally against it all the anarchic passions that ferment in the human heart and which, in ordinary times, are restrained by the predominance of a complete social regime. Thus first of all the dogma of unlimited freedom of conscience was forged to destroy the theological power, next that of the sovereignty of the people to overturn temporal government, and finally that of equality to break up the old social classification; not to mention the less important secondary ideas, which constitute the critical doctrine, and each of which tended to demolish a corresponding piece of the old political system.

Everything that develops spontaneously is necessarily legitimate for a certain time, since by the very fact of its spontaneous development it satisfies some need or other in society. So I am very far from underestimating the utility and even the absolute necessity of the critical doctrine in the last three centuries. Furthermore, I believe that this doctrine will inevitably survive, contrary to all appearances, until the direct establishment of a new social system, and that throughout this time it will exert a necessary influence, since only then will the existence of the old system be seen to be irrevocably ended. But if, in this sense, the influence of the critical doctrine should be viewed as still necessary, in a certain degree, to the development of civilization, it is nevertheless today, from a much more important point of view, the main obstacle to the establishment of the new political order, for which it at first helped prepare the way.

By an irresistible necessity, the only way in which the different dogmas that constitute the critical doctrine could acquire all the energy necessary completely to fulfil their natural destiny was by assuming an absolute character, which necessarily makes them hostile not only to the system they had to destroy, but to any social system at all. Thus, once the destruction of the old political order was fully consummated, the influence of critical principles worked to create in society a disposition – sometimes involuntary, sometimes deliberate – to reject all true organization. At the same time the habit contracted over three centuries of applying this doctrine to all social questions naturally induced leading minds to take it as the basis of reorganization, when the catastrophes provoked by the destruction of the old regime brought to the fore the necessity of a return to order. It was then that there appeared the strange phenomenon – inexplicable for anyone who has not followed historical development – of moral and political disorder erected into a system, and presented as the culmination of social perfection. For each of the dogmas of the critical doctrine, when taken in an organic sense, amounts precisely to laying down the principle (again, from the organic point of view) that society must not be organized.

It would be easy to demonstrate, for each of the modern political dogmas, that this judgement is not in the least exaggerated. But I do not propose now to undertake the direct and complete examination of the critical doctrine. I have sketched it here only to indicate clearly the point of view from which I consider this theory. For my present object, I must limit myself to viewing it in its most important principle, that is as it relates to the fundamental law of the division between the spiritual power and the temporal power.

Of all the revolutionary prejudices engendered over the last three centuries by the decay of the old social system, the oldest, the most entrenched, the most widespread, and the general foundation of all the others, is the principle by virtue of which no spiritual power should exist in society; or, what amounts to the same thing, the opinion that completely subordinates this power to the temporal power. Kings and peoples, who are in conflict, more or less openly, on all other parts of the critical doctrine, are wholly in agreement on this point of departure. In countries where Protestantism triumphed, this annihilation or absorption of the spiritual power has been proclaimed regularly and openly. But the same principle in essence has been no less genuinely re-established, though less directly, in states which have continued to call themselves Catholic, where we have seen the temporal power entirely subjugate the spiritual hierarchy, and where the clergy themselves have voluntarily submitted to this transformation, hastening to relax the ties uniting them with their central government in order to nationalize themselves. In short, to bring home just how strong and universal this opinion is by reference to a recent occurrence, it is enough to recall that in our own time we have seen some very distinguished philosophers who, having tried to struggle against this prejudice, have found that their own party consisted only of dogged opponents.

After the general explanation I have given above, I have no fear of being accused of underestimating the temporary utility – indeed necessity – of this seminal idea of the critical doctrine, or of any of the others, in effecting the transition from the old social system to the new. But as I think that, if the demolition of the first system

New starts in spiritual domain

had to begin in the spiritual domain, the same course must necessarily be followed in the establishment of the second, I am led to a direct examination of this fundamental principle of the critical doctrine, so as to recall minds – as far as it lies in me – to the true elementary notions of general politics, forgotten for three centuries, insofar as they are applicable to the present state of society. This is the goal of this essay, in which I shall seek to demonstrate the necessity of instituting a spiritual power, distinct and independent of the temporal power, and to determine the main characteristics of the new moral organization appropriate to modern societies.

First I must prepare reflective minds to place themselves at a vantage point so alien to their present habits. To this effect I think I must indicate a series of observations which, without yet dealing with the question in itself, seem to me capable of drawing attention to this subject, by making people sense empirically that the universal tendency of modern publicists and legislators towards a political organization without a spiritual power leaves an immense and baneful lacuna in the social order.

The experience of the past could testify to the necessity of the division between the spiritual power and the temporal power in two different ways: whether by comparing the state of the human race under the rule of Catholicism and feudalism with that in which the essentially temporal organizations of Greece and Rome maintained it; or by showing the disadvantages produced, from the beginning of the sixteenth century, by the suppression of the spiritual power, or – what is politically equivalent – its usurpation by the temporal power. Although it was possible to derive essential information from the first class of observations – information directly applicable to the present question – nevertheless the great difference of periods would so complicate it as to make it incapable of producing the sense of self-evidence I want above all to establish here; and besides I have given sufficient indication of the bases of this comparison at the outset of this essay. Thus in what follows I shall confine myself exclusively to the second species of facts, whose testimony, being more direct and more tangible, must be more decisive. It therefore remains for me to consider briefly what are the main political disadvantages that can be attributed with certainty to the dissolution of the spiritual power in modern society. An investigation of such importance would naturally demand some very lengthy expositions.

But the reader, once situated at the proper vantage-point, will by himself easily be able to supply the details which I am prevented from giving here.

In order to introduce into this series of observations only those facts that are capable of establishing clear and irresistible conviction, I purposely set aside the consideration of great catastrophes, even though in the last analysis they are to be traced back to the spiritual disorganization of society, because – in spite of this origin – their return can justifiably be regarded as impossible from now on. I confine myself to the examination of the usual state of civilized peoples over the last three centuries, and as it still remains today.

If we first consider the most general political relationships, we can see that for as long as the Catholic system retained its great vigour, relations between state and state were subject, throughout Christian Europe, to a regular and permanent organization which was capable of habitually maintaining among them a certain voluntary order and imparting to them, when circumstances demanded, a collective purpose, as in the vast and important undertaking we know as the Crusades. In short, people were then able to contemplate what M. de Maistre calls, with profound aptness, the miracle of European monarchy.[2] No doubt, given the state of civilization at that time, this government was very incomplete. But from this point of view, as from the national point of view, is not the most imperfect government in the long run much preferable to anarchy? What has happened in this respect since the absorption of papal power? The different European powers have returned, in their relations one to the other, to the savage state; the kings have had engraved on their canons the inscription, from that time on precisely true, *ultima ratio regum*. What expedient has been thought up to fill the immense void left here by the nullification of spiritual power? No doubt we must do justice to the very worthy efforts of diplomats to produce and maintain what was called the European balance of power, in the absence of a real bond; but one cannot help smiling at the hope of constituting a true government of states by that route. It is obvious that the system of the balance of power, considered in its total life-span, has occasioned more wars than it has prevented. The upheaval produced by the French Revolution has reduced it to dust,

anything over anarchy

[2] J. de Maistre, *Du pape* (1872 edn), p. 295.

and each state has remained in a situation of continuous anxiety about a general invasion on the part of one or other great power. At the time of writing this essay, is not the whole of Europe on the verge of fearing – no doubt wrongly – that the whole system of foreign relations might be compromised by the death of one man?[3]

We must add to the foregoing that, following a very judicious remark made by M. de Maistre, the influence of the spiritual power, in the respect in which I am considering it, must be judged not only by the tangible good it produces, but above all by the evil it prevents, which is not as easy to demonstrate. A memorable example, indicated by that philosopher, can cast light on the importance of this observation.

In the formation of the colonial system which followed the discovery of America, there were two nations, quintessential rivals, each potentially jealous of the other for the most important colonial possessions on the globe, and in perpetual contact on a vast scale. Yet they did not have a single war for this cause, whereas all the other European powers disputed almost insignificant outposts with the most relentless obstinacy. How could such a great result have been brought about? By a single act of the spiritual power, even then shaken in its existence. All that was needed was a simple bull from Alexander VI, who, from the outset, had equitably traced a general demarcation line between the colonial establishments of Spain and those of Portugal.[4]

I repeat, everything that has happened had to happen, and I am certainly as far as anyone from any sterile regret about the past. But I may be allowed to observe, with the great Leibniz,[5] the fact of the large gap left in the organization of Europe by the inevitable dissolution of the former spiritual power, and to deduce that, in this first respect, the establishment of a new moral government is imperi-

---

[3] Tsar Alexander I of Russia died on 2 December 1825, according to the Gregorian calendar. His death was followed by a period of uncertainty over the succession. His successor, Nicholas I, was markedly less sympathetic to the cause of Greek independence than Alexander had been.

[4] The reference here is to the bull *Intra cetera* of 1493.

[5] See G. W. Leibniz, 'Observations on the Abbé de St Pierre's "Project for perpetual peace" ' in Leibniz, *Political Writings*, ed. Patrick Riley (2nd edn 1988), p. 180. Leibniz had an acute sense of the importance of the 'republic of Christendom' for European concord, and devoted much of his life to schemes of Christian reunion.

ously demanded by the present state of the civilized nations. Turning our sights now to the internal organization of each people, the same necessity becomes still more tangible, for a mass of reasons of which I shall restrict myself to mentioning the most general.

The decay of theological philosophy and of the corresponding spiritual power left society without any moral discipline. Hence this series of consequences which I shall note in the order of their mutual dependence.

1 The most complete mental anarchy. Since each mind tends to form, of its own power, a system of general ideas, without fulfilling any of the essential preconditions, it has gradually become absolutely impossible, in the mass, to obtain any real and durable agreement between just two minds on even the simplest of social questions. If this anarchy could be limited to its ridiculous side, the harm would be unimportant, and satire would be enough to confine it within proper limits. But because it is consequently so easy to imagine the pros and the cons on the majority of points where certainty is so highly important to good order – and because the pros and the cons are more or less equally plausible – the effects are altogether more serious.

To get a proper sense of the depth and universality of this intellectual anarchy, we should note that it does not today exist only among the supporters of the critical doctrine, in whose minds it has come to constitute a fundamental dogma; but, what is much more conclusive, we can also observe it, though naturally to a much lesser degree, among the supporters of the retrograde doctrine, where it is – contrary to the tendency of their thought – an involuntary result of the general and irresistible course of the human mind. First, we can observe among them a great primary division, which often degenerates into direct opposition, between the defenders of Catholicism and those of feudalism. Furthermore, if we consider only the former, whose opinions are necessarily more compact, we can tell that if they converge on a large enough number of points to be seen as forming a single school, they nonetheless present very basic divergences on fundamental questions, which would end up by leading them in practice to wholly incoherent results, if the present social state permitted an extended application of their doctrines. This is what is revealed by a close examination of the theories produced along these lines by the principal thinkers, M. de Maistre, M. de la Mennais, M. de Bonald and M. d'Eckstein. Their various opinions all basically manifest a very palpable degree of individuality on the most important points.[b]

2 The almost total absence of public morality. On the one hand, the destination of each individual in society is no longer determined by any generally respected maxims, and practical institutions have had to conform to this intellectual situation, so the blossoming of individual ambitions is no longer really contained by anything except the irregular and fortuitous power of the external circumstances particular to each individual. On the other hand, the social sentiment searches in vain, whether in private reason or in public prejudices, for exact and settled notions on what constitutes the general good in each case that presents itself, and so it ends up degenerating little by little into a vague philanthropic intention, incapable of exerting any real influence on the conduct of life. Through this dual influence, each individual is gradually led to make himself the centre of the great social relationships, and as the notion of private interest alone remains wholly clear amidst all this moral chaos, pure egoism naturally becomes the only motive with enough energy to direct active existence.

This result, so palpable today in public morality, even extends to a certain point into private morality. The latter fortunately depends on many other conditions than firm opinions. Natural instinct, which speaks much more clearly in this case than in the previous one; the ever-growing power of the habits of order and work, which so strongly tend to repulse the idea of vice; the general improvement of conditions, produced by the continual development of industry, which makes temptations less acute and less frequent; the universal softening of manners, resulting from the progress of civilization; all these causes must undoubtedly go far towards counterbalancing the immorality which the absence of settled principles of conduct today

---

[b] The most logical philosopher, among all those who today write along these lines, M. de la Mennais, has very recently been led into a solemn offence against fundamental principles, by explicitly invoking freedom of worship. [Comte is probably referring here to Lamennais's *De la religion considérée dans ses rapports avec l'ordre politique et civil*, published in two volumes in May 1825 and February 1826. In that work, Lamennais – still persuaded that the only hope of social regeneration lay in the church – expounded the view that the alliance of church and state posed an insuperable obstacle to that process of regeneration.]

tends to engender. Yet even in this respect the absence of organization produces unquestionable effects, though they are harder to disentangle. Let each of us, setting aside at the outset the crude cases where the evil is too palpably obvious not to be stifled in its germ, consult our daily life and investigate whether real life does not reflect the state of flux which today characterizes most ideas of duty, whether in the different family relations, or in the ordinary and mutual relations of superiors and inferiors, or in the reciprocal relations of producers and consumers, etc.

Furthermore, in this respect an indirect observation can up to a certain point exempt us from the need for immediate verification. This is the fact of the ascendancy obtained more or less universally, at least in practice, by the moral theories which claim to explain all the sentiments of man by tracing them back exclusively to personal interest. Considered speculatively, they are repulsed by the moral instinct, but in the real world they have become the permanent mode of explanation, and they still retain among philosophers a credit which is only too faithful an index of the true state of society. The dominant opinion among them today that penal legislation is, in the last analysis, the only effective means to ensure the morality of the lower classes clearly confirms this observation.

3 The social ascendancy increasingly accorded, for three centuries, to the purely material point of view, is again an obvious consequence of the spiritual disorganization of modern peoples. As practical power has, since the sixteenth century, nullified or ever more subordinated theoretical power, the same spirit has correspondingly insinuated itself into all elements of society. All in all, we have gradually come to consider immediate utility almost exclusively, or at least to place it in the forefront. Thus, for example, in the reasoned appraisal of the sciences, we have increasingly underestimated their philosophical importance, and they have been evaluated only in respect of their practical services.

This essentially material spirit is apparent above all in England, where, through the concourse of special causes, this sort of provisional social organization, formed from the sixteenth century onwards, has acquired more solidity than on the continent; it is still more completely dominant in the United States, where spiritual disorganization has been pushed infinitely further than anywhere else.

Now that the course of events has brought about the age of constitutions, the same characteristic has asserted itself most strikingly in this new sphere of activity. Attention has been exclusively directed towards the material part of this great work. People have concerned themselves directly with recasting all practical institutions; they have gone so far as to regulate in the tiniest detail the forms of the deliberative assemblies, without thinking to establish first of all some new social doctrines; without even trying to determine precisely the spirit of the new political system. Even today when, thanks to experience, society is entering upon new directions, at least in the sense that it is definitively renouncing metaphysical constitutions, it is to be feared that the influence of the same habits will set back true reorganization a long way.

It is undoubtedly with the re-establishment of a moral order that this vast operation must necessarily begin, for the reorganization of minds is at once more urgent and better prepared than the regulation of social relations. Nevertheless, it is probable that the disposition – still too pronounced among the peoples – to call for institutions immediately, or in other words to seek to reconstruct the temporal power before the spiritual power, will initially be a potent obstacle to the adoption of this natural course which alone is efficacious.

4 I must now indicate, as the last general consequence of the dissolution of the spiritual power, the establishment of that sort of modern autocracy that has no precise analogy at all in history, and which, in the absence of a more accurate expression, may be designated under the name of ministerialism or administrative despotism. Its distinctive organic characteristic is the centralization of power pushed further and further beyond all reasonable limits, and its general means of action is systematized corruption. Both result inevitably from the moral disorganization of society.

A very well-known law of nature establishes conclusively, in politics, that the only way not to be governed is to govern oneself. It is applicable to masses as well as to individuals, to things as to persons. It signifies, in its most extended sense, that the less energy moral government has in society, the more indispensable it is for material government to gain in intensity, to prevent the entire decomposition of the social body. For example, in a population as large as that of France, where no moral bond any longer joins the different parts

smaller communities emerge

strongly enough, how could we imagine that the nation would not dissolve into smaller and smaller partial communities, if in the absence of a common spirit, a central temporal power did not hold all social elements in an immediate and continuous dependence? Such an effect would be only the continuation of the influence of the same principle which, as I indicated above, decomposed the old European society into independent nationalities. Thus temporal centralization has come about more and more, as moral disorganization has become more complete and more tangible. The same cause which made this result essential tended, from another point of view to make it inevitable, since the nullification of the spiritual power destroyed the only legal barrier which could have contained the encroachments of the temporal power.

legally immoral

As for corruption erected into a permanent means of government, this deplorable consequence results still more clearly than the first from the annihilation of the spiritual power. One could sense it in seeing this shameful regime emerge in the country where the degradation of moral authority has been most strongly constituted in a legal manner. But direct proof of it can easily be obtained.

where is it?

In a population where the indispensable cooperation of individuals in public order can no longer be achieved by the voluntary and moral assent accorded by each to a common social doctrine, there remains no other expedient for maintaining any kind of harmony than the sad choice between force and corruption. The first means is incompatible with the nature of modern civilization, since the temporal character of society has ceased to be essentially military and become essentially industrial. Wealth, which by the institution of property was at first the regular measure of force, being its permanent result, has in recent centuries increasingly become its principal and constant source. In this respect it could be designated very precisely by the name of virtual force. Whence it came about insensibly that, as a means of discipline, violence was in the end transmuted into corruption. To the extent that the present state of societies rejects the first mode, it lends itself to the second, ever since the moral disorganization began clearly to take effect.

Governments can act on individuals only by employing on a grander scale the same procedures that individuals recognize among themselves as the most effective in influencing one another day by day. Thus, when personal interest is considered, in private relations, as the only motive in whose energy one can ordinarily place sufficient trust, is it surprising that the central power is led to use the same means of action? This distressing result must not be imputed to rulers any more than to the ruled; it stems from their common faults; or, more exactly, it is the difficult but fortunately momentary consequence of the temporary state of anarchy into which society was necessarily plunged during the transition from the theological and military system to the positive and industrial system.

If the picture I have just sketched of the general effects gradually produced, since the sixteenth century, by the moral disorganization of society is judged to be in conformity with observation, and if the facts are recognized to derive from the cause I assign to them – as I firmly hope – they will no doubt lead people to understand that the establishment of a new spiritual power is of capital importance, even more from the national than from the European point of view.

To prevent, as far as possible, any inaccurate interpretation of my thought, I declare here, from this first point of view, as I have already done from the second, that in my opinion this state of anarchy, whose pernicious consequences I with all true observers deplore, has been not only an inevitable result of the decay of the old social system, but also an essential condition for the establishment of the new one. If we again take up, from this latter perspective, the direct examination of the four general facts set out above, I could prove, for each of them, that if it seems a revolting monstrosity when conceived as a permanent state (which is where the critical doctrine logically leads us, if it is taken in an organic sense), this is not at all the case when it is considered as a purely transitional state. I shall confine myself to outlining this new analysis for the first fact, which is the basis of all the others.

The profound anarchy which today reigns in the intellect is not only justified historically by the necessary decay of the old social system, but it will remain inevitable and even indispensable up to the moment when the doctrines intended to serve as the foundation for the new organization have been adequately formed. On the one hand, as long as this sort of moral interregnum lasts it will be impossible in fact to discipline the intellect. On the other hand, if before the end of this era we were to attempt to move directly to the unity of minds, in the absence of suitable doctrines this could only be through material and arbitrary means; and since the free development of thought would be prohibited, we should be able neither to form doctrines nor to put ourselves in a position to adopt them; and hence the very operation of reorganization would come to a halt.

Thus I am convinced that I can appreciate as much as anyone all the real worth of the critical doctrine; but I do ask that we should no longer mistake its true nature. The time has come when we can give a rational account of the course that has been followed; pure routine is no longer essential. It is possible to retain for critical principles all the influence which they still need to exercise for some time, without being thereby obliged to conceive them as organic and thus slumber in an artificial sense of security in the face of the serious dangers of various kinds with which society would be threatened by a pernicious prolongation of the present anarchy. If this intellectual disposition perhaps surpasses the capacity of the majority of minds, in my eyes it must at least be the habitual point of view, henceforth, of the thinkers who wish to devote their powers to the great social operation of the nineteenth century.

By the totality of the considerations set out so far, I hope I have sufficiently prepared all thoughtful readers for a direct treatment of this fundamental question of the spiritual power, the dawning of which today inspires so many puerile and chimerical fears. I can therefore proceed without hesitation to the immediate examination of the question.

The present state of opinions in relation to the fundamental principle of the necessity of a spiritual power presents the impartial observer with a singular and even painful contrast. On the one hand, those who take the cause of true liberty, of civilization, those in short who declare themselves to be particularly progressive in tendency, and who indeed are up to a certain point, those who are dominated by the desire – legitimate in itself but not at all thought out – to avoid theocracy at all cost, thereby follow a path which, if it could be followed to its end, would inevitably lead, if it is to escape complete anarchy, to the most degrading despotism, that of force devoid of any moral authority. On the other hand, those who are accused of reactionary tendencies, and who in truth merit this accusation in some respects – not in their philosophic intentions but in the inevitable consequences to which the complete application of their doctrines would lead – are in essence the only ones whose theories suitably restore human dignity, by constituting moral superiority as the corrective and the regulator of force or wealth.

By the various considerations indicated above, I have sought to demonstrate that the social state of the most civilized nations today imperiously demands the formation of a new spiritual order, as the first and principal means of ending the revolutionary period which began in the sixteenth century and has for thirty years been at its conclusion. It is now the time to examine directly the nature of the spiritual organization appropriate to modern societies. A question so fundamental, which is intimately bound up with all the great political questions, could only be treated properly in a special work addressed exclusively to the most austere minds. But although the very brief remarks to which I am here confined are certainly insufficient to go into this question as closely as it deserves, yet they will perhaps contribute to attracting to this subject the attention of serious men, which is at present my essential goal.

To get a full idea of the new moral order, we must consider separately the functions which the spiritual power must fulfil, in abstraction from its proper constitution, and then the general character which its organization must have to correspond closely to the nature of modern civilization. The following expositions are exclusively devoted to the first kind of considerations, which can be reduced essentially to the analysis of the principal different points of view from which society needs spiritual government. Later, I shall examine the second part of the question. This division is determined by the natural course of public reason, which will no doubt arrive at a strong sense of the necessity of a new moral power, before it clearly understands its true organization. Having thus set out the overall shape of the new spiritual order towards which modern societies are tending to move, I shall in a later work[6] consider the general course by which this great movement of reconstruction must by the nature of things be brought about, setting out from the point it has reached today.

To begin with, it would be easy to form empirically a clear idea of the attributes of modern spiritual power, by observing attentively those of the Catholic clergy in the era of its greatest vigour and its

---

[6] This was never written.

most complete independence, that is from about the middle of the eleventh century to around the end of the thirteenth century. No doubt the philosophical bases of these two powers, and the corresponding social relations, in consequence of their respective modes of influence, are completely different in nature and even, in many respects, absolutely opposite. But as regards the extent and intensity of their influence, which is the essential point to determine here, we can say that for each of the social relationships which it was within the competence of the Catholic clergy to rule upon, there corresponds, in the new political system, an analogous attribution for the modern spiritual power. It is even probable that, because the new system must establish itself in a much more peaceful manner than the old, and in a more enlightened era, in which its nature, much more worked out in advance, must for that reason alone be better understood, the intervention of the spiritual power must be more explicit and more complete, because it will encounter less resistance in the corresponding temporal power. Nevertheless, however valuable this comparison may be in terms of the precision it entails, which it would be very difficult to obtain in any other way, it can only be profitable to thinkers capable of abstracting from the extreme difference between the two states of civilization, or rather of according it only its rightful share of influence, and who at the same time have studied the past in a frame of mind sufficiently distanced from the pernicious prejudices generally inspired today by the critical doctrine against the spiritual regime of the Middle Ages. This parallel would therefore lead almost inevitably, in the majority of readers, to false applications, which would give a very erroneous idea of my opinion. Thus, although I have thought it proper to point it out for those capable of utilizing it, I shall proceed without further delay to a direct exposition by immediately considering the functions of modern spiritual power.

Although it might be useful, and even in certain cases necessary, to consider the idea of *society* in abstraction from that of *government*, it is universally recognized that these two ideas are in reality inseparable. That is, the lasting existence of any real association necessarily presupposes a constant influence, sometimes directive and sometimes repressive, exercised within certain limits by the whole upon the parts, in order to get them to converge towards the general order from which by their nature they are always tending to stray to some degree, and from which they would deviate indefinitely if they could be left entirely to their own impulses. This influence of the whole consists of two sorts of actions, the one material and the other moral, which are quite heterogeneous whether in their bases or in their modes, although they always coexist. The first bears immediately on acts, to prescribe some and to prevent others: it is founded in the last resort on force or – which amounts to the same thing – on wealth, which has become its equivalent among modern peoples, to the extent that the progress of civilization has conferred upon industrial pre-eminence the civil power that was originally attached to military superiority. The second consists in the regulation of opinions, propensities, wills, in a word of tendencies: its basis is moral authority, which results in the last analysis from the superiority of intelligence and enlightenment. It is thus that the two great species of inequality on which any society is established contribute to the maintenance of social order.

Since civilization has been sufficiently advanced for these two general branches of government to be capable of being assigned to different classes, as occurred in the Middle Ages, the distinction between them has become apparent to everyone's eyes, and the names of temporal power and spiritual power have been created to designate it; and for that very reason alone it is desirable to retain them, at least provisionally, in the new social state, although their structure still essentially recalls the social state for which they were formed.

The spiritual power therefore has as its distinctive object the government of opinion, that is the establishment and maintenance of the principles which are to govern the different social relations. This general function divides into as many parts as there exist distinct classes of relations; for there is, so to speak, no social fact in which the spiritual power does not exercise a certain influence when it is well organized, that is in close harmony with the corresponding state of civilization. Its main attribution is therefore the supreme direction of *education*, whether general or special; but above all the first, taking this word in its widest sense, meaning – as it should – the whole system of ideas and habits necessary to prepare individuals for the social order in which they are to live, and to adapt each of them, as far as possible, for the particular station he is to fill there. It is in this great social function that the influence of the spiritual power stands out most clearly, for it belongs to it alone, whereas in all the other cases its influence is more or less confused with that of the temporal power. It is in this sphere that it gives decisive proof of its strength, and at the same time lays the most solid foundations for its general authority. *Education* would even embrace the totality of the national functions of the spiritual power if, by an improper use of this expression, we followed the example of a number of philosophers and included not only the preparation of youth, but also the influence – so important – exercised on grown men, which is the necessary complement and inevitable sequel of the former. This second class of spiritual functions consists in unceasingly representing in active life – whether to individuals or to the mass – the principles with which they have been imbued, and recalling them to the observation of these principles when they stray from them, insofar as moral means are effective for that purpose.[c]

These are, in summary, the general functions of the spiritual power, considered in an isolated nation. But relations between peoples assign a new class of attributions to it, which are only the sequel to the foregoing, transferred to a larger scale. Considered abstractly, in territorial terms the jurisdiction of the spiritual power would know no other limits than those of the habitable globe, if all fractions of the human race had reached more or less the same state of civilization, since spiritual association is obviously capable, by its nature, of an indefinite extension. But considered in reality it only embraces all peoples (as, for example, those of Europe) whose social state is sufficiently similar for there to exist between them a certain degree of permanent community, but whose differences are suffic-

[c] Apart from these two kinds of function, the spiritual power also obviously exercises, as a learned corporation, a direct or indirect consultative influence in all social operations. The pernicious and incomplete system of education we have before us leads us today to think of this as an important or even the chief kind of attribution; but it essentially belongs to one or other of the two foregoing functions, when we consider a well-ordered social system, and that is why I do not make express mention of it in this brief summary. For, when education is as it should be, it almost never happens that individuals or masses really need in practice general principles other than those on which they have been brought up; they simply need to be reminded of them, and to have their application explained, because they naturally tend to forget them and to misunderstand them. When the general or particular needs of society really require new principles, it is for the spiritual power, which must provide them regularly as the class charged with the cultivation of theoretical knowledge, to introduce them as appropriate into the system of education.

iently great to require temporal governments, distinct and independent of each other. For as soon as this similarity exists, continuous relations are inevitably established; whence result at the same time the possibility and the necessity of a certain common direction, destined to regularize those relations by subjecting them to general and uniform principles.

We should not be astonished that Catholic philosophers should have seen in this European government the principal and characteristic attribute of the spiritual power: it belonged wholly and exclusively to the spiritual power and was thus its clearest and most tangible attribute. No doubt, in each determinate social state, the association of any number of men under the same spiritual regime always necessarily precedes their union under the same temporal government. That is just as true on the national scale as on the European scale. But this truth is infinitely easier to demonstrate in the second case than in the first, for in the latter these two powers constantly coexist; whereas in the former, by the nature of things, spiritual association is always in full force long before the onset of any temporal association, so that in the old political system the first alone could exist; and it is still uncertain even whether the second will ever exist in any system whatever.

This is therefore the second incontestably great object of the exercise of spiritual power: the union of all European peoples, and in general of the greatest possible number of nations, in the same moral communion. This function, which completes the picture of its attributes, can be reduced, like the previous ones, to the continuous establishment of a uniform system of education for the different populations, and of the regular influence which is its necessary consequence. It is thus that the spiritual power naturally finds itself invested, in relation to the different peoples and their temporal leaders, with the share of authority that is indispensable for it if they are to be led, voluntarily or involuntarily, to subject their disputes to its arbitration, and to receive from it a common impulse, in cases which demand collective action.

Thus, in short, the lives of individuals and peoples consist alternately of speculation and action, or, in other words, of tendencies and results. These two orders of facts are intertwined in a thousand different ways in real life. Spiritual power has as its proper and exclusive object the immediate regulation of the former, temporal power that of the latter. Each of the two powers acts legitimately whenever it confines itself strictly to its natural sphere of activity, at least insofar as the distinction is humanly possible. When one of them oversteps the mark and usurps some function of the other, there is an abuse, which does not mean that such usurpations in one direction or the other have not been and might not even again momentarily become inevitable and necessary in certain circumstances; but they never constitute the normal state. This is the typical order towards which political combinations must always tend; although it can unquestionably be foreseen that the imperfection of human organization, whether in terms of intellect or passions, absolutely forbids any hope – in this case as in any other – of ever obtaining complete success.[d]

Once this general definition of the spiritual power in any social state has been laid down to settle our ideas, it becomes easier, by applying the foregoing considerations to particular cases, to see that this power, properly reorganized, has no less an influence to exercise in the system of modern civilization than in that of the Middle Ages. I do not here need to concern myself particularly with the latter, with regard to which I refer readers to the works of the Catholic philosophers, and especially of M. de Maistre, who, in his *Traité du pape*, has presented the most methodical, most profound and most accurate exposition of the old spiritual organization.[e] Here

[d] Philosophically considered, spiritual influence and temporal influence will always, by their nature, be wholly distinct; but considered politically, the distinction, even approximate, is not always possible, because there exists a mass of secondary matters of government – which this is not the place to enumerate – in which they are inevitably united more or less equally in the same hands. The fundamental principle of the division of the two powers simply demands that no individual or class should possess both in a high degree. This is not only practical, but has long been inevitable, especially in the modern social system.

[e] In defending the Catholic system, the philosophers of the retrograde school, and particularly M. de Maistre who can today be regarded as its leader, have presented some very important general considerations on the spiritual power, considered in any society whatever. But these abstract conceptions, though capable of providing useful clues to those who wish to treat this fundamental question from its true perspective, lack both the precision and the generality necessary to establish a methodical opinion. We constantly observe in them that radical illogicality which consists in directly transferring to modern societies considerations exclusively drawn from observation of the societies of the Middle Ages which were so essentially different. Linked, moreover, as they always are, to the project of restoring a system whose destruction – already almost completely consummated – is henceforth irrevocable, they tend, in the present state of minds, much more to fortify

it is essentially a matter of considering the spiritual power in the social state proper to modern nations, which I see as characterized, from the temporal point of view, by the total preponderance of industrial activity.

In the positive domain, social organization, whether considered in its overall shape or in its details, is nothing other than the regularization of the division of labour, taking this expression not in the extremely narrow sense the economists have given it,*f* but in its wider sense, that is as applying to all the different coexisting classes of work, whether theoretical or practical, which can be conceived as contributing to the same final goal, and including national specialisms as well as individual specialisms. The greater and greater separation and specialization of private activities – whether between individual and individual, or between people and people – in fact constitute the general means to the improvement of the

the general prejudice against any spiritual power than to uproot it. One can even observe that the sentiment, involuntary though quite incomplete, of this total disharmony with their age, inspires in these philosophers a sort of hesitancy and timidity on this subject, which makes itself felt even in their judgements on the past.

From a philosophical point of view, then, these works therefore have essentially only a historical utility, as they are eminently suited to bring out the true general character of the old system, and to arouse a worthy appreciation of the immense benefits for which the human race is indebted to it. In this respect, the conceptions of the reactionary school retain all their value, being fully and directly applicable to an order of facts for which, or rather according to which, they were systematized. But, in relation to the moral reorganization of present-day societies, the question must be regarded, in spite of all these words, as quite unaffected.

Nonetheless it should be added that the political influence of the reactionary school is, from this crucial point of view, very useful today, and even necessary for a certain time, though in an indirect and in a sense negative way. For on the one hand it forms an essential obstacle to preserve society from the total preponderance of critical doctrines, which would prevent any real organization. At the same time, it acts as a no less essential stimulus to force modern civilization at last to produce the moral system appropriate to it, and to give it all the coherence it must have if it is to be capable of replacing the old one. In this sense, the influence of the reactionary school is just as necessary as that of the critical school, though in a different way, and it must naturally survive for the same length of time.

f The economists have been led by the imperfect nature of the investigations assigned to them by the general course of the human mind to consider the social state from a very incomplete point of view, and so we can easily understand that they could see only the narrowest and least important applications of the principle of the division of labour of which they were, properly speaking, the inventors. We must observe, in honour of Adam Smith, that not only was he the first to conceive this great principle in a clear and positive manner, but he presented it from a much more elevated point of view than any of his successors.

human race, and by a necessary and continuous reaction they are also its permanent result.[g] It is by that means that society naturally tends to become more and more extensive, and that it must in the end embrace sooner or later the entire human race, if the time allowed by the totality of the laws of the world to the progressive activity of our species is sufficiently prolonged. All real progress that has taken place or that could occur in social organization can be regarded, from this point of view, as ultimately resulting in the establishment of a better distribution of work. For the social order would obviously be perfect, whether from the point of view of private well-being or from that of the smooth harmony of the whole, if each individual (or each people) could, in all cases, devote himself to the precise kind of activity that is most appropriate for him, whether by his natural dispositions or by his antecedents or by the special circumstances in which he is placed; which, considered from another angle, would be precisely a perfect division of labour. No doubt such an order could not exist completely in any era. But the human race continuously tends to approach it more and more, without it ever being possible to determine how far away it is at any one time. It is above all in the social state that asserts itself more and more among modern peoples that this tendency is most direct and most tangible. For industrial activity, compared with military activity, is characterized by the admirable quality that its full and free development in an individual or in a people does not necessarily at all suppose its compression in other individuals or other peoples; on the contrary, not only does it allow universal competition, but it even inevitably provokes it within certain limits; whence it naturally results that men and nations are continually pushed into forming associations that are more and more extensive and more and more peaceful.

But if, considered from this first angle, the division of labour is the general cause of human improvement and of the development of the social state, considered from another angle – no less natural – it shows a continuous tendency to deterioration and dissolution,

---

[g] The considerations set out in this paragraph and in the next are by their nature just as applicable to the theoretical domain as to the practical domain. But I thought I should here direct them essentially towards the latter, in order to deduce from them more clearly the necessity of the spiritual power, which is now my main goal.

which would finally halt all progress if it were not incessantly combated by the ever-growing influence of government, and above all of spiritual government. For in fact the necessary result of this constantly developing specialization is that each individual and each people is habitually confined to a more and more limited perspective, and inspired by interests that are more and more particular. So if on the one hand the mind is stimulated, on the other hand it grows narrower;[h] and in the same way, what sociability gains in breadth, it loses in energy. By this means, men and peoples become less and less capable of grasping, by their own faculties, the relation between their own special action and the totality of social action, which at the same time is becoming ever more complex; and on the other hand they feel increasingly prompted to isolate their particular cause from the common cause, as the latter from day to day becomes less perceptible. These disadvantages of the division of labour obviously tend, by the nature of things, to increase continually, just as much as its advantages. So the first would cancel out the second, if their course were entirely free. Whence the absolute necessity of continuous action produced by two forces, one moral and the other physical, whose special role is constantly to recall to the general point of view minds which by themselves are always disposed to diverge, and to bring back into line with the common interest activities which unceasingly tend to distance themselves from it. At the same time as such intervention is essential, it becomes possible and even inevitable, insofar as the natural development of the various kinds of inequality which necessarily result from the division of labour tends by itself to establish the hierarchy – whether spiritual or temporal – that is necessary to this kind of action. This is the truly elementary point of view of the general theory of government, whose whole art thus consists in regularizing in each era this spontaneous hierarchy which forms within society, in such a way as to diminish, as far as possible, the harmful influence of the division of labour in comparison with its useful influence.

These considerations apply specially to the system of modern civilization, just as much as the opposite considerations set out

[h] A number of economists – among others M. Say – have perceived this inevitable effect of the division of labour when pushed too far, but only in the same subordinate cases which were the exclusive subject of their observations. [J.-B. Say, *Traité d'économie politique* (6th edn 1841), p. 99.]

above. This social state being the one in which the division of labour is pushed furthest, and where – much more than in any other – it must inevitably experience continual growth, whether between individuals or between peoples, the disadvantages associated with this division are necessarily more pronounced there, just as its advantages are. It is as inferior to the social state of antiquity from this first angle as it is superior from the second, which furnishes plenty of material for the speechifying of those who wish to praise or to criticize one or the other in an absolute sense, and who can do either indifferently according to the point of view they assume. Who, indeed, has not observed that, from the points of view of generality of mind and political energy, ancient peoples are as superior to the moderns as they are inferior from the points of view of extent of knowledge and universality of social relations? We can see, from what precedes, that there is nothing accidental in this contrast, whose source it is no doubt important to explore further in order to banish for good the pernicious endeavours aiming at combining, in the new social order, two kinds of pre-eminence which are mutually exclusive.

However it may be, the last kind of consideration set out above, which explains the general function of government, conceived according to its broadest purpose and especially within the system of modern civilization, obviously applies particularly to the spiritual power; it shows that in the new social state the action of this power must in the nature of things be more extensive and less intense than in any previous state. Since in fact the general disadvantages of the division of labour inevitably grow more and more, from the same necessity which produces the general development of civilization, society therefore has more and more need – especially among modern peoples – to feel the influence of this speculative corporation which, because it makes its distinctive specialism the consideration of the general point of view, has the role of constantly bringing that point of view before individuals and peoples. At the same time, the spiritual power is disinterested, by nature and through the independence of its social position, in this practical movement from which so many reasons for divergence and isolation stem; and so it is splendidly suited to identify its particular interest with the common interest, of which it can be regarded as the proper organ, in the majority of cases. But to complete this general survey, it is

essential to distinguish more precisely – in the continuous development of government's collective action – between the spiritual
direction and the temporal direction of society.

If we observe the mechanism of human societies closely enough,
we can recognize – as I pointed out above – that in each political
system the formation of the spiritual power has always necessarily
preceded the development of the temporal power, even in systems
where these two powers have been united in the same hands. It is
thus – to take the most convincing example – that the Roman constitution was in origin as essentially theocratic as that of the Etrus-
cans; and although it later assumed so different a character, the
patricians always saw the fundamental basis of their power in their
authority as a sacerdotal corporation. Generally, indeed, spiritual
association founded on communion of doctrines and the homogeneity of sentiments that results from it must in the nature of things
precede temporal association, which is founded on conformity of
interests; since the latter cannot exist without the former (interests
never being able by themselves to be sufficiently uniform to dispense with a certain similarity of principles), whereas we can conceive the possibility of associating on the basis of similarity of principle alone, provided that the opposition of interests is not too
extreme. But a truly complete and stable society, whether between
individuals or peoples, can exist only where the two conditions are
to a certain extent satisfied simultaneously. As civilization develops,
each of the two kinds of association increases in extent while diminishing in energy, as I have explained. But the original difference
stemming from their innermost nature always makes itself felt
between them, in the sense that because the temporal association
cannot wholly maintain itself on its own without the cooperation of
the spiritual power, whereas the spiritual association logically can
exist to a certain extent on its own and without the aid of the temporal power, the spiritual power increases its domain as society gets
more complicated, instead of the domain of the temporal power
seeing its own diminish. In fact only those who cannot be ruled
spiritually are ruled temporally; that is, we govern by force only
those who cannot be adequately ruled by opinion. And as men
become civilized, they become on the one hand more sensitive to
moral motives, and on the other more disposed to amiable reconciliation of interests. That is why the action of the temporal power is

continually decreasing, and why it must be less in the new social state than in all previous states; whereas the action of the spiritual power increases, and must be greater in the system of modern civilization than in any other. We can thereby see how deeply pernicious is the disposition which critical doctrines have in our day introduced into so many minds and which leads people to conceive the new social order without a spiritual power. On the contrary, that power must exercise a much greater political influence here, in its natural sphere of activity, than the temporal power will exercise in its; for the latter tends to become less and less important, and to reduce itself more and more – at least as long as civilization remains in the ascendant – to a purely civil hierarchy; though probably this latter effect can never in any era be absolutely complete. Having thus conceived the general influence of the modern spiritual power, by contemplating the overall shape of its various functions, whether national or European, we must complete this survey by considering them in their main details.

The first division of this aggregate of functions – the one to which I think I must restrict myself here – consists, as I have said, in distinguishing in the spiritual power two great classes of attributions: the first national, the other European. Let us begin by considering the first.

We have seen that, from this angle, the action of the spiritual power consists essentially in establishing by means of *education* the opinions and habits which are to direct men in their active life, and then in maintaining the practical observation of these fundamental rules by means of a regular and continuous moral influence exercised either on individuals or on classes. It is therefore a case of examining the main reasons which, contrary to current prejudices, require, in the new social state, a moral government bearing on ideas, propensities and conduct, whether in the individual domain or the collective domain.

Dogmatism is the normal state of the human mind, the state to which by nature it tends, continuously and in all sorts, even when the mind seems to be distancing itself from it most. For scepticism is only a state of crisis, the inevitable result of the intellectual interregnum which necessarily occurs whenever the human mind is called to change doctrines, and at the same time an essential means employed whether by the individual or the species to permit the transition from one dogmatism to another; that constitutes the only fundamental utility of doubt. This principle, which can be verified for all classes of ideas, is applicable *a fortiori* to social ideas, as they are at once the most complicated and the most important ideas. Modern peoples have obeyed this imperious law of their nature, even in their revolutionary period, since whenever it was necessary really to act – even if only to destroy – they were led inevitably to give a dogmatic form to ideas which were in essence purely critical.

Neither individuals nor the human race are destined to waste their lives in sterile argumentative activity, continually discoursing upon the course of conduct they should follow. It is essentially to *action* that the totality of the human race is called, except for a minute fraction, which is principally devoted by nature to contemplation. Nevertheless, any action presupposes prior principles of direction which individuals and masses have neither the capacity nor the time to establish, or even to verify, other than by applying them to the majority of cases. This is, from a straightforwardly intellectual point of view, the fundamental consideration which decisively justifies the existence of a class which, pre-eminently active in the speculative domain, is constantly and exclusively occupied in providing all the rest with general rules of conduct with which they can no more dispense than they are capable of forming them; and which, once accepted, allow them to employ all their reasoning capacity in applying them judiciously in practice, in doing so making use of the knowledge of the contemplative class, when deduction or interpretation present too many difficulties.

This need for spiritual leadership appears no less clearly if we cease to consider man only as an intelligent being, and envisage him also from the moral angle. For even if we admitted that each individual or each corporation could by their own faculties form the plan of action most suited either to their own well-being or to the smooth harmony of the whole, it would remain certain that this doctrine – because it must most often be to some degree in opposition to the most energetic impulses of human nature – could by itself exert practically no influence on real life. It therefore needs, so to speak, to be quickened by a regularly organized moral force which, bringing it before the mind of each individual in the name of all, will stamp it with all the energy resulting from this universal assent which is alone capable of overcoming or even sufficiently counterbalancing the power of antisocial propensities which are naturally preponderant in man's constitution.

Whatever may be the progress of civilization, it will still be true that if the social state is, in certain respects, a continual state of individual satisfaction, it is also, from other no less necessary points of view, a continual state of sacrifice. In more precise terms, in any particular act there is for each individual a certain degree of satisfaction without which society would not be possible, and a certain degree of sacrifice without which it could not be maintained, given the opposite tendencies of individuals, which are to some degree absolutely inevitable. The relative intensity of the first kind of sensations no doubt can increase, and indeed it does constantly increase, which constitutes the progressive improvement of human conditions; but the opposite kind always necessarily exist, and indeed their absolute intensity also increases without ceasing, by that growing ardour of our desires which our organization invariably links to the growth of pleasures, as an inevitable compensation and an indispensable corrective.

The greatest imaginable social perfection would obviously consist in each individual always fulfilling in the overall system the particular function to which he is best suited. And even in this extreme case, which is purely imaginary (although we are constantly approaching it), men would need a moral government, because no one could spontaneously contain his personal propensities within limits consistent with his own condition. For nature and society will to the end of time by common accord assign to different individuals roles which confer unequal satisfaction. Natural aptitudes and social roles present an infinite variety, whether in kind or in intensity. By contrast, the propensities that are habitually predominant are more or less the same from these two points of view in all men, or at least in all men they are energetic enough to inspire in each individual the spontaneous desire for all the pleasure he can observe in others, whatever may be the difference in their conditions. Whence, therefore, the need for special action to develop the natural morality in man, to reduce as far as possible the impulses of each individual to the scale required by the harmony of the whole, by making people accustomed from childhood to the voluntary subordination of private interest to the common interest, and by never ceasing to reproduce consideration of the social point of view in active life, with all the necessary emphasis. Without this salutary influence, which stifles evil at its source, society would be constantly obliged to act materially on individuals, whether by direct violence or by interest, to repress the effects of the tendencies it had allowed to develop freely; and hence the maintenance of order would soon become impossible when this temporal discipline had become stretched to its limits. But happily, in the nature of things, the absolute conception of such a mode of government – at once barbaric and illusory – is and can only be a pure supposition. In reality, temporal repression has never been and will never be anything but the complement of spiritual repression, which in no era could wholly suffice for the needs of society. If, in accordance with the natural course of civilization, the first does not cease to diminish, it is on the inevitable condition that the second increases in the same proportion.

Thus, whether from the intellectual angle or from the moral angle, it is established that, in any regular society, the notions of good and evil destined to direct the conduct of each person in the different social relations (and even in purely individual life, insofar as it can influence these relations) can be reduced to what is *prescribed* or *prohibited* by positive precepts, established and maintained by a suitably organized spiritual authority, the aggregate of these precepts constituting the guiding social doctrine.[i] By this means we can explain that old experience of the human race whose general result has been systematized by Catholic philosophy in accordance with that profound though essentially empirical knowledge of our nature which is its distinctive quality: we can directly present *faith* as a fundamental virtue, the immutable and necessary basis of private or public happiness; faith, or the disposition to believe spontaneously, without prior proof, in the dogmas proclaimed by competent authority; which is indeed the indispensable general

---

[i] In the foregoing reasoning, I have specially considered the action of government as repressive rather than as guiding, so as better to adapt my demonstration to the habits that today so generally predominate in political speculations. But the same reasons obviously apply, with even more force, when we do not restrict ourselves to conceiving government in its passive role – having as its object the maintenance of order – but consider it in its active role, charged with getting all partial activities to contribute to one and the same general goal, which is in my eyes its main function, especially in the social system appropriate to modern peoples. Readers who have properly understood the two classes of considerations set out above will easily be able to transfer them to this new aspect of the question.

condition allowing the establishment and the maintenance of true intellectual and moral communion.

In principle, the whole influence of the individual on the regulating doctrine is limited, in the normal state of things, to deducing from it the practical rule applicable to each particular case, consulting the spiritual organ in all doubtful cases. But as for the *construction* of the doctrine, from whichever angle we may consider it, no individual has any other legitimate right than to seek its partial rectification when experience has demonstrated that, from any point of view, it does not adequately meet its practical goal. It is to the spiritual power, thus alerted, that it naturally belongs to effect suitable changes in the doctrine, having verified their necessity. This is, at least, the regular order of things. On any other assumption, society would have to be regarded as being in a true state of revolution, more or less complete. This state, which is necessary in certain determinate eras, though it is always transitory, is subjected to special rules of a quite different nature, with which therefore I do not have to concern myself here, for I am simply prescribing for the normal state.[j]

The two kinds of general considerations set out above apply specially to the social state towards which modern peoples are tending. For, in this new state, characterized by a more complete and ever-growing separation of the different functions, each person – whatever capacity he may have – is only capable of spontaneously conceiving an extremely small portion of the doctrine he needs to guide him, whether industrially or socially; and at the same time his own interest, which has become more partial, naturally tends more fre-

---

[j] In the inevitably gradual tendency of public reason to recognize the need for reorganization, there is of course a temporary state, already attained by a certain number of minds, in which the necessity of a social doctrine is accepted, though the importance of a class invested with appropriate authority and having as its special and permanent role to bring the doctrine to life is misunderstood. But this semi-conviction, which is politically sterile since it strictly amounts to desiring the end without willing the means, cannot fail to round itself off promptly, once it has become sufficiently widespread. For, having really understood the intellectual, moral and political necessity of a general doctrine, we cannot take long to sense – independently of the fact that any doctrine presupposes founders – that from each of these three points of view, it absolutely requires interpreters, who, on the other hand, appear spontaneously; so that the idea of *function* and that of *organ* are as inseparable, by the nature of things, in social physics as in physiology.

quently to distance itself from the common interest, though to a lesser degree.

The evident tendency of modern societies towards an essentially industrial state, and consequently towards a political order in which the temporal power will belong permanently to the predominant industrial forces, is today beginning to be generally felt, and the natural course of things will display it more from day to day. The inevitable impetus produced by the awareness of a truth which is so important, though partial, disposes our minds to underestimate or even to neglect the moral reorganization of society; it tends to maintain the habit engendered by the critical doctrine, and particularly sustained by political economy, assigning priority in social matters to the purely material point of view. As we consider too exclusively the immense moral and political advantages which incontestably belong to the industrial mode of existence, we end up by exaggerating them in our own minds to the point of imagining that they almost entirely release us from any real spiritual organization; or, at least, that this will no longer have more than a secondary importance, once social relations have become purely industrial, and are no longer affected – as they still are today – by institutions and habits derived from the military antecedents of society.

We, however, are not to look upon this great fact as artists swayed by the attractions its appearance holds for human imagination, but as observers who, without allowing ourselves to admire it or to curse it, accept it as a fundamental datum in all modern political speculations. We must strive, as far as possible, to study it from all angles. And in this rational spirit we can easily tell that the regulative and guiding influence of the spiritual power is no less necessary in the sphere of industrial relations than it has been in the sphere of military relations, though not wholly in the same way. I restrict myself here, on this subject, to some general points, reserving the right to complete and develop them should controversy demand it.

Even supposing – what is in any case absolutely impossible – that the temporal order corresponding to this new state of society can be wholly established without the intervention of a spiritual power, it remains true that, deprived of this conservative influence, such an order would be quite unable to maintain itself. If it is certain that besides the general causes of disorder which are inherent in any society and which necessitate moral government, the military system displays others that are particular to it, this is also incontestable for the purely industrial system; it is just that these special causes are not the same in the two cases, and consequently they do not have the same intensity.[k]

By their nature it is no doubt much easier to reconcile individual interests in the new mode of existence than in the old one. But this fortunate characteristic, which makes it much easier to establish the moral rule, does not in the least exempt us from it, since their opposition, though it has become less intense, has not at all disappeared, and it has even become more extensive insofar as contacts have multiplied. Thus, to choose the most important example, although it is much to the advantage of the social order that the hostility between employers and workers is replacing that which existed between warriors and slaves, it is no less real. We would hope in vain to destroy it by means of temporal institutions which, binding more closely the material interests of these two classes, would diminish the arbitrary influence exercised by each of them on the other. Never will a permanent state be solidly established on simple physical antagonism, which is all that such institutions could regularize. Though no doubt very useful, they would always be insufficient because they would necessarily allow employers to continue to seek to – and even to be able to – abuse their position to reduce wages and work; and workers to seek to obtain by violence what an industrious life could not procure for them. The solution of this serious difficulty necessarily demands the continued influence of a moral doctrine imposing reciprocal duties on employers and workers, in conformity with their reciprocal relations. And this doctrine can obviously only be founded and maintained by a spiri-

---

[k] M. Dunoyer, in a recently published work, has noted, by means of some most luminous observations on the various successive states of civilization, the tendency of present-day societies, considered from the temporal point of view, towards the purely industrial state; but he was able to guard himself against the commonplace exaggeration which leads people to imagine that this new mode of existence is endowed with absolute perfection. He devoted the last chapter of his book to a conscientious and rigorous analysis of the main disadvantages characteristic of industrial society. Although this enumeration is conceived with a very different aim from my present considerations, and is executed in a wholly different spirit, I refer the reader to it, to provide the details which I am precluded from giving here. [The text referred to here is Charles Dunoyer's *L'Industrie et la morale considérées dans leurs rapports avec la liberté*, 1825.]

tual authority situated at a vantage-point sufficiently general to embrace an overview of these relations, and at the same time sufficiently disinterested in the practical movement not to be habitually suspected of partiality by either of the two enemy classes between which it has to interpose itself. Analogous observations can be made about the other great industrial relations, such as those between farmers and manufacturers, or between either of those and merchants, or between all of them and bankers. It is clear that in these different respects interests that are left entirely to their own guidance, without any other discipline than that resulting from their own antagonism, always end in direct opposition.[*l*] Whence results, therefore, the fundamental necessity of a moral rule, and consequently of a spiritual authority, which are essential if the interests are to be contained within limits so that, instead of coming into conflict, they converge; limits which they are constantly tending to transcend. It would, moreover, be easy to establish that this moral influence, considered from these two angles, must besides play a major and essential role in the establishment of temporal institutions intended to complete this regularization of social relations.

It would be expecting too much of the power of the proofs of political economy to demonstrate the necessary conformity of the different industrial interests if we were to hope that this might ever be sufficient to discipline them.[*m*] Even if we were to accord these demonstrations all the logical latitude – which is in any case much

---

[*l*] The commercial and manufacturing crisis which is currently devastating the country in which industrial activity is most developed – a crisis which could at any moment assume a more or less serious political character – is well suited to prove to impartial observers the need for government to exert some action on industrial relations as it did in the past on military relations. No doubt these irritants are in their nature transient. But social order and individual happiness by common accord demand more direct, more explicit, in a word more regular guarantees against the ever-imminent renewal of these grievous oscillations – guarantees which do not make each individual judge in his own case, and which do not require minds that are customarily situated at very particular vantage-points spontaneously and consistently to adopt a general point of view.

[*m*] The fundamental vice of political economy, considered as a social theory, consists in this: having discovered, from some particular points of view which are very far from being the most important, the spontaneous and permanent tendency of human societies towards a certain necessary order, it believes itself entitled to infer that it is useless to regularize that order by positive institutions; whereas this great political truth, conceived as a whole, only proves the possibility of organization, at the same time as it leads us to a worthy appreciation of its vital importance.

exaggerated – which economists have given them, it would still be certain that man does not solely or even mainly act on the basis of calculations, and in the second place that he is not always or even normally capable of calculating accurately. Nineteenth-century physiology, confirming or rather explicating universal experience, has positively demonstrated the frivolity of these metaphysical theories which represent man as an essentially calculating being, moved by the sole motive of private interest.

Thus morality, whether private or public, will necessarily be fluid and without force as long as we posit exclusive consideration of private utility as the point of departure for each individual or each class. This is nevertheless where the industrial spirit by its nature inevitably leads, like any other purely temporal spirit, when it arises in isolation and without undergoing the regulative moral influence which is only to be found in the action of a properly organized spiritual power. If it were possible to conceive of society delivered entirely and exclusively to an impetus directly derived from temporal activity alone, the new political order (if we could then give it this name) would have no real advantage over the old (also considered according to the same abstract hypothesis) other than the substitution of monopoly for conquest, and despotism founded on the right of the wealthiest for despotism founded on the right of the strongest. These would be the extreme but logical consequences of a purely temporal social organization, if such a hypothesis could ever be realized. But fortunately, however pernicious our political views may be, the nature of things preserves society from the absolute influence of its own aberrations, and the order which in the end establishes itself is always superior to that which human combinations had built in advance.

The necessity of a spiritual order in the new social state manifests itself not only in respect of relations between individuals or between classes, but also in purely personal morality. One general consideration, derived from the study of human nature, shows first of all, as the majority of philosophers have observed in all ages, that the most solid foundation for social virtues is to be found in the habitual practice of individual virtues, since it is by that means that man most decisively proves his power of overcoming the vicious impulses of his organic propensities. But independently of this universal reason, the inevitable influence which purely individual acts exercise indirectly on the whole, in any system of social relations, is especially marked in the modern system, and it consequently provides another reason for the moral regulation of society. To cite only one example, it is generally recognized, since Mr Malthus's works, that the constant tendency of population to increase more rapidly than the means of subsistence, a tendency which is above all characteristic of industrial societies, demands a certain permanent repression of man's most energetic propensity; and this could obviously occur to a sufficient degree only by means of moral authority, whatever may be the incontestable influence of temporal means in containing this instinct within appropriate limits.

Up to now, for the general reason set out above, I have only considered the preventive or repressive action of the spiritual power in the new system of social relations. Its importance is still more apparent when we consider its directive action as well.

Even if we were to accept for the purpose of hypothesis that in the new social state the maintenance of order can take place spontaneously without any special regulative influence, it would remain incontestable that in order to act collectively, as the nature of the system calls them to do in a large number of cases, individuals and classes need to be directed by common dogmas, which the spiritual power establishes in the course of social education and then constantly reproduces in real life. The need for doctrine is all the greater, in this respect, as – because the classification of individuals in this system is necessarily far looser than in the old system – each person is so much less prepared by nature for the particular station he is to fill. When stations in life were essentially hereditary, domestic education could be regarded, so to speak, as a sufficient preparation. It is not so when stations tend essentially to be allocated in conformity with individual aptitudes. Public education, whether general or special, now acquires much more importance, as the sole rational means of determining these aptitudes, originally so indistinct in most cases, and at the same time of developing them properly. So the action of the spiritual power then becomes all the more indispensable to establish and to maintain a social classification consistent with the spirit of the system. If we consider the multitude of wasted vocations, of professional failures, which today result from the absence of intellectual and moral direction, if we try to calculate the deplorable consequences which derive from them, whether for individuals or for society, we can grasp the importance of the fore-going consideration.

These are, in summary, the main grounds which assign to modern spiritual power a large and fundamental influence; considering it only in its national attributions.

The same general considerations are precisely applicable to the necessary action which spiritual power must exercise for the regulation of relations between people and people. I therefore think I can release myself here from having explicitly to set out this line of thought, which any careful reader will easily be able to elaborate by sticking to the fundamental point of view determined by the foregoing reasoning.

The whole radical difference between the two cases consists in the greater generality of the second kind of social relations. But if this distinction shows the regulative action of spiritual power to be necessarily less intense in the European than in the national domain, at the same time it presents it as even more strictly indispensable – in proportion to the importance of the relations – and above all as less susceptible to be replaced by any other influence.

As relations between peoples are at once much more extensive and much more continuous in modern civilization than in that of the Middle Ages, it becomes all the more important to regulate them. The collective activity of European society, which in the old system occurred only at very distant intervals, must become very frequent if not strictly permanent in the new system. It is brought about either by operations of common utility, which demand the cooperation of two or more peoples; or by the overall influence, partly repressive, which the most civilized nations must exercise over those which are less so, in the common interest of both. These different causes will perhaps even be powerful enough to instigate the formation of a certain degree of temporal sovereignty, extending at once over several of the most advanced peoples. But what is obviously incontestable, on any hypothesis, is that they immediately necessitate the establishment of a social doctrine, common to the different nations, and consequently a spiritual sovereignty capable of maintaining this doctrine by organizing a European education and then applying it as appropriate in actual relations. Until that time the European order will be constantly on the point of being compromised, in spite of the influence – both despotic and inadequate, though for all that essential on a temporary basis today – exercised by the imperfect coalition of the old temporal powers, which can offer no solid guarantee of security, since it is, by its innermost nature, always on the point of dissolution.

I think I should point out here, as in the previous case, but more briefly, the false political conceptions that are tending to be produced today by an incomplete view of the temporal future of society, which presents relations between people and people as sufficiently regularized by the simple fact that the different nations have reached the stage of purely industrial life. No doubt this new mode of existence has the fortunate quality of facilitating the moral association of nations, like that of individuals or classes; but no more in the former than in the latter case does it release us from that moral association, and indeed it makes it more necessary, insofar as it multiplies and extends relations. Let us accept for a moment that the European temporal order could entirely shed its military character to acquire a purely industrial character, without this change being preceded and inspired by an appropriate spiritual reorganization; which certainly implies a contradiction. But even on this abstract assumption, it remains incontestable that this system could have no solidity if the various nations were permanently abandoned to temporal impulsions alone, without subordinating them to any common moral doctrine established and maintained by some spiritual power. For the particular interest, conceived as the unique and direct basis of a plan of conduct, is still less capable of serving as the solid foundation for the morality of peoples than for that of individuals and classes. Indeed, even if we continue to assume that conduct can be exclusively or chiefly guided by calculation (which is no more true of nations than of individuals), the relation between the well-being of each and that of all is certainly at the same time less real and less perceptible in the European domain than in the national domain. It is very difficult, and consequently extremely rare, for the real happiness of an individual to accord completely with very pronounced antisocial conduct; that is much easier, and consequently much more common, for a nation, even in the industrial mode, as experience has proved only too much since the foundation of the colonial and protectionist system; so much so that this is still the dominant opinion. In the same way, from the intellectual point of view, an individual could at a pinch, by ceasing to lead an active life, place himself at a national vantage-point, and could grasp it up to a certain point, if his mental powers were sufficient; but that is altogether more difficult when it is a case of having to raise it to a European point of view, and a social organization which permanently demanded such an effort on the part of a very large number, or even only of the leaders of the national temporal orders, would obviously be impossible.

The economists' exaggerated theories of the necessary and constant identity of the industrial interests characteristic of the different nations, even if they were absolutely accurate, would inevitably be even more powerless to regularize the relations of peoples than those of individuals with the sole aid of the conviction they were able to produce. It is in vain that the most advanced peoples today seek, more or less firmly, to abandon the protectionist regime. If this result were ever attained, the spirit of industrial antagonism would not fail to reproduce itself in new forms which it could easily create, if it were possible for each nation indefinitely to continue to allow no other rule of conduct than the satisfaction of its own interest, without recognizing any moral duty towards others. The only power truly capable of containing this natural rivalry of peoples within its necessary limits, and of utilizing it by reducing it – at least in principle – to legitimate emulation, is that of a general doctrine concerning the actual relations of nations, a doctrine established and habitually proclaimed by a spiritual authority which, addressing each people in the name of all, finds in this universal assent the necessary support for getting its decisions accepted.

Thus as a final result of all the foregoing considerations we can verify in detail the fundamental proposition established above in general terms. Whether from an active or a passive point of view, and for both general and special reasons, the social state towards which modern peoples are moving requires – just as much as that of the Middle Ages did – a spiritual (that is, intellectual and moral) organization which is at once European and national.

I shall later examine in the same spirit the main aspects of the nature of this organization, which so far, through unavoidable abstraction, I have left indeterminate so as not to make impracticable a demonstration which is already so profoundly complicated. This new exposition, quite apart from its great intrinsic importance, will perhaps dissipate the obscurity which is to a certain degree inevitably attached to this abstract point of view, in most minds; and above all it will destroy the false interpretations which current habits have generally led people to conceive whenever the spiritual power was in question. Such are at least my hopes.

Essay 6
Examination of Broussais's Treatise on Irritation[1]

Since the end of the sixteenth century, the human mind has experienced a general and continuous revolution whose object has been the gradual and total recasting of the entire system of human knowledge, which is henceforth to be built upon its true foundations, observation and reasoning. This fundamental revolution, prepared by the successive works of all previous centuries, especially from the Arabs on, was definitively caused and immediately begun by the great new impetus simultaneously imparted to human reason by Descartes's ideas, Bacon's precepts and Galileo's discoveries. Since that memorable time, the human mind, in all the branches of its knowledge, has constantly tended more and more to liberate itself completely and for ever from the dominance previously exercised by theology and metaphysics, completely to subordinate imagination to observation; in a word, to constitute the definitive system of positive philosophy.

The different branches of human knowledge have not all participated at the same speed in this important renovation. They had to undergo it in turn, according to the degree of complexity and of mutual dependence of the phenomena they consider. Physiology, being of all the parts of natural philosophy the one which studies

---

[1] This essay first appeared in the *Journal de Paris*, August 1828. F. J. V. Broussais's *De l'irritation et de la folie* was published in 1828.

the most complicated and the least independent phenomena, necessarily had to remain longer than any other under the yoke of theological fictions and metaphysical abstractions. Thus it was only in the second half of the last century, and after astronomy, physics and chemistry had become positive sciences, that physiology began in its turn to experience this great and salutary transformation, through the immortal works of Haller, of Charles Bonnet, of Daubenton, of Spallanzani, of Vicq-d'Azyr, of Chaussier, of Bichat, of Cuvier, of Pinel, of Cabanis, etc.

But, for this revolution to be complete and effective, it had to extend equally to intellectual and affective phenomena, which necessarily had to participate in it later than other animal phenomena, given their greater complexity, and given their immediate connection with theological and metaphysical theories which attached them to the constitution of society. Thus the papers published at the beginning of this century by Cabanis on the relations of the physical and the moral were the first great direct attempt definitely to bring within the domain of positive physiology this branch of study which had up to then been exclusively abandoned to theological and metaphysical methods.[2] The impetus given to the human mind by these memorable investigations has not at all slowed down. The works of M. Gall and his school have singularly strengthened it, and above all imparted to this new and latest portion of physiology a noble quality of accuracy, by providing a determinate basis for discussion and investigation. Today we can say that this revolution, although it has not yet become popular, is finally consummated in all minds that are truly in tune with their times, which all look upon the study of intellectual and affective functions as inseparably linked to that of all other physiological phenomena, and necessarily pursued by the same methods and in the same spirit.

However, some men, misunderstanding in this respect the current and irrevocable direction of the human mind, have for ten years been trying to transplant German metaphysics among us, and to constitute under the name of *psychology* a pseudo-science independent of physiology, superior to it, and to which alone would belong the study of the phenomena specially called *moral*.[3] Though these

---

[2] *Rapports du physique et du moral de l'homme*, 1802.
[3] Comte is directing his attack against Victor Cousin, whose critique of sensationalism depended crucially on the validity of the psychological method, or self-observation, which was intended to give Cousin's philosophy scientific authority.

retrograde attempts are not capable of checking the development of real knowledge, since the ephemeral enthusiasm they still excite essentially stems only from strange and accidental circumstances, it is certain that they exercise a baneful influence, retarding in many minds the development of the true philosophical spirit, and wastefully consuming a great deal of intellectual activity.

This situation has been profoundly sensed by M. Broussais. Without exaggerating the evil, he has properly understood how important it is to oppose the vague and chimerical direction in which people are today seeking to lead French youth. Thus he believed he should interrupt his great work in general pathology to make plain the emptiness and nullity of psychology. This is the general and essential goal of his new work, as he clearly declares in a very noteworthy preface, where he is not afraid to rise above those pious accusations of materialism with which our psychologists, following the example of our theologians, their predecessors, have continued to shroud their adversaries. In this respect, independently of the distinguished merit of his work, M. Broussais has, in publishing it, undertaken a true act of courage, worthy of the recognition of all good minds, and whose value cannot be properly felt other than by those who know how much today's scientists, though feeling for metaphysical theories the profound disdain that they must necessarily inspire in all intellects nourished on positive studies, carefully avoid opposing in public discussion the domination that those theories claim to exercise today.

M. Broussais's work completely achieves the chief goal the author set himself. Entering the discussion more deeply than any physiologist has hitherto done, he has immediately focused scrutiny on the supposed method of interior observation recommended by psychologists as the basis of the science of man.

The ascendancy acquired by the positive sciences since Bacon is today such that psychologists, to raise metaphysics from the ruins into which it has fallen, have found themselves obliged to present their works as also based on observation. To this effect they have thought up the distinction between external facts, the domain of the ordinary sciences, and interior facts or facts of consciousness, which are proper to psychology. M. Broussais shows how frivolous this supposed distinction is. In the fifth chapter of the first part, he sets out a physiological analysis – singularly notable for its depth, for its subtlety – of the state of a mind meditating on its own acts. This analysis makes wholly evident the impossibility of reaching any real discovery by this illusory mode of exploration. I regret that I can only cite a few passages from it.

'Let us now examine', he says, 'what physiologists can find in their consciousness, by proceeding to this kind of investigation. They are sure to come across sensations originating in the intestines which constantly correspond with the brain: not only hunger, sexual desires, cold, head, definite pain, or pleasure, which can be traced back to some part or other of the body; but they will also notice a mass of vague, indeterminate sensations, which will sometimes lead them to sadness, sometimes to joy, sometimes to action, sometimes to rest, one day to hope, the next to despair and even to loathing of life. They will find all that without suspecting where it comes from; for physiologists are the only ones who can teach them. If they take all these interior sensations for revelations of the divinity they call consciousness, they can increase their wealth by taking, after the manner of the Orientals, a certain dose of opium combined with spices, etc.'

Notwithstanding M. Broussais's expert handling of this discussion, it seems to me that he could have tackled the question still more directly, by proving immediately that such interior observation is necessarily impossible.

In fact, man can observe what is external to him; he can observe certain functions of his organs other than the thinking organ. He can even, up to a certain point, observe himself in respect of the different passions he experiences, because the cerebral organs on which they depend are distinct from the observing organ properly so called, and even that supposes that the state of passion is not very pronounced. But it is obviously impossible for him to observe himself in his own intellectual acts, for the organ observed and the observing organ are in this case identical, so by whom would the observation be made? The psychologists' illusion in this respect is analogous to that of the old physicians who thought they could explain vision by saying that luminous rays traced *images* of external objects on the retina. Physiologists judiciously pointed out to them that, if luminous impressions acted as images on the retina, another eye would be needed to watch them. It is the same with the supposed interior observation of intelligence. For that to be possible, the individual would have to be able to divide himself into two parts, of which one would think and the other, during that time, would watch him think. Thus man cannot directly observe his intellectual operations; he can only observe the organs and the results. From the first point of view, we are brought back to physiology; from the second, the great results of human intelligence being the sciences, we are brought back to the philosophy of the different sciences, which is not at all separable from these sciences themselves. From no point of view is there any room for psychology or the direct study of the soul independent of any external consideration.

In the parallel, so satisfying and so decisive, that M. Broussais establishes between physiology and psychology, we might wish that he had brought out more vividly the inferiority of the latter, which, even if we accepted its supposed methods as suitable for exploration, only considers the adult and perfectly healthy man, and makes total abstraction of animals, and even of man in an imperfect state of development or in a state of disturbed organization; whereas in any physiological reflections, the point of view of man in the normal state is always admirably combined with that of the totality of the animal series, and with that of the pathological state. This contrast, which M. Broussais only indicates in a fragmentary way, if presented with the clarity and vigour of exposition which characterize him, would have formed a useful contrast with that loftiness of view, that depth of conception on which our psychologists singularly congratulate themselves.

A more serious omission committed by M. Broussais consists in not indicating clearly enough the immense difference that exists between the physiological doctrine of intellectual and moral man and the theories of the metaphysicians of the last century, who saw in human intelligence only the action of the external senses, thus setting aside any predisposition of the internal cerebral organs. The very well-argued critique of this ideology by Condillac and Helvétius is what alone gives some foundation to the influence of present-day psychology, which in any case merely popularizes in obscure and emphatic declarations what physiologists such as Charles Bonnet, Cabanis, and chiefly MM. Gall and Spurzheim had for a long time expounded on this subject much more clearly and above all much more accurately. M. Broussais will no doubt rush to remove this single resource from psychology, or from what he so judiciously calls *ontology*. I confidently point out this important improvement for a second edition, an honour which a work such as his could not fail to receive soon. The omission which I point out to him surely stems only from the obvious haste with which his work was composed; for psychologists cannot say that he anywhere shows himself to be the definite supporter of eighteenth-century metaphysics.

A general examination of M. Broussais's book gives rise to a final philosophical consideration of great importance: that the author has not circumscribed any more precisely than his physiologist predecessors the true sphere of physiology.

When Cabanis was the first directly to claim the study of moral phenomena as falling within the domain of physiology, he did not carefully enough separate – or rather he inaptly confused – the study of the individual man and that of the human race considered in its collective development. It seemed to him that both without distinction ought equally to form part of the same science, physiology. This confusion was maintained by MM. Gall and Spurzheim; it still survives in the minds of almost all physiologists who are seriously concerned with the portion of their science that relates to moral phenomena. M. Broussais has done nothing to eradicate it, although from a number of passages in his book he seems to have seen its chief vice.

It is in fact clear that the study of the individual and that of the race, though by nature having such close relations that they might be considered as two parts of a single science, are nevertheless sufficiently distinct, and above all both sufficiently developed, to be necessarily cultivated separately, and consequently conceived as forming two sciences, physiology properly so called and social physics. The second is no doubt founded on the first, which provides it with its positive point of departure and its permanent guide. But it nonetheless constitutes a separate science, having its own special methods and getting its own observations from the history of the development of human society. It would be absolutely impossible to treat it simply as a direct deduction from the science of the individual (except for animals, whose social development is so limited that it does not demand separate study). If physiology is not yet completely and definitively constituted, if the scope of that science is not precisely determined, the main cause is that this distinction is not yet regularly established and unanimously accepted. This fluid state of the science, even in the loftiest minds, could alone – if it continues – give real and lasting force to the psychologists' critique and their pretensions, although it is in any case obvious that the study of social phenomena does not any more belong to their metaphysical methods than does that of individual phenomena.

These are the principal philosophical reflections suggested to me by M. Broussais's book, considered in relation to the general goal the author has set for himself.

In spite of the observations which I thought I ought to present in this connection, this book is wholly worthy of its illustrious author. I hope, for the credit of a public which people are today striving to turn back towards metaphysics, that it will obtain a success that measures up to its importance. It should contribute powerfully to supporting the natural course of human mind, by generally discrediting vague and chimerical speculations which retard the progress of real knowledge. Since Cabanis's papers and the works of MM. Gall and Spurzheim, no work has appeared that is so capable of demonstrating the emptiness and nullity of this illusory science of personified abstractions which M. Cuvier characterized so well by saying that it employs metaphors in place of reasoning, and which M. Broussais himself defined so happily as *a trick of the imagination more or less analogous to poetry*. He helps us to appreciate the true worth of this assemblage of incoherent opinions which necessarily vary, not just from one individual to another, but in the same individual, according to the different inclinations his organization experiences. Above all he tends to eliminate for ever that mystical spirit, so flattering to proud ignorance, which inspires an instinctive repugnance for any special and positive study, by giving a few senseless abstractions precedence over all real knowledge, and which tends to plunge us back into the state of infancy by re-establishing the rule of theological conceptions among us in a new form.

M. Broussais can be regarded as the founder of positive pathology, that is of the science which connects the disturbance of vital phenomena to the lesion of organs or tissues. Since the era when physiology began to form a true science – that is, around the middle of the last century – several of those who co-operated in this great movement of the human mind, and above all Morgagni and Bonnet, had engaged in important work on the location of diseases. But this work did not alter the general spirit of pathology which continued to represent the greater number of the most important diseases as independent of any alteration in the normal state of the organs. These investigations could not have a very great influence on science before the establishment of the fundamental distinction between organs and tissues, due to the genius of Bichat, since it is above all through tissues and not through organs that lesions must be studied. M. Broussais, setting out from the general anatomy founded by Bichat, constituted pathology on its true foundations, by making it consist of the examination of the alterations of which the various tissues are susceptible, and the phenomena that result. He was the first to recognize clearly and to proclaim aloud that almost all known diseases are only symptoms, and that there could be no disturbance of functions without lesion of organs, or rather of tissues.

If M. Broussais had confined himself to establishing this general principle, he would no doubt have avoided the majority of the criticisms to which his works have been subjected; but he would not have accomplished the important renovation in the scientific system which his school is producing, and which is chasing metaphysics from its last refuge. For that it was essential not only to represent every disease as deriving – at least in principle – from some organic lesion, a proposition which was by its nature hardly contestable; but to determine the precise location of each of the diseases which were regarded as having no special location. That is what M. Broussais accomplished, chiefly by reducing the six supposedly essential fevers to inflammations of the mucous membrane of the stomach and the intestines, which doctors had up to then neglected. It is not for me to investigate whether M. Broussais did not later exaggerate the influence of gastritis or gastroenteritis on the production of the various morbid symptoms; this was almost inevitable. But impartial minds, which would be led to criticize such exaggerations, must have regard to the philosophical necessity which M. Broussais faced of assigning an organ to each recognized ailment, in order to establish the discussion on positive foundations. We must bear in mind that, even if he was mistaken as to the real location of such-and-such a disease, it was much preferable both for pathology and even for therapeutics to conceive a location different from the true one than not to conceive one at all. M. Broussais will thus have pointed our minds to the true path of observation, on which, by combating his ideas, we can only serve the progress of science.

The first part of the work now published by M. Broussais is a treatise on irritation. It can be regarded as an exposition of the noblest generalizations of the author's doctrine. Never has there been so direct and satisfying a conception of the fundamental relation between physiology and pathology; and it is his profound sense of that relation that best characterizes M. Broussais's mind.

Setting out from the great general truth glimpsed by Brown, that life can only be sustained by excitation, a truth which M. Broussais made his own by the important use he made of it, he represents all diseases as consisting essentially of an excess or lack of excitation of the various tissues, above or below the degree that constitutes the normal state. This conception casts a great deal of light on the nature of diseases, showing them to be produced by a simple change of intensity in the action of the very stimulants that are essential to the maintenance of health.

Having established that most often there is an excess rather than a lack in the excitation of the organs, and even that the diminution of the action of the stimulants of an organ ordinarily determines the irritation of the other organs – as, for example, the stomach relative to the brain – M. Broussais distinguishes three degrees in the abnormal excitation of organs: over-excitation properly so called, subinflammation and inflammation. He sets out the characters of these three states in the main organic systems, and especially in the nervous system, which in accord with the majority of present-day physiologists he presents as the general agent of the sympathies. M. Broussais pushes the physiological analysis of the different tissues even further than has hitherto been done, for he considers the organic elements of which all tissues are composed, and he reduces them to three: fibrin, gelatine and albumin, in each of which he examines the phenomena of irritation. This conception will later bring a great and invaluable simplicity to the first foundations of physiology and pathology.

I must not neglect to point out a considerable improvement introduced by M. Broussais's physiological doctrine: the disappearance of those vital properties accepted or rather maintained by Bichat, which leave a certain metaphysical character in the fundamental ideas of physiology. M. Broussais replaces them with the uniform property of irritability, which exists in all tissues, but which in each manifests itself through different phenomena. This conception tends to purify physiology of the remains of metaphysics which Bichat tried to preserve. At the same time, he definitively assigns to the physics of living bodies a character that is clearly distinct from that of the physics of inorganic bodies, for the point of view of irritation embraces everything that is characteristic of the state of life. This consideration was not less indispensable for constituting a true positive physiology, and it had not up to then been precisely fulfilled by physiologists, who had striven completely to free their science from metaphysical conceptions.

This first part of M. Broussais's work abounds in lofty and new insights. I shall reproach him only for a certain obscurity in his exposition, and especially for an almost total absence of method in the coordination of ideas. The rather ill-contrived blending of physiological conceptions and pathological conceptions introduces a sort of confusion which must make it difficult, even for an attentive and educated reader, to grasp the general spirit of this notable piece of work; but this imperfection can be remedied in a new edition, if M. Broussais, as I do not doubt, feels the necessity of nurturing further his major ideas, of determining their character more precisely, and of assessing more exactly the scope of each of them. We must not lose sight of the serious general reason which induced the composition of this work: the necessity of combating ontology, which again seeks to take hold of the mind of the present generation. In this respect we can excuse a vice in his method which the author would certainly have avoided if he could have devoted the right amount of time to reflecting about his work. Nevertheless, M. Broussais must not forget that this work contains the chief seminal ideas of a general treatise on life, considered either in its normal state or in its abnormal state. It is important for his fame that he should himself erect this monument which is necessary to the future progress of science.

If he reflects again about his work, M. Broussais will no doubt also feel that when he dealt with the nervous system he did not accord enough importance to the fundamental distinction between the two nervous systems, the cerebral and that of the ganglions. He did not pay enough regard to the distinctive characteristics of the latter, as much from the physiological as from the pathological point of view. We should also wish that M. Broussais had paid more attention to comparative anatomy, and that he had explicitly undertaken to bring his view on human organization into harmony with the totality of the animal series, for this is today the indispensable condition for any large conception of physiology, and he no doubt fulfilled it implicitly.

I have few things to say on the second part of this work, which deals with madness. It is a very natural application of the principles established in this first part on the special irritation of the brain. This application, very well done, sheds much light on the principles themselves. Its execution is much more satisfying than that of the previous part. It adds nothing very fundamental to the present state of this important branch of pathology. But the knowledge acquired hitherto on this subject is summed up with a clarity and a methodological perfection far superior to those displayed by any of the existing treatises, and that is to render science a very essential service. There is nothing one might read that is better suited to keeping one free or curing one of the psychological contagion. As for what is personal to the author in the substance of his ideas, I have noticed that in placing – along with all present-day physiologists – the location of madness in the brain, he characterizes much more precisely than they have done the state of cerebral irritation which brings about derangement. He also sets out some new and very well-judged considerations on the information that we can expect from post-mortem examinations. He demonstrates that because the state of inflammation which disorganizes the tissues – and which, consequently, leaves after death the only tangible traces to which we ordinarily pay attention – is only the highest degree of the state of irritation which disturbs normal functions, it is quite possible that this disturbance can take place as the effect of over-excitation, without which we could after death discover inflammatory modifications. M. Broussais thus indirectly destroys the only reasonable objection raised against positive pathology by the metaphysical pathologists of the Montpellier school who, noting the absence in certain cases of lesions in the corpse, conclude in favour of the existence of so-called *essential* diseases.

Persons who, on the strength of vulgar prejudices to which scientists ought to be impervious, picture M. Broussais as subordinating everything to the stomach in the animal economy, will acquire, by reading this work, a fairer idea of the breadth and nobility of his mind. He sets out all the intensity of the great sympathetic influence exerted by the digestive intestines over all organs, and particularly over the brain, an influence which has not always been properly appreciated by physiologists who have devoted themselves to the special study of the nervous system. But we cannot detect any trace of a preoccupation with this subject in his book; he does not expound anything beyond the most authenticated observations.

In dealing with monomanias, M. Broussais finds and grasps the opportunity to pay worthy homage to the important work of MM. Gall and Spurzheim and of the phrenological school on the brain. I must congratulate him on this act of justice, which is at the same time an act of courage, for even today scientists need courage to pronounce publicly in favour of doctrines that are so contrary to official opinions. In this doctrine, very imperfect as it still is, M. Broussais has seen how much light it casts on the study of man. He seems to have sensed the extent to which this important reformation supports the general revolution of the human mind for the establishment of a wholly positive philosophy.

M. Broussais, however, raises several objections to M. Gall's current doctrine. Most seem to me ill-founded. Only one is really solid: the reproach of not taking account of the extreme influence exercised on the brain by the digestive and generative intestines. It is certain that this influence, considerably exaggerated by physiologists before MM. Gall and Spurzheim, has been much too neglected by the phrenological school, and that, in this respect, the fundamental ideas of the new doctrine of the brain need to be subjected to fuller elaboration.

In relation to the real treatment of madness, the considerations set out by M. Broussais add little to the mass of accepted knowledge; but the therapeutic treatment of this ailment is conceived and expounded in a much more rational way than in any of the existing treatises. The author finds the ordinary treatment too inactive. He thinks, with reason, that major blood-lettings, carried out opportunely at the onset of the disease, can immediately avert the development of madness, as is the case with severe peripneumonia or gastritis. M. Broussais rightly insists, with all the authors who have written since Pinel, on the importance of moral treatment. But one cannot help being surprised that in recommending asylums as an essential condition for that purpose he does not point out the extreme negligence with which this essential part of medical treatment is generally conducted in these institutions.[4] No doubt M. Broussais was not able to observe carefully enough the way in which the majority of these establishments are run; he thought they were constituted and administered as they ought to be and could be. If he had studied them for himself, he would have convinced himself that, in spite of the promises of their directors, they in fact abandon the whole of the intellectual and affective part of the treatment to the arbitrary action of subordinate and unrefined agents, whose conduct almost always aggravates the disease they ought to be helping to cure.

These are the main reflections I wanted to present here about M. Broussais's new work. I have not sought to make it known in depth, but only to characterize its spirit accurately, and to make all those who are interested in the progress of the physiological sciences see the necessity of studying it. I have sought to direct public attention towards this book as a piece of work capable of contributing to the general development of human reason, and effectively opposing the mystical direction which a number of writers alien to the true spirit of our age are today striving to impart to the study of man. The publication of this important piece of writing must consolidate M. Broussais's renown, and make people appreciate the real scope of his ideas. Hitherto, he was essentially known only as a reformer in pathology and in therapeutics. Now he emerges as a physiologist and philosopher. He proves that there is a unity in his mind, in that his applied ideas derive from theoretical conceptions marked with the same character. In short, he shows himself destined, by the overall shape of his work, to appear to posterity as one of the men who have most effectively contributed – directly or indirectly – to the formation and the triumph of positive philosophy, the general and definitive culmination of the great evolution of the human mind.

---

[4] Comte himself had spent eight months in Esquirol's clinic following his mental breakdown in 1826, but was released uncured. This remark reflects Comte's resentment at his treatment.

Index of names

Albert the Great, theologian, 180
Alembert, Jean-Baptiste Le Rond d',
  xxix
Alexander I, Tsar of Russia, 195n
Alexander VI, Pope, 195
Alexander the Great, 177
Appollonius, 178
Archimedes, 176n, 178
Aristotle, 164, 177
Arnaud, Pierre, xxx
Augustine of Hippo, 179

Bacon, Francis, 14, 32, 154n, 155, 167,
  228, 230
Bacon, Roger, 8, 180
Barthez, Paul-Joseph, 146
Berlin, Sir Isaiah, xv
Berrêdo Carneiro, Paulo E. de, xxx
Berthollet, Claude-Louis, 151
Bichat, Xavier, 127, 229, 235–6
Birkbeck George, 185
Blainville, Henri de, xxiv, xxvi–xxviii
Bonald, Louis de, xiii, xvi, 197
Bonaparte, Napoleon, Emperor of
  France, 94, 100
Bonnet, Charles, 229, 232, 235
Broussais, François, xxiv, xxvi–xxvii,
  230–40
Burdin, Jean, xix

Cabanis, Pierre-Jean-George, xxv–xxvii,
  132, 136, 229, 232–4
Charlemagne, 6
Charles VII, King of France, 38

Chaussier, François, 229
Clement of Alexandria, 71n
Colbert, Jean-Baptiste, 12, 33
Columbus, Christopher, 99
Condillac, Etienne Bonnot de, xxvi, 232
Condorcet, Jean-Antoine-Nicolas Caritat,
  Marquis de, xiv–xvi, xix, 2, 115–18,
  121–2, 125–7, 165
Constant, Benjamin, viii, ix, xvii, xxi
Copernicus, Nicholas, 5, 179
Cousin, Victor, xxv–xxvi, xxx, 229n
Cuvier, Georges, 229, 234

Daubenton, Louis Jean-Marie, 229
Descartes, René, 32, 155, 167, 228
Destutt de Tracy, Antoine-Louis-Claude
  de, xxvi
Dunoyer, Charles, viii, 220n
Dupin, Charles, 185
Durkheim, Emile, vii

Eckstein, Ferdinand d', 197
Eichthal, Gustave d', viii, 66n, 166n
Esquirol, Jean-Etienne Dominique, 240n

Ferguson, Adam, xiv
Franklin, Benjamin, 18
Furet, François, ix

Galileo, 15–16, 18, 32, 155, 167, 179, 228
Gall, Franz Joseph, 229, 232–4, 239
Guizot, Françcois, viii, ix, xvii–xviii

Haller, Victor Albrecht von, 229

Index of subjects

Academies, 33–4

Capacity
  and power, 9
  scientific and industrial, 20–43
Cause, causation, 146, 153
Centralization, xxii, 188, 199–200
Charter (of 1814), 12n
Civilization
  and natural laws, 93–100: foundation
    of social science, 103
  progressive oscillations of, 102–3
  states of, 103–6, 116–21
Climate
  influence of, according to
    Montesquieu, 114
Communes
  enfranchisement of, xvii, 6–7, 11, 19,
    21–5, 29, 43, 52, 92–3
  political role of, 11–14, 17, 23–31,
    35ff., 43–5
Constitutions, inefficacy of, 63
Corruption, as means of government,
  200–1
Critical doctrine, 49–50, 57, 191–3
  of the kings, 52–4
  of the peoples, 53, 57, 67–8
  prejudice against spiritual power,
    192
Crusades, 194

Education
  role of spiritual power in, 205–6
  and teaching of morality, 34n

Encyclopaedia, 166–7
English constitution, as model, 18–19
Enlightenment, x, xii, xv–xvi, xxv

Feudal-theological system, xx
  decay, 10–20
  formation, 5–10
Freedom of conscience, 17–18, 55–6

Greece
  ancient, 175–8
  modern struggle for independence,
    53

History, hisotrians, 98–9, 116, 142–3
Holy Alliance, 53

Idéologues, xii, xvi, xxv–xxvi
Imagination
  and observation in the positive state,
    86–90
  role in the positive state, 109–12
Industrialists
  and practical work of social
    reorganization, 76

Kings, errors of, 50–3

Law of the three states, xvii–xx, 81–5,
  96, 145–55
Legists incompetence in social
  reorganization, 73–4

243

Cambridge Texts in the History of Political Thought

Titles published in the series thus far

Aristotle *The Politics* and *The Constitution of Athens* (edited by Stephen Everson)

Arnold *Culture and Anarchy and Other Writings* (edited by Stefan Collini)

Astell *Political Writings* (edited by Patricia Springborg)

Augustine *The City of God against the Pagans* (edited by R. W. Dyson)

Austin *The Province of Jurisprudence Determined* (edited by Wilfrid E. Rumble)

Bacon *The History of the Reign of King Henry VII* (edited by Brian Vickers)

Bakunin *Statism and Anarchy* (edited by Marshall Shatz)

Baxter *A Holy Commonwealth* (edited by William Lamont)

Beccaria *On Crimes and Punishments and Other Writings* (edited by Richard Bellamy)

Bentham *A Fragment on Government* (introduction by Ross Harrison)

Bernstein *The Preconditions of Socialism* (edited by Henry Tudor)

Bodin *On Sovereignty* (edited by Julian H. Franklin)

Bolingbroke *Political Writings* (edited by David Armitage)

Bossuet *Politics Drawn from the Very Words of Holy Scripture* (edited by Patrick Riley)

The British Idealists (edited by David Boucher)

Burke *Pre-Revolutionary Writings* (edited by Ian Harris)

Christine de Pizan *The Book of the Body Politic* (edited by Kate Langdon Forhan)

Cicero *On Duties* (edited by M. T. Griffin and E. M. Atkins)

Comte *Early Political Writings* (edited by H. S. Jones)

Conciliarism and Papalism (edited by J. H. Burns and Thomas M. Izbicki)

Constant *Political Writings* (edited by Biancamaria Fontana)

Dante *Monarchy* (edited by Prue Shaw)

Diderot *Political Writings* (edited by John Hope Mason and Robert Wokler)

The Dutch Revolt (edited by Martin van Gelderen)

The Early Political Writings of the German Romantics (edited by Frederick C. Beiser)

Early Greek Political Thought from Homer to the Sophists (edited by Michael Gagarin and Paul Woodruff)

de Maistre *Considerations on France* (edited by Isaiah Berlin and Richard Lebrun)

Malthus *An Essay on the Principle of Population* (edited by Donald Winch)

Marsiglio of Padua *Defensor minor* and *De translatione Imperii* (edited by Cary Nederman)

Marx *Early Political Writings* (edited by Joseph O'Malley)

Marx *Later Political Writings* (edited by Terrell Carver)

James Mill *Political Writings* (edited by Terence Ball)

J. S. Mill *On Liberty*, with *The Subjection of Women* and *Chapters on Socialism* (edited by Stefan Collini)

Milton *Political Writings* (edited by Martin Dzelzainis)

Montesquieu *The Spirit of the Laws* (edited by Anne M. Cohler, Basia Carolyn Miller and Harold Samuel Stone)

More *Utopia* (edited by George M. Logan and Robert M. Adams)

Morris *News from Nowhere* (edited by Krishan Kumar)

Nicholas of Cusa *The Catholic Concordance* (edited by Paul E. Sigmund)

Nietzsche *On the Genealogy of Morality* (edited by Keith Ansell-Pearson)

Paine *Political Writings* (edited by Bruce Kuklick)

Plato *Statesman* (edited by Julia Annas and Robin Waterfield)

Price *Political Writings* (edited by D. O. Thomas)

Priestley *Political Writings* (edited by Peter Miller)

Proudhon *What Is Property?* (edited by Donald R. Kelley and Bonnie G. Smith)

Pufendorf *On the Duty of Man and Citizen according to Natural Law* (edited by James Tully)

The Radical Reformation (edited by Michael G. Baylor)

Rousseau *The Discourses and Other Early Political Writings* (edited by Victor Gourevitch)

Rousseau *The Social Contract and Other Later Political Writings* (edited by Victor Gourevitch)

Seneca *Moral and Political Essays* (edited by John Cooper and John Procope)

Sidney *Court Maxims* (edited by Hans W. Blom, Eco Haitsma Mulier and Ronald Janse)

Spencer *The Man versus the State* and *The Proper Sphere of Government* (edited by John Offer)

Stirner *The Ego and Its Own* (edited by David Leopold)

Thoreau *Political Writings* (edited by Nancy Rosenblum)
Utopias of the British Enlightenment (edited by Gregory Claeys)
Vitoria *Political Writings* (edited by Anthony Pagden and Jeremy Lawrance)
Voltaire *Political Writings* (edited by David Williams)
Weber *Political Writings* (edited by Peter Lassman and Ronald Speirs)
William of Ockham *A Short Discourse on Tyrannical Government* (edited by A. S. McGrade and John Kilcullen)
William of Ockham *A Letter to the Friars Minor and Other Writings* (edited by A. S. McGrade and John Kilcullen)
Wollstonecraft *A Vindication of the Rights of Men* and *A Vindication of the Rights of Woman* (edited by Sylvana Tomaselli)